W9-AYE-024

John Maynard Keynes

Great Thinkers in Economics Series

Series Editor: **A.P. Thirlwall,** Emeritus Professor of Applied Economics, University of Kent, UK.

Great Thinkers in Economics is designed to illuminate the economics of some of the great historical and contemporary economists by exploring the interactions between their lives and work, and the events surrounding them. The books will be brief and written in a style that makes them not only of interest to professional economists, but also intelligible for students of economics and the interested lay person.

Titles include:

William J. Barber
GUNNAR MYRDAL

Paul Davidson
JOHN MAYNARD KEYNES

Peter D. Groenewegen
ALFRED MARSHALL

Forthcoming titles include:

Esben Sloth Andersen
JOSEPH A. SCHUMPETER

Michael Szenberg and Lal Ramrattan
FRANCO MODIGLIANI

Charles Rowley
JAMES McGILL BUCHANAN

Michael A. Lebowitz
KARL MARX

John King
NICOLAS KALDOR

Alessandro Roncaglia
PIERO SRAFFA

Julio Lopez and Michaël Samuel Assous
KALECKI'S THEORY OF CAPITALIST ECONOMIES

Gerhard Michael Ambrosi
ARTHUR C. PIGOU

J. R. Stanfield
JOHN KENNETH GALBRAITH

Warren Young and Esteban Perez
ROY HARROD

G. C. Harcourt and Prue Kerr
JOAN ROBINSON AND HER CIRCLE

Roger Middleton
ROBERT SOLOW

Gavin Kennedy
ADAM SMITH

Gordon Fletcher
SIR DENNIS HOLME ROBERTSON

Great Thinkers in Economics
Series Standing Order ISBN 978–1–4039–8555–2 (Hardback)
978–1–4039–8556–9 (Paperback)
(*outside North America only*)

You can receive future titles in this series as they are published by placing a standing order. Please contact your bookseller or, in case of difficulty, write to us at the address below with your name and address, the title of the series and the ISBN quoted above.

Customer Services Department, Macmillan Distribution Ltd, Houndmills, Basingstoke, Hampshire RG21 6XS, England

---

John Maynard Keynes

Paul Davidson

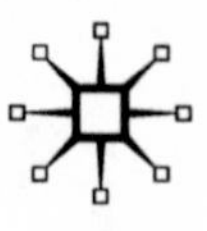

First published 2007 by
PALGRAVE MACMILLAN
Houndmills, Basingstoke, Hampshire RG21 6XS and
175 Fifth Avenue, New York, N.Y. 10010
Companies and representatives throughout the world

PALGRAVE MACMILLAN is the global academic imprint of the Palgrave Macmillan division of St. Martin's Press, LLC and of Palgrave Macmillan Ltd. Macmillan® is a registered trademark in the United States, United Kingdom and other countries. Palgrave is a registered trademark in the European Union and other countries.

ISBN-13: 978-1-4039-9623-7 hardback
ISBN-10: 1-4039-9623-7 hardback

This book is printed on paper suitable for recycling and made from fully managed and sustained forest sources. Logging, pulping and manufacturing processes are expected to conform to the environmental regulations of the country of origin.

A catalogue record for this book is available from the British Library.

A catalog record for this book is available from the Library of Congress.

10 9 8 7 6 5 4 3 2 1
16 15 14 13 12 11 10 09 08 07

Transferred to Digital Printing 2008

To Louise, Robert, Diane, Greg, Chris, Emily, Arik, Gavi, and Zakkai

Contents

List of Figures

List of Tables

Preface

> In economics you cannot *convict* your opponent of error, you can only *convince* him of it. And even if you are right you cannot convince him ... if his head is already filled with contrary notions.
>
> — Attributed to John Maynard Keynes

The purpose of this book is to convince the reader, whether an intelligent layperson, a student of economics, or even a professional economist, that what passes as the conventional economic wisdom espoused by the talking heads on television or written about in the mass media and mainstream professional economics journals is not applicable to the world in which we live. I hope to demonstrate that the revolutionary economic analysis of John Maynard Keynes, the greatest thinker in economics in the 20th century, is the most apt description of our market-oriented, money-using entrepreneurial economy.

The less the reader has been exposed to traditional economic analysis, the less his/her head is filled with what Harvard Professor John Kenneth Galbraith described as the "conventional wisdom" and "innocent frauds" of orthodox economists. Consequently, convincing the lay reader of how a monetary economy really operates will be an easier task for me than convincing an economics student, while the hardest task will be convincing the professional economist who professes the conventional wisdom by rote. Accordingly, although I have tried to provide a clear exposition, I have found it necessary occasionally to introduce technical jargon and tools into the discussion in order to jog the minds of students and their professors. The most difficult of these technical discourses I have relegated to the appendix to chapter 6. I suggest that the lay reader can readily skip this appendix without loss.

The first three chapters of this book briefly describe Keynes's early development into a traditional orthodox economist, and how the economic realities of World War I and its aftermath convinced Keynes that the economics that he taught and practiced was deficient. Chapters 4 through 6 describe how, after more than a decade of thought, Keynes was able to differentiate his analysis from classical economic theory. Chapter 7 summarizes Keynes's view of the economic system in which we live. The lay reader will find the discussion in chapter 7 so obviously correct that he/she will be amazed to learn that mainstream professional economists do not accept this description and analysis. Chapters 8–10 develop Keynes's analysis to solve the economic problems of the 21st-century global economy. Chapter 11 deals with the problem of inflation and explains how Keynes's analysis leads to recommendations for fighting inflation that differ dramatically from the innocent fraud perpetrated by central bankers who claim to be able to inflation-target. Finally, chapter 12 explains how the anti-communist (McCarthyism) witch hunt immediately after World War II, plus the mathematization of the discipline of economics, led to obfuscation as to what was Keynes's revolutionary theory, and why it has not become the handmaiden of all professional economists.

Hopefully, when enough people have read this book, Keynes's analysis will again affect economists and government policymakers' thoughts, and we will make strides toward eliminating the major faults of the economic system in which we live, namely, the inability to provide jobs for all who are willing, able, and capable of working and the growing inequalities of incomes and wealth that have affected both the developed and less developed nations of our globalized economy.

1
An Introduction to Keynes and His Revolutionary Views

Dear reader, may I ask you who you believe was the greatest Englishman of the 20th century – a man whose efforts enabled the possibilities for democracy and a civilized society to flourish on our planet? Some may answer Winston Churchill, but it is the purpose of this volume to convince you that the Englishman was John Maynard Keynes, an economist who never held elected political office.

Keynes was not an ivory tower academic economist. Besides his teaching position at Cambridge University, as Bursar of Kings College in Cambridge, Keynes made important investment decisions involving the College's portfolio. Keynes also served on the boards of several insurance and investment companies and in so doing obtained firsthand knowledge of the behavior of participants in financial markets. Moreover, his experience as a civil servant in the India Office between 1906 and 1908, as well as his service in the Treasury during the two world wars, enabled Keynes to recognize the need to convert theoretical prescriptions into politically acceptable, workable plans. Keynes was truly an economist of the real world.

Churchill fought to preserve the British Empire and in so doing created a bulkhead that produced sufficient time for the United States to join the conflict against Hitler. Churchill's economic policies, however, were based on a 19th-century classical economic theory that has a propensity to produce an economic system with two outstanding faults: (1) a failure to provide persistent full employment for all who want and are qualified to work at the going wage and (2) an arbitrary and inequitable distribution of income and wealth that often creates living conditions for the poor and lower middle class that are unnecessarily uncivilized (cf. Keynes, 1936a, p. 372). To Keynes, the existence of human distress resulting from the inability of the economic system to persistently generate a fully employed economy, and the gross inequalities of income and wealth under the existing economic system, should not go unheeded. If at all possible, institutions and policies should be developed to abolish these faults of the economic system in which we live (see Harrod, 1951, p. 192).

Through his economic teachings, writings, and advising to governments, Keynes developed and championed a revolutionary economic theory to overthrow the 19th-century classical economic theory that had dominated economic thought for more than 130 years. Even though his revolutionary theory was misunderstood by most professional economists, Keynes's policy prescriptions were followed by post–World War II governments to develop prosperous economic conditions. The result was an era of historically unprecedented real economic growth that lasted for a quarter of a century – from the end of World War II until the early 1970s.

Development economist Irma Adelman has called this quarter century the "golden age of economic development" for all nations that organized its economic system on capitalist principles. During this "golden age", these nations experienced no significant unemployment problems. Moreover, the income and wealth of these nations grew more rapidly than they ever had in the history of mankind. Existing inequalities were reduced, and almost all residents of these countries experienced substantial improvements in their living standards. This record of economic performance promoted the possibility that a globalized civilized society could be achieved – perhaps as early as the end of the 20th century.

Unfortunately, as we will see, Keynes's revolutionary theory was never completely understood by the post–World War II political leaders, their economic advisors, mainstream academic economists, and economics textbook writers during the last half of the 20th century. Consequently, by the 1970s, a counterrevolution occurred in both economic theory and policy. The result was that by the mid-1970s the last vestiges of Keynes's policy proposals were being rejected by most mainstream professional economists and economic advisors to governments. Keynes's policy recommendations were superseded by more orthodox classical prescriptions that were supported by a hi-tech version of the old 19th-century classical economic theory resurrected by economic theorists under the claim that their approach made economics a "hard science". Keynes's policies were rejected on principle, although sometimes followed in practice, especially in the form of "military Keynesianism" by conservative United States presidents (e.g., Ronald Reagan and George W. Bush) who, by encouraging massive increases in military and defense expenditures, produced huge budget deficits that provided strong short-term growth stimulus for the United States economy.

Nevertheless, the reintroduction of the classical theory's *laissez-faire* approach as an overriding principle for the government relationship toward market behavior reversed the progress that had been made in reducing the two major faults of the capitalist economic system. Since 1973, real economic growth for many developed and less developed nations has slowed significantly. Persistent unemployment problems and increasing inequalities of income and wealth again haunted the global economies of the late 20th century and early 21st century.

This book will attempt to explain how Keynes was able to free his mind from the bonds of traditional classical economic theory with its Panglossian philosophy. As Keynes (1936a, pp. 33–4) put it:

> The celebrated *optimism* of traditional economic theory, which has led to economists being looked upon as Candides, who, having left this world for the cultivation of their gardens, teach that all is for the best in the best of all possible worlds provided we will let well enough alone. ... For there would obviously be a natural tendency towards the optimum employment of resources in a Society which was functioning after the manner of the classical postulates. It may well be that the classical theory represents the way in which we should like our Economy to behave. But to assume that it actually does so is to assume our difficulties away.

Keynes was not one to assume our difficulties away.

In 1945, at a dinner given in his honor by the Royal Economic Society, Keynes offered a toast to "economics and economists who are the trustees, not of civilisation, but the possibilities of civilisation" (Harrod, 1951, pp. 191–2). The great thinker that he was, Keynes freed his mind from the binds of the classical analysis that was the conventional wisdom of economists of his (and our) time. He was able to reorient economic analysis in his mind toward a realistic analysis of the economic world in which we actually live. By so doing, Keynes was the best trustee for a stable, peaceful, and civilized global economy available for all mankind.

I. Keynes's early intellectual surroundings

John Maynard Keynes was born on June 5, 1883, the first of the three children of John Neville Keynes, a Cambridge University don, and

Florence Ada Keynes. The Keynes family, residing at 6 Harvey Road in Cambridge, England, represented a Victorian family "living in moderate circumstances, but solid comfort, the house well staffed with domestic servants, the passing days full of [intellectual] activity and the future secure" (Harrod, 1951, p. 1). As a young boy, Maynard Keynes was brought up with what Harrod has called the "presuppositions of Harvey Road" (Harrod, 1951, pp. 183, 192–3), which embodied the stable values of a Victorian civilization that "assumed peace, prosperity, and progress to be the natural order of things" (Skidelsky, 1996, p. 2).

In Cambridge, at the end of the 19th century, the belief in religion as the predetermination of one's life and one's society was being replaced by the notion that by studying the principles of the "moral sciences" one could recognize the source of social order and wisdom (Greer, 2000, p. 20). At that time, Cambridge's Moral Sciences Tripos examination was composed of studies in moral philosophy, political philosophy, logic, psychology, and economics.

While Maynard Keynes was growing up, visitors at the Keynes family's Cambridge residence included some of the most famous economists and philosophers of the day. Intellectual discussions in the moral sciences were daily exercises at 6 Harvey Road. The learned discussions that must have occurred there during Keynes's childhood and adolescent days surely had an impact on the developing mind of the young Maynard Keynes.

One of the suppositions of Harvey Road was that the search for knowledge by a small but influential intellectual group of moral scientists provided the guidelines for government to follow to achieve peace, prosperity, and progress under the principles of a *laissez-faire* system where governments would not interfere in markets, since it was assumed that unfettered markets permitted individuals to pursue their self-interest and in doing so promote the social good.

Unfortunately, World War I and its economic aftermath would dispel these rosy Harvey Road expectations. Consequently, as a young man in his twenties, Keynes recognized there was a problem with this Panglossian *laissez-faire* philosophy in economics. Nevertheless, Keynes never lost faith in the view that an intellectual group of moral scientists would light the pathway to continuous progress and improvement of the human condition. It is therefore not surprising that through his writings and teachings, Keynes would urge the creation of economic institutions and policies that, with the exercise of intelligence by *pro bono* managers, would establish a civilized, peaceful society that created conditions of prosperity and progress for all its inhabitants without destroying the market economy system.

II. Keynes's intellectual development

In 1897, at the age of 14, Keynes won a scholarship to Eton, one of Britain's most prestigious public schools. At Eton, Keynes was an outstanding student who excelled at mathematics, classics, and history (Skidelsky, 1996, p. 18). In 1902, Keynes was enrolled as an undergraduate student at King's College, Cambridge. There Keynes came under the influence of the philosopher G. E. Moore, whose *Principia Ethica* (1903) became a "manifesto of modernism" to Maynard Keynes and his generation of intellectuals. In an essay written in 1938 entitled "My Early Beliefs", Keynes noted that the effect of Moore's book "dominated, and perhaps still dominates, everything else" in establishing his views of the world (Keynes, 1949, p. 81).

Keynes wrote that "under the influence of Moore's method ... you could hope to make essentially vague notions clear by using precise language about them and asking exact questions" (Keynes, 1949, p. 88). It was this drive for a precise taxonomy and exposition that permitted Keynes to break away from the grip of orthodox classical economics that he had been exposed to at Cambridge as a student of the leading economist of the day, Alfred Marshall. The influence of Moore's method lead Keynes to his revolutionary way of thinking about economics that could only be brought about by Keynes's ability to create a new taxonomy regarding the vague notion of savings held by classical economic theorists.

As Keynes's first biographer, Roy Harrod (1951, p. 463–4), noted:

> It is true to say that the Keynesian scheme consisted in essence in a set of new definitions and a re-classification. He asked us to look upon the multifarious phenomena of business life, and order them in our mind in a different way. ... Classification in economics, as in biology, is crucial to the scientific structure. It is not by the intrinsic importance of the considerations which gave him [Keynes] his points of departure that he must be judged, but by what he achieved when he made the departure [from 19th century economic theory]. The older school [*sic*] were concerned to argue that new considerations could perfectly well be accommodated within the old conceptual framework ... a new conceptual framework was not called for. Such an inference was fallacious.

Harrod (1951, p. 463) observed: "The real defect with the classical system was that it deflected attention from what most needed attention. It was Keynes' extraordinarily powerful intuitive sense of what was important that convinced him the old classification was inadequate. It was his highly developed logical capacity that enabled him to construct a new classification of his own. It took him ten years to do so".

In the end, Keynes provided a scientific taxonomic structure for economic analysis which, at least for a while, allowed economists and advisors to government to transform their thinking about the causes of unemployment and economic growth.

How many of today's eminent economists would be willing to work for a decade on developing a new taxonomy (following Moore's dictum regarding precise language and developing exacting questions) to understand the shortcomings of the well-established classical theory that is taken to be the absolute truth by the leaders of the economics profession? Yet for Keynes, the pursuit of knowledge "meant philosophy and economics and more the first than the second" (Skidelsky, 1996, p.17). Consequently, Keynes, the philosopher-economist, was a "great thinker" willing to devote his time to develop a precise classification system and language to explain the causes of the two great faults of the economic system we live in – unemployment and the arbitrary and inequitable distribution of income and wealth (Keynes, 1936a, p. 372). Writing in the midst of a period of mass unemployment, it was obvious to Keynes that any significant movement toward full employment would not only increase the aggregate income of the community, but would also significantly increase the income of the majority of the poorer members of society – the unemployed workers. Thus, adoption of Keynes's analysis and full employment policies were likely to reduce income inequality. Keynes, however, did not believe in a complete equality of incomes. He wrote:

> For my own part, I believe that there is social and psychological justification for significant inequalities of income and wealth, *but not for such large disparities as exist today*. There are valuable human activities which require the motivation of money-making and the environment of private wealth ownership for their full fruition. Moreover, dangerous human proclivities can be canalised into comparatively harmless channels by the existence of opportunities for money making ..., which, if they cannot be satisfied in this way, may find their outlet in cruelty, the reckless pursuit of personal power and authority, and other forms of self-aggrandisement. It is better that a man should tyrannise over his bank balance than over his fellow-citizens. ... But it is not necessary ... that the game should be played for such high stakes as at present. Much lower stakes will serve the purpose equally well, as soon as the players are accustomed to them. The task of transmuting human nature must not be confused with the task of managing it.
>
> (Keynes, 1936a, p. 374, emphasis added)

2
How the Great War and Its Aftermath Affected Keynes's Thinking

Upon graduation from Cambridge in 1906, Keynes scored second on the Civil Service Exam. In a letter dated October 4, 1906 to his friend Lytton Strachey, Keynes noted that in this Civil Service Exam "real knowledge seems an absolute bar to success. I have done worst in the only two subjects of which I possessed a solid knowledge, Mathematics and Economics. ... For Economics I got a relatively low percentage and was 8th or 9th in order of merit – whereas I knew the *whole* of both ... in a real elaborate way" (Skidelsky, 1983, p. 175). Harrod (1951, p. 121) points out that later on Keynes explained his poor performance in economics by saying, "I evidently knew more about economics than my examiners".

His second ranking in this exam permitted Keynes to choose to accept a position as a clerk in the India Office. In the short time that Keynes worked at the India Office, he gained the knowledge of how a government office operates as well as an interest in Indian affairs and especially in the Indian monetary system (Harrod, 1951, p. 130). This experience would have a profound effect on his later professional work and his development of a serious economic theory of the role of money in the economy.

Two years later, on his 25th birthday (June 5, 1908), Keynes resigned from the India Office to take a special lecturer position at Cambridge University. This lectureship was privately financed by A.C. Pigou, the successor to Alfred Marshall as the professor of economics at Cambridge. At Cambridge, in the years before World War I, Keynes lectured on the topic of Money, Credit and Prices. Harrod notes that although Keynes's lectures were on economic theory, and though he used the language of the financial markets in his discussions, "his explanations were in every case impeccably lucid. ... Even in his lectures on Principles ... there was more factual illustration than is usual in such courses" (Harrod, 1951, p. 145).

While working at the India Office, Keynes used his spare time to work on the theory of probability (Skidelsky, 1983, p. 206) – a subject he had initially written about in his fellowship dissertation at Cambridge. He would continue for almost 15 years to spend his spare time on this subject until he finally published his *Treatise on Probability* (1921).

The development of Keynes's view on probability would later permit him to differentiate his theoretical approach to the concept of uncertainty from the theories of Marshall, Pigou, and other leading classical economists of his time, as well as from those of modern orthodox economists. For these classical theorists, "uncertainty plays a minimal role in the decision making of economic agents, since rational utility-maximizing individuals are [assumed] capable of virtually eliminating uncertainty with the historical information at hand" (Greer, 2000, p. 33).

Unlike the old 19th- and 20th-century classical economics orthodoxy (as well as what passes for mainstream economics in the 21st century) Keynes regarded "both probability theory and economics as branches of logic, not of mathematics, which should employ methods of reasoning appropriate to the former, including intuition and judgment, and incorporating a wide knowledge of non-numerical facts" (Skidelsky, 1983, p. 222). This view was to play an important role in separating Keynes's economic analytical framework from those of the orthodox theorists.

With the outbreak of World War I, Keynes, unlike many of his best friends from Cambridge, thought it was his duty to assist the war effort (Harrod, 1951, p. 78). In the September 1914 issue of *The Economic Journal*, Keynes, who was the editor, published a masterful article on "War and the Financial System, August 1914". Although this article made quite a stir in Whitehall, Keynes did not get a job with the government until January 1915, when he was made an assistant to Sir George Paish, the Special Advisor to the Chancellor of the Exchequer, Lloyd George. With a change of government in May 1915, Reginald McKenna became the Chancellor of the Exchequer, and Keynes was appointed to the Treasury's No. 1 Division – the section "centrally concerned with the financial direction of the war" (Skidelsky, 1983, p. 303).

Keynes's work at the Treasury, during the war years, educated him in the importance of controlling expectations if one wanted to affect the exchange rate. At the outbreak of World War II, Keynes noted the importance of maintaining a stable exchange rate when he wrote about his experience in the Treasury during the World War I: "To have abandoned the peg would have destroyed our credit and brought chaos to business; and would have done no real good" (Harrod, 1951, p. 204).

This early experience had a strong effect on Keynes's vision for the post–World War II international payments system and the need for stable exchange rates.

The following is an amusing incident that illustrates why Keynes's experience during World War I led him to recognize the flimsy basis of market-price asset valuation in financial markets. During the war, the English were in dire need of Spanish pesetas for purchasing war-related imports from Spain. With great difficulty, Keynes managed to obtain a small sum of pesetas and duly reported this to a relieved Secretary of the Treasury who "remarked that at any rate for a short time we had a supply of pesetas. 'Oh no!' said Keynes. 'What!' said his horrified chief. 'I've sold them again: I'm going to break the market'. And he [Keynes] did" (Harrod, 1951, p. 203).

For most of the war, Keynes's primary responsibility in the Treasury was to try to manage the crisis in external finance of the many military and civilian imports that Britain needed. This experience was to put him in good stead when, during World War II, he headed the British delegation to the Bretton Woods conference on developing a postwar international payments system.

In January 1916, the British government introduced military conscription. Most of Keynes's Bloomsbury friends became conscientious objectors. Keynes argued with his friends that since Britain was already immersed in the war, it was essential to work to establish world affairs on a new and better basis so that this terrible bloodshed would never happen again.[1] Keynes "was now solemnly pledged to do all that in him lay to secure a durable peace and a new pattern of international relations" (Harrod, 1951, p. 215). As Skidelsky (1983, p. 316) indicates, this implicit pledge contributed to the passion with which he condemned, in his book *The Economic Consequences of the Peace* (1919), the victorious Allied government leaders for the terms they demanded from Germany in the Versailles Peace Treaty.

The Armistice of November 1918 contained a rider, inserted by the French and the British, requiring the Germans to pay "for all damage" done to the civilian population and to their property (Skidelsky, 1983, p. 354). As early as 1916, Keynes had written a memo that any reparations demanded must not damage Germany's productive capacity, for ultimately it was Germany's ability to sell her exports abroad that would finance any reparations demanded. Unfortunately, as Keynes recognized, the postwar reparations demanded by the French, and supported by the British Prime Minister Lloyd George, would overwhelm the German economy.

Keynes believed that the magnitude of reparations that the Allies demanded was intolerable. "The British and French wanted to milk Germany partly for the purpose of paying" the French and British war debts to America (Skidelsky, 1983, p. 367). Keynes recognized that if the Americans could be convinced to scale down their claims on the Allies, the size of the reparations imposed on Germany might be reduced to a more manageable level. Keynes argued for an all-round cancellation of debts. He suggested that attempts to collect all the debts and reparation claims could destroy the capitalist system. If total cancellation was not politically possible, then Keynes recommended that Allied governments accept German reparation bonds "in final discharge of the debts incurred between ourselves" (Skidelsky, 1983, p. 368). In Keynes's use of the phrase "final discharge of debts incurred" we see the seeds of Keynes's liquidity preference theory of money – the theory that was to be the basis of the 1936 Keynesian Revolution against the classical economic orthodoxy.

Keynes's recommendation was an attempt to "prevent Germany being immediately stripped of all her working capital and would assist the European Allies to carry their heavy burden. It was indeed a sort of Marshall Plan, albeit on a smaller scale" (Harrod, 1951, p. 246). Unfortunately, Keynes's suggestions were not acceptable to either the French, the British, or the Americans.

When the Treaty of Versailles was signed, Keynes resigned from his position at the Treasury. Keynes wrote to the Prime Minister, "I am slipping away from the scene of nightmare. I can do no more good here. I've gone on hoping even through these last dreadful weeks that you'd find some way to make the Treaty a just and expedient document. But now it's apparently too late. The battle is lost" (Skidelsky, 1983, pp. 374–5).

During the summer and early fall of 1919, Keynes wrote a book entitled *The Economic Consequences of the Peace* to explain his disillusionment with the process of producing the peace treaty. This book was published in December 1919. Harrod (1951, p. 253) has hailed it as "one of the finest pieces of polemic in the English language". Skidelsky (1983, p. 384) has stated that the book "has the claim to be regarded as Keynes's best book". Although the book was an explanation of the reparations problem, it was not written as a technical treatise. "The writing is angry, scornful, and, rarely for Keynes, passionate: never again were his denunciations of bungling and lying, or his moral indignation, to ring so loud and clear. ... The result is a personal statement unique in twentieth century literature. Keynes was staking the claim of the economist to be Prince. All other forms of rule were bankrupt. The economist's vision of welfare, conjoined to a new standard of technical excellence, were to be the last barriers to chaos, madness and retrogression" (Skidelsky, 1983, p. 384).

Keynes's war experience "marked the start of Keynes's career as a radical economist" (Skidelsky, 1983, p. 401). Skidelsky notes that Victorian England had relied on a belief in God to maintain social cohesion and civilized progress. By the turn of the century, Cambridge dons and philosophers had proclaimed the death of God, which meant the end of a false belief, and the advent of a new belief in science as the mode of progress. The devastating World War I had suggested that science did not necessarily lead to a progressive civilized society. "The rest of Keynes's life was spent trying to bring back the vision of a civilized society" (Skidelsky, 1983, p. 402).

For Keynes it was the creative artists, such as his friends in Bloomsbury (Lytton Strachey, Virginia Woolf, Vanessa Bell, Duncan Grant, etc.), that were the true trustees of civilization.[2] Nevertheless, a prosperous, growing economic system was a necessary condition for the artists' civilizing influence to flourish. Good advice from economists, therefore, was a necessary condition for encouraging the possibility of a civilized society.

During the Victorian period, when Keynes was growing up, the presuppositions of Harvey Road implied that everything was already in place to ensure a prosperous, growing, and well-functioning civilized economic system. World War I brought this faith in a *laissez-faire* economic system crashing down, and with it the hopes for a civilized society. Between 1922 and 1936, the unemployment rate in Britain fell below 10 percent in only one year. In 1927, it was 9.7 percent. This long period of unemployment distress in Britain seemed to destroy all hope for advancing a civilized society.

The British economic experience of the 1920s made it obvious to Keynes that orthodox classical theory could not provide the guidelines to provide for the civilized system that underlay the presuppositions of Harvey Road. Classical economic theory argued that "there would obviously be a natural tendency toward the optimum employment of resources in a Society which was functioning after the classical postulates" (Keynes, 1936a, p. 33). When the unemployment rate appeared to be stuck near or above 10 percent for almost 14 years, it was apparent that the classical theory argument was not applicable to the world of experience. To a man of Keynes's creative abilities it became obvious that what was necessary was a new economic theory to provide an understanding of an economic system that was able to perpetuate widespread unemployment. Intelligent application of this new theory would once again set mankind on the road to a more civilized society. The path to creating this new economic theory would be a long and arduous one. It would take Keynes more than a decade to develop his revolutionary ideas.

Keynes's vigilant observation of the postwar economic scene made him well aware of the failings of the existing economic system. Nevertheless, until the 1930s Keynes was still partially a prisoner of the classical economic theory that he had been taught and that he had taught at Cambridge University. The moral of Keynes's book *The Economic Consequences of the Peace* (1919) was that it was foolishness and ignorance that led the Allied governments to create such a dreadful economic situation, not the application of the principles of classical economic theory. In 1919, Keynes still believed that intelligent management could have avoided the dreadful peace agreement and reestablished the conditions that would permit classical economic theory to operate for the improvement of both the victorious Allied nations and the defeated Germany.

By August 1920, over 100,000 copies of the *Economic Consequences of the Peace* had been sold in Britain and America, and the book had been translated into German, Dutch, Flemish, Danish, Swedish, Italian, Spanish, Rumanian, Russian, Japanese, and Chinese (Skidelsky, 1983, p. 394). With the success of such large book sales, Keynes gained world-wide public attention. Keynes then recognized that his creative abilities could be channeled into making the economic system once again a haven for the creative artists. Keynes was to seize this opportunity "not only to assert his own claim to attention but [also] the claim of economic science to shape the future" (Skidelsky, 1992, p. 3).

3

Keynes's Middle Way: Liberalism is Truly a New Way

The question of whether unfettered individual self-interest decision making in economic affairs can promote the social good has vexed philosophers and economic thinkers for a long time. Based on Adam Smith's 1776 writings about the "invisible hand" in the *Wealth of Nations*, classical economic theory had developed a large superstructure to explain that a system of *laissez-faire*, where the role of government was not to interfere with the economic activities of the marketplace, would result in the maximum welfare of the community. The worldly wisdom of economists and politicians during the Victorian age was that an economy prospers best when market forces are unhampered by government actions. Government may raise taxes to pay for a military defense and to enforce law and order on the community, but the State should never try to influence total economic activity.

The Economic Consequences of the Peace (Keynes, 1919) seemed to suggest that following the conditions laid down by the Treaty of Versailles, a *laissez-faire* economic system could not produce the progress claimed by classical economic theory. Accordingly, some observers thought that Keynes must support the opposite extreme, a system where government made the major production decisions in order to achieve a social good – a truly socialist system. Keynes, however, was not sympathetic to a truly socialist system.

At the time of the publication of *The Economic Consequences of the Peace*, Keynes did not have an alternative economic theory to juxtapose against classical theory. In *Economic Consequences*, Keynes's argument was that in the 19th century there had been four forces: (1) population, (2) organization, (3) the psychology of society, and (4) the relation of the old world (Europe) to the new (America) that had led to a precarious balancing of forces between labor and capital, savings and consumption, the trade balance and international capital flows between Europe and America that permitted a *laissez-faire* policy to provide a tolerable economic system of progress (Skidelsky, 1992, p. 220). In *Economic Consequences*, Keynes suggested that this balance of forces had broken down by the time of World War I, and that the Treaty of Versailles had destroyed all possibilities of restoring such a balance. Consequently, something else had to be done.

Keynes always believed that if a situation of distress in any form should occur, it should not go unheeded. The post–World War I *laissez-faire* economic system created great distress for its inhabitants. Keynes argued that institutional arrangements could be developed that could work with market forces to relieve this distress and promote the general welfare. Keynes did not believe in eliminating market forces altogether – as one would under a socialist system. Hence, he could not accept a true socialist solution.

As the decade of the 1920s developed, and the distress of mass unemployment without relief became the persistent experience of the British economy, Keynes recognized that the opposite extreme of complete *laissez-faire* was not an acceptable prescription. Accordingly, it was necessary to develop a new economic theory: (1) to explain what caused this tragic economic malady in our entrepreneurial system and (2) to provide an alternative to the two extremes of *laissez-faire* and state socialism. The alternative required showing how the government, together with market forces, could move to end unemployment and provide full employment for all who were willing and able to work at the going market wage rate. Keynes's view was not, as many have claimed, a Middle Way between *laissez-faire* capitalism and the socialist view of absolute government control of the production and exchange economy. It was truly a New Way (cf. Skidelsky, 2000, p. xvii).

During the decade of the 1920s, in Britain, the two major political parties were Labour and the Tories. Keynes's economic views were at odds with both of these parties. Only the Liberal Political Party held any possibility for accepting Keynes's economic ideas. Keynes's temperament and conviction would make him a Liberal throughout his life. Nevertheless, Keynes did not get involved in developing Liberal policies until Lloyd George became the leader of the Liberal Party in 1926 (Skidelsky, 1992, p. 21). Keynes tried to turn the Liberals away from *laissez-faire* toward a system which would preserve a free economy where individual initiative is welcomed, while permitting government intervention where economic distress was significant and persistent (Harrod, 1951, p. 334).

In 1923, Keynes published a book entitled *A Tract on Monetary Reform*. Although still under the influence of classical theory, in this book Keynes argued for a system of price stability without a return to the Gold Standard. At that time, it was widely believed by economists and politicians that the Gold Standard was a respected and sacrosanct mechanism that had been responsible for the wonderful progress exhibited by 19th-century capitalism.

Keynes argued that price stability was necessary for contractual predictability, which in turn promoted economic stability. Since the entrepreneurial system that we call capitalism was a production and exchange system organized by the use of monetary contractual agreements between buyers and sellers, price stability was, therefore, an essential condition for the operation of a progressive civilizing economic system. In *A Tract On Monetary Reform* (1923), Keynes relied on the Cambridge version of the classical quantity theory of money to explain how price stability could be established. Keynes argued that the price level depended on the interaction of two decisions: (1) the decision of the central bank on how much money to create and (2) the decision of the public as to the quantity of money they wanted to hold as a store of value rather than spend on goods and services. The central bank, therefore, had to be prepared to offset unanticipated changes in the public's desire to hold money as a store of value by increasing (decreasing) the quantity of money when people desired more (less) money to hold as a store of value.

Keynes, however, recognized that the Cambridge version of this classical quantity theory of money was valid only in the long run. In one of his most famously quoted remarks, Keynes wrote: "But this *long run* is a misleading guide to current affairs. *In the long run* we are all dead. Economists set themselves too easy, too useless a task if in tempestuous seasons they can only tell us that when the storm is long past the ocean is flat again" (Keynes, 1923, p. 65). The difficult, but useful, task that economists should undertake is to establish what economic actions should be taken when the economy exhibits instability in the short run in which we live. Unfortunately, the classical economic theory shed no light on this problem.

When Winston Churchill returned Britain to the Gold Standard in April 1925 at the old exchange rate, Keynes argued that this was a gross error that overvalued the English pound sterling by approximately 10 percent. This meant, according to Keynes, that in order to maintain markets overseas, Britain would have to reduce its money costs of production, and therefore money wages, by 10 percent. In a *laissez-faire* system this wage reduction could only be accomplished by sufficient and persistent massive unemployment that would weaken the labor's ability to defend the existing wage rate structure. Accordingly, Keynes believed that Britain was in for a prolonged period of intensifying unemployment. Keynes did, however, note that this unemployment distress necessary to lower wages could be "short-circuited by means of a 'national treaty' to reduce wages and other incomes by agreement" (Skidelsky, 1996, p. 58). This fleeting discussion of the possibility of an "incomes policy" agreement would be resurrected by some Post Keynesian economists in the 1960s and 1970s, under the title of a "tax based incomes policy" that could be used as an institutional weapon against the opposite problem that threatened the economies of the 1970s – the problem of inflation.

In a column for *The Nation*, in May 1924, Keynes suggested that the distress of massive unemployment in Britain needed a "drastic remedy". He readily endorsed government spending on the construction of capital facilities in Britain such as roads, electricity, grids, housing, etc. (Keynes, 1924, pp. 219–23). This 1924 column marks the beginning of Keynes's revolutionary view that there could be a role for the government to buy socially useful things from private industry to create market demand and thereby relieve unemployment distress in the private sector of the economy. At the time, however, Keynes had not developed an economic theory that would support such a proposal for active government spending.

For the next 12 years, Keynes would struggle to throw off the vestments of the classical theory and to create his own new taxonomy and revolutionary economic theory to explain the persistent existence of widespread unemployment in a modern, money-using, entrepreneurial economy. Only by understanding the cause of mass unemployment could one develop a prescription for alleviating the problem. The classical theory that Keynes had inherited could only promise that in the long-run things would come out all right. It could not satisfactorily explain how to relieve the economic distress that was happening in the short run in which we live.

Thus Keynes embarked on a process of creation. Keynes's first major attempt to explain the normal operations of a money-using, entrepreneurial economy was a two-volume work entitled *A Treatise on Money* (1930). In the more than five years Keynes spent in writing this *Treatise*, he found an excellent critic in his Cambridge colleague, Dennis H. Robertson. While writing the *Treatise*, Keynes and Robertson had long and animated discussions. In fact, Robertson had just written a book on the subject of unemployment, price stability, and the role of the banking and monetary system entitled *Banking Policy and the Price Level* (1926).

Robertson's arguments were a stimulus for Keynes's thinking and, in many ways, a trailblazer for Keynes's new ideas. Keynes's *Treatise on Money* developed Robertson's innovative ways of thinking about savings and investment. Robertson, however, was always the classical theorist and would not deviate too far from the classical path. Accordingly, Robertson's influence led to the failure of Keynes's *Treatise on Money* to break away completely from the classical theory grounding and create a new revolutionary analysis which could save the world from the Great Depression. Instead, it forced Keynes into semantic arguments and circumlocutions with other economists to explain the cause of the persistent distress of massive unemployment that existed in the real world.

In the animated Robertson-Keynes discussions, it became obvious that for Robertson fluctuations in economic activity, i.e., the business cycle, were "real" phenomena that were independent of the quantity of money and credit. Although Keynes originally accepted Robertson's argument that an investment boom is usually triggered by "real" factors such as new inventions, Keynes did not accept the argument that it was "overinvestment in real plant and equipment" that inevitably led to crisis and collapse. For Keynes, the business cycle was inherently connected with the operation of the banking system and it could be prevented, or at least controlled, by controlling the volume of bank credit (Skidelsky, 1983, vol 2, p. 278).

Despite their long and lively discussions, it was clear that, by 1931, Robertson and Keynes's theoretical views began to significantly diverge. "During such a [creative] endeavour the basic tempo of the soul is different. By some mysterious process the thought gathers, forms itself, defines itself. It must be protected from too much dialectic and debate. Mr. D. H. Robertson's subtle criticisms, which in the early days proved very simulating to Keynes, seemed to become in the end an impediment to the final fruition of his ideas. ... Creation is a subtle and precarious activity" (Harrod, 1951, p. 367).

The result was that Keynes and Robertson became adversaries regarding the basic economic theory. While Robertson would never completely abandon the fundamental postulates of classical theory, Keynes would overthrow three specific classical theory axioms that prevented classical theory from being applicable to the problems of the real world. Only after Keynes rejected these classical axioms could he produce his revolutionary *The General Theory of Employment Interest and Money* (1936a).

4
The Before and After of Keynes's General Theory

> It seems to me that economics is a branch of logic: a way of thinking. ... One can make some quite worthwhile progress merely by using axioms and maxims. But one cannot get very far except by devising new and improved models. This requires ... vigilant observation of the actual working of our system. Progress in economics consists almost entirely in a progressive movement in the choice of models.
>
> —J. M. Keynes (1938)

I. Keynes's revolutionary theory versus mainstream classical theory

On New Year's Day, 1935, Keynes wrote a letter to George Bernard Shaw. In this letter he stated:

> To understand my new state of mind, however, you have to know that I believe myself to be writing a book on economic theory which will largely revolutionize not I suppose at once but in the course of the next ten years the way the world thinks about economic problems. When my new theory has been duly assimilated and mixed with politics and feelings and passions, I cannot predict what the final upshot will be in its effect on actions and affairs, but there will be a great change and in particular the Ricardian Foundations of Marxism will be knocked away.
>
> I can't expect you or anyone else to believe this at the present stage, but for myself I don't merely hope what I say. In my own mind I am quite sure.

13 months later, in February 1936, Keynes's book *The General Theory of Employment, Interest and Money* was published. This book, coming in the midst of the Great Depression and a world war that soon followed, induced innovative Keynes-like thinking in economic policy discussions. Unfortunately, mainstream economists failed to adopt the logically consistent innovative theoretical analysis laid down by Keynes as the basis of the nontraditional postwar policies prescriptions. Instead, what was called "Keynesianism" in most postwar professional writings and popular economics textbooks was a modernized version of the pre-Keynesian 19th-century classical system larded over with some verbal Keynesian terminology.

Keynes's biographer, Lord Robert Skidelsky, recognized this reversion of mainstream postwar Keynesianism to more orthodox classical theory when he wrote (Skidelsky, 1992, p. 512) that "the validity of Keynes's 'general theory' rests on his assertion that the classical theory ... is, as he put it in his lectures, 'nonsense'. If it [the classical theory] were true, the classical 'special case' would in fact, be the 'general theory', and Keynes's aggregative analysis not formally wrong, but empty, redundant. It is worth noting ... that mainstream economists after World War II treated Keynes's theory as a 'special case' of the classical theory, applicable to conditions where money wages ... were 'sticky'. Thus his theory was robbed of its theoretical bite, while allowed to retain its relevance for policy".

The best known of these post–World War II Keynesians who treated Keynes's theory as a special case where wages are sticky was Professor Paul Samuelson of MIT, who, partly in response to the anti-communism witch hunt (McCarthyism) that prevailed in the United States after World War II, implicitly boasted of the classical theoretical foundations of his interpretation of Keynes's theory by calling his version "Neoclassical Synthesis Keynesianism". (In chapter 12 *infra* we will provide the evidence to explain why Keynes's revolutionary theory was never understood or adopted by those economists who called themselves "Keynesians" – including several Nobel Prize winners – who laid claimed to Keynes's mantle after World War II.)

In the first three decades following World War II, the resulting Neoclassical Synthesis Keynesianism[1] (or what is sometimes referred to as Old Keynesianism or American Keynesianism) conquered mainstream academic discussions as completely as the Holy Inquisition conquered Spain (to paraphrase one of Keynes's more colorful expressions relating to Ricardo's influence on economic theory). By the 1970s, however, the logical incompatibilities of this "Keynesian" synthesis of classical theory and Keynes's policy prescriptions were becoming evident as the

Neoclassical Synthesis Keynesians struggled to develop an anti-inflation policy as real-world economies suffered from inflation while experiencing significant levels of unemployment.

In the 1970s, the logical inconsistencies between the macroeconomics of American Keynesianism and its classical (or neoclassical) microfoundations became apparent in the failure of Neoclassical Synthesis Keynesianism to provide a logically consistent theory of inflation. Consequently, most mainstream economists abandoned "Keynesianism" and regressed to a more logically consistent mathematical classical theory – the Walras-Arrow-Debreu general equilibrium model – for both its microfoundations and its macroeconomic implications. The complex mathematical structure of this general equilibrium system approach made it difficult for its proponents to recognize that its axiomatic base made it an unsatisfactory tool for understanding the operations of the economic world of experience (see Davidson, 2003).

Keynes had begun work on his revolutionary *General Theory* book in 1932. Unlike the United States, Great Britain had been suffering from a great recession with very high unemployment rates since the end of World War I. On the other hand, except for a brief recession at the beginning of the 1920s, the roaring 1920s had been a period of unbridled prosperity in the United States. In 1929, only 3.2 percent of American workers were unemployed.

The New York stock market had climbed to unprecedented highs, and everybody seemed to be getting rich. It is no wonder that English economists, and not the American economics professionals, were more concerned about the problem of chronic and persistent unemployment when the United States plunged into the Great Depression of the 1930s.

Just a few days before the stock market crash of October 24, 1929, one of the most eminent American economists of the time, Professor Irving Fisher of Yale University, told an audience that the stock market had reached a high plateau from which it could only go up. Then, suddenly, the bottom fell out. It is said that Professor Fisher, who put his money in what he believed in, lost between $8 million and $10 million in the stock market crash. The Great Depression had hit America.

From 1929 through 1933, the American economy went downhill. It seemed as if the economic system was enmeshed in a catastrophe from which it could not escape. Unemployment went from 3.2 percent in 1929 to 24.9 percent by 1933. One out of every four workers in the United States was unemployed by the time Roosevelt was inaugurated as president of the United States, in March 1933. A measure of the standard of living of Americans, the real gross national product (GNP) per capita, fell by 52 percent between 1929 and 1933. This meant that, by 1933, the average American family was living on less than half of what it had earned in 1929. The American capitalist dream appeared to be shattered.

The economics experts of those times, including Professor Irving Fisher, still invoked classical economic theory to argue that the high levels of unemployment being experienced in the United States in the early 1930s could not persist. The economy would soon right itself as long as the government did not interfere with the workings of a free market system.

A wonderful example of this classical prescription is revealed in the memoirs of Herbert Hoover, the president of the United States during the onset of the Great Depression. Mr. Hoover had won praises as a kind and caring person for his efforts to help feed the people of Europe devastated by the effects of World War I. Hoover obviously was a person who would try to alleviate a situation where humans experienced economic distress not of their own doing. In his memoir, President Hoover noted that whenever he wanted to take positive action to end the Depression and create jobs, his Treasury Secretary, Andrew Mellon, always cautioned against government action and offered the same advice. "Mr. Mellon had only one formula. Liquidate labor, liquidate stocks, liquidate the farmer, liquidate real estate. It will purge the rottenness out of the system ... People will work harder, lead a more moral life"(Hoover, 1952, p. 30).

In contrast, Keynes argued that the persistent unemployment was not the fault of the unemployed or intransigence of workers to accept lower wages or the result of market imperfections such as monopolies or trade unions. Rather, the cause was nested in the public's desire for liquidity and the peculiar but essential properties possessed by money and other liquid assets. The bad economic times of the Great Depression induced people to spend less out of whatever income they received and try to remain as liquid as possible. The result was a persistent, weak market demand for the products of industry, so that entrepreneurs could not profitably sell all the output they were capable of producing with their existing plant, equipment, and a fully employed labor force.

Whenever market demand weakens, entrepreneurs are forced to lay-off workers and close factories. The resulting unemployment and poverty, Keynes argued, could not be automatically cured by Mr. Mellon's suggestion that high levels of unemployment played a useful function of "purging the rottenness [monopoly elements] out of the system". It was, Keynes argued, weak market demand for output and not monopoly or other imperfections on the supply side of product or labor markets that was the fundamental cause of persistent unemployment during the

Great Depression. The cure lay in government taking an active role in promoting an increase in the aggregate demand for the products of industry.

Classical economic theory, on the other hand, provided the rationale for the *laissez-faire* or "no government intervention in the marketplace" philosophy that dominated economic discussions of how to cure the unemployment problem and promote prosperity. For classical theorists and government policy decision makers such as Secretary of the Treasury Andrew Mellon, the *laissez-faire* doctrine is likened to the writings of a Deity that no good economist or pious government official would question.

It is claimed that, in 1751, the Marquis d'Argenson was the first writer to use the phrase *laissez-faire* in his argument for removing the visible hand of government from the economic affairs of the nation. The Marquis wrote that "To govern better one must govern less". Although the phrase *laissez-faire* does not appear in the writings of the founding fathers of classical economic theory such as Adam Smith or David Ricardo, the idea is there. The pursuit of self-interest of individual buyers and entrepreneurs, unfettered by government interference, is at the heart of the philosophy of classical economics.

In his 1776 classic, *The Wealth of Nations*, Adam Smith wrote:

> It is not from the benevolence of the butcher, the brewer, or the baker that we expect our dinner, but from regard to their own self-interest. We address ourselves, not to their humanity but to their self love, and never talk to them of our necessities, but of their advantage. ... Every individual is continually exerting himself to find out the most advantageous employment for whatever capital he can command. It is his own advantage, indeed and not that of society which he has in view. ... He intends only his own gain, and he is in this, as in many other cases, led by an invisible hand to promote an end which was no part of his intention. By pursuing his own interest he frequently promotes that of the society more effectually than when he really intends to promote it.
>
> (Smith, 1776, p. 14)

Following Adam Smith's invisible hand paradigm, classical theorists insist that if the government intervened in economic matters during any "temporary" period of unemployment, then the economic situation would deteriorate, and the economy would take a longer time to right itself. If the government did not interfere with the invisible hand of the market during this transient period of unemployment, then only the weak and inefficient would be weeded out (or liquidated to use

Andrew Mellon's term), leaving a stronger, more powerful economy to carry on. In true Social Darwinian fashion, what was being asserted was that the Great Depression was merely Nature's way of weeding out the economically weak and providing for the "survival of the fittest". When the economic system righted itself, it would regenerate full employment and prosperity for all the fittest survivors.

In the very first paragraph of his book *The General Theory*, Keynes challenged this orthodox dogma when he wrote:

> I have called this book the *General Theory of Employment Interest and Money*. ... The object of such a title is to contrast the character of my arguments and conclusions with those of the classical theory of the subject, upon which I was brought up and which dominates economic thought, both practical and theoretical of the governing and academic classes of this generation, as it has for a hundred years past. I shall argue that the postulates of the classical theory are applicable to a special case only and not to the general case. ... The characteristics of the special case assumed by the classical theory happen not to be those of the economic society in which we actually live, with the result that its teaching is misleading and disastrous if we attempt to apply it to the facts of experience.
>
> (Keynes, 1936a, p. 3)

Keynes explicitly tailored the exposition of his book to change the minds of his "fellow economists" while hoping "it will be intelligible to others." Keynes's purpose was to persuade "economists to reexamine critically certain of their basic assumptions. ... The matters at issue are of an importance which cannot be exaggerated. But if my explanations are right, it is my fellow economists, not the general public, whom I must first convince" (Keynes, 1936a, pp. v–vi).

Keynes believed that the fatal flaw of the classical system lay in the very restrictive "basic assumptions", i.e., the fundamental axioms that are necessary to demonstrate the self-correcting tendency of an unfettered competitive market economy system. Unfortunately, as will be explained *infra*, it was not clear to the economists of the 1930s what classical axioms Keynes wished to jettison and why he felt they must be overthrown. Consequently, although Keynes affected economists' vision of what policies government could pursue to relieve the problem of unemployment, Keynes failed to change the minds of his fellow economists on the underlying economic theory.

For several years before publication, Keynes circulated drafts of his work to some world-famous professional colleagues in England (e.g., Dennis

Robertson, Ralph Hawtrey, and Frederick Hayek). Keynes took extraordinary time and effort to elicit comments from these professional colleagues and respond to these comments. Hayek, who had written a savage review of Keynes's 1930 two-volume *A Treatise in Money*, published his own explanation of the Depression in Britain, in his book *Prices and Production* (Hayek, 1931). Hayek's arguments and explanations were especially important in forcing Keynes to rethink his approach and to ultimately develop a logical distinction between a real exchange (neutral money) economic system that represented Hayek's "special case" of a general theory and Keynes's money-using, market-oriented entrepreneurial system developed from Keynes's general theory (Skidelsky, 1992, p. 458).

Through this process of intellectual argument and discussion,[2] Keynes's new theory slowly emerged, even though many ramifications of Keynes's general theory remained obscure to even its inventor. Prodded by Hayek's attacks, Keynes developed his new theory as a methodological attack on classical theory for its lack of clarity and the restrictiveness of its underlying axioms.

Keynes wrote of Hayek's classical theory masterpiece, *Prices and Production*, that this book was "one of the most frightful muddles I have ever read. ... It is an extraordinary example of how, starting with a mistake [an unrealistic axiom], a remorseless logician can end in Bedlam. Yet Dr. Hayek has seen a vision, and though when he woke up he has made nonsense of his story by giving wrong names to the objects which occur in it, his Kubla Kahn is not without inspiration and must set the reader thinking" (Keynes, 1931, p. 252).

Hayek argued that any temporary unemployment that occurred would end when the market would self-correct any supply-side imperfection that prevented instantaneous money wage and price flexibility. If there was unemployment, classical theory holds that even if there is not instantaneous flexibility in wages and prices, in the long run market forces would cause wages and prices to fall sufficiently to restore full employment. Keynes, on the other hand, argued "We must not regard the conditions of [rigid wage and price] supply ... as the fundamental sources of our troubles. ... [I]t is in the conditions of demand which our diagnosis must search and probe for an explanation" (Keynes, 1934, p. 486).

Hayek's writings made it clear to Keynes that his dispute with classical economists required Keynes to create a new taxonomy that would reject some fundamental axioms that were the basis of classical theory's argument that the existence of flexible wages and prices was all that was necessary to assure a *laissez-faire* economy always reverted to a full-employment prosperity.

As a result of these ongoing discussions, and intellectual confrontations with his professional economics colleagues, Keynes became fully aware of the arguments that his fellow economists would marshal to defend the classical orthodoxy against his revolutionary assault. If Keynes was to convince his professional colleagues of the errors of their ways, Keynes had to develop persuasive arguments to rebut the many adverse comments he received.

The British experience of high levels of unemployment since World War I had convinced Keynes that the capitalist system was unlikely to survive unless proper policy actions were taken as soon as possible. What was needed to galvanize professional support for his policy suggestions was something other than a tedious and contentious professional formalization of his model. Rightly or wrongly, in 1936, Keynes felt that rhetorical exposition rather than a formal mathematical model was needed. Keynes (1936a, p. 297) argued that

> The object of our analysis is, not to provide a machine, or method of blind manipulation, which will furnish an infallible answer, but to provide ourselves with an organized and orderly method of thinking out particular problems. ... It is a great fault of symbolic pseudo-mathematical methods of formalising a system of economic analysis ... that they expressly assume strict independence between the factors involved and lose all their cogency and authority if this hypothesis is disallowed; whereas, in ordinary discourse, where we are not blindly manipulating but know all the time what we are doing and what the words mean, we can keep "at the back of our heads" the necessary reserves and qualifications and the adjustments which we shall have to make later on, in a way in which we cannot keep complicated partial differentials "at the back" of several pages of algebra which assume that they all vanish. Too large a proportion of recent "mathematical" economics are mere concoctions, as imprecise as the initial assumptions [axioms] they rest on, which allow the author to lose sight of the complexities and interdependencies of the real world in a maze of pretentious and unhelpful symbols.

Besides being an excellent logician, Keynes was a master expositor and essayist. Accordingly, he developed his general theoretical analysis as an essay in persuasion just at the time when the economics profession was becoming more imbued with the belief that if economics was to be a hard science there was a necessity of presenting economic arguments in terms of formal mathematical models. The generation of young economists in

America coming of age in the 1930s who later became the leaders of the profession in the 1940s and 1950s tended to think primarily in terms of mathematical formalizations. These mathematical-oriented economists had, and their students and followers still have, great difficulties in comprehending the logical analytical foundation of Keynes's *General Theory* essay in persuasion.

Keynes stated that classical theorists who "demonstrated" that instantaneous flexible money wages was the cure for any unemployment were engaged in an "*ignoratio elenchi*" (Keynes, 1936a, p. 259), i.e., of offering a proof irrelevant to the proposition of what caused unemployment in the world in which we lived.[3] Keynes argument was that the classical theorist's "proof" that an economy with flexible wages and prices would automatically find its way to a full-employment equilibrium was not a proof at all; it was merely a reflection of the restrictive axioms that made classical theory only applicable to a "special case" of an unrealistic always fully employed economy.

Keynes (1936a, p. 16) stated that

> The classical economists resemble Euclidean geometers in a non-Euclidean world who, discovering that in experience straight lines apparently parallel often meet, rebuke the lines for not keeping straight – as the only remedy for the unfortunate collisions which are occurring. Yet in truth, there is no remedy except to throw over the axiom of parallels and to work out a non-Euclidean geometry. Something similar is required today in economics. We need to throw over ... postulate[s] of the classical doctrine and to work out the behaviour of a system in which involuntary unemployment in the strict sense is possible.

In developing his general economic theory analog to non-Euclidean geometry, Keynes threw over three restrictive classical axioms to provide an analysis of a money-using, market-oriented entrepreneurial system that could display persistent levels of involuntary unemployment.

II. Axioms and theory building

The best way to evaluate any economic theory is to consider the theorist as a magician. Theorists rarely make logical errors in moving from axioms to conclusions, any more than professional prestidigitators drop the deck of cards while performing a card trick. Today's economic theorists are proficient at creating the illusion of pulling policy conclusion rabbits out of their black hat mathematical model of the economy. The more surprising the policy rabbits pulled from the hat, the greater the audience enjoyment of the economist's performance, and the greater the applause and rewards.[4]

A careful examination of the rabbits that a classical theory economist-magician puts into the hat backstage is required to evaluate the relevance of the policy rabbits pulled from the black hat on stage. The policy rabbits pulled from the classical economists' hat cannot be criticized if the axiomatic rabbits initially being put into the hat have been judged acceptable by the audience. In other words, before accepting the conclusions of any economist's theory as applicable to the world in which we live, the careful student should always examine and be prepared to criticize the applicability of the fundamental axioms of the theory. In the absence of any mistake in logic, the axioms of the theory determine its conclusions. Remember, that the dictionary definition of an axiom is *"a statement universally accepted as true ... a statement that needs no proof because its truth is obvious"*. Consequently, economic theorists do not question the axioms underlying their theory, even though differences in theories are normally due to different underlying axioms.

III. The neutral money axiom

Neutral money was a fundamental axiom of 19th-century classical theory. The neutral money postulate is that changes in the quantity of money in the economy have absolutely no effects on the aggregate level of employment and production in the system. In a neutral money economy, employment and output are determined solely by nonmonetary factors in the economic system. By the early 20th century, this neutrality of money presumption became one of the basic axioms of the prevailing orthodoxy in economics textbooks. Even today, neutral money remains one of the fundamental axioms of modern mainstream economic theory. For those who are trained in classical economic theory, therefore, the neutrality of money is an article of faith, requiring no proof or justification.

For example, in a moment of surprising candor, Professor Oliver Blanchard, a prominent member of the economics faculty of the Massachusetts Institute of Technology and the prestigious National Bureau of Economic Research, has characterized all the macroeconomic models widely used by mainstream economists as follows:

> All the models we have seen impose the neutrality of money as a maintained assumption. This is very much a matter of faith, based on theoretical considerations rather than on empirical evidence.
> (Blanchard, 1990, p. 828)

In other words, even though there is no empirical evidence underlying the fundamental classical presumption of neutral money, all mainstream macroeconomic models, including those used by the Federal Reserve, the Council of Economic Advisors, the National Bureau of Economic Research, etc. are based on the neutral money axiom. This unshakable belief in neutral money is merely the creed (dogma) of mainstream economists that permits them to claim that if governments individually and via international cooperation remove all regulations from markets, i.e., "liberalize all markets", then the national and global economy will achieve its goal of full-employment prosperity. Since this conclusion requires the neutral money axiom as a foundation, mainstream economists are assuming what they pretend to be proving.[5]

In 1933, Keynes explicitly indicated that the "monetary theory of production" he was developing explicitly rejected the classical neutrality of money assumption as applicable in either the short run or the long run. Keynes (1933a, pp. 408–11) wrote:

> An economy which uses money but uses it merely as a *neutral* link between transactions in real things and real assets and does not allow it to enter into motives or decisions, might be called – for want of a better name – a *real-exchange economy*. The theory which I desiderate would deal, in contradistinction to this, with an economy in which money plays a part of its own and affects motives and decisions and is, in short, one of the operative factors in the situation, so that the course of events cannot be predicted either in the long period or in the short, without a knowledge of the behavior of money between the first state and the last. And it is this which we ought to mean when we speak of *a monetary economy*. ... Booms and depressions are peculiar to an economy in which ... money is not neutral. I believe that the next task is to work out in some detail such a monetary theory of production. That is the task on which I am now occupying myself in some confidence that I am not wasting my time.

Here, in Keynes's own words, is his claim that a theory of production for a money-using economy must reject what mainstream economists have always believed is a "universal truth", the neutrality of money. This neutrality axiom had been the foundation of classical economic theory for 125 years before Keynes. No wonder Keynes's *General Theory* was considered heretical by most of his professional colleagues who were wedded to the classical analysis. Keynes was delivering a mortal blow to the very foundation of classical faith. No wonder Keynes's original analysis and the further elaboration and evolution of Keynes's system by Post Keynesian economists in recent decades has not been understood by the majority of economists who, as Professor Blanchard has expressly noted, are ideologically bonded to the classical traditional axiom of neutral money.

Since, by definition, a theory is more general if it requires fewer restrictive axioms than an alternative theory, Keynes's analysis provides a more general theory than classical theory (including general equilibrium theory) since Keynes threw out the neutral money axiom and two other axioms (see *infra*) that are the foundation on which all mainstream economic theories are based. As a matter of logic, however, it is not necessary for those who reject restrictive axioms to justify doing away with them. Rather, the onus is on those who insist on utilizing these additional axioms as part of the foundation of their theory to demonstrate the reasonableness of their additional basic assumptions. It would be extremely difficult for mainstream theorists to justify their use of the neutrality of money axiom. Blanchard's statement that there is no empirical evidence for the neutrality of money should be sufficient to expunge this dogma from economic analysis.

Once the neutrality of money is rejected as a necessary axiomatic building block, then an organizing principle for studying the level of employment and output in a market economy involves: (1) comprehending the role of money as a means of settling contractual obligations and (2) understanding the essential role that liquidity plays in determining the flow of production and employment in the economic system in which we live.

James K. Galbraith has noted that the first three words of the title of Keynes's book *The General Theory of Employment, Interest and Money* (1936) "are evidently cribbed from Albert Einstein" (Galbraith, 1996, p. 14). Einstein's general theory of relativity had displaced Newton's classical theory in physics, which had maintained the separation of time and space. Einstein demonstrated that the time-space continuum is, in essence, the extension of non-Euclidean Riemannian geometry of curved spaces. Keynes hoped to mimic Einstein's revolutionary general theory of relativity and displace the classical economic theory that maintained the separation of market outcomes and the money supply implied by the neutral money axiom. Keynes wanted to replace this axiomatic separation with the equivalent of a market-money curved space continuum, i.e., where money and market outcomes continuously interact.

To accept Keynes's logic and its Post Keynesian development, however, threatens the Panglossian conclusion that, in the long run, all is for the best in this best of all possible worlds where an unfettered market economy assures full employment and prosperity for all those who want to work. Keynes's *General Theory* uses fewer restrictive axioms than classical theory and thereby allows for the possibility that an entrepreneurial system might possess some inherent faults, such as its "failure to provide for full employment" (Keynes, 1936a, p. 372) even in the long run. Keynes's logic is just as antithetical to the classical Social Darwinistic classical economic theory as the view on the origin of human life as asserted by the "scientific theory of evolution" is to the "intelligent design" view of some fundamentalist Christian religions' axiomatic belief in biblical explanation of the creation of human life.

Keynes's general theory suggests that this inability of the entrepreneurial system to provide full employment can be ameliorated by developing corrective fiscal policies and regulatory institutions for stabilizing financial markets via monetary policies. *There can be a permanent role for government to correct systemic economic faults of the entrepreneurial system in which we live,* while preserving the freedom of entrepreneurial decision making and innovation.

In addition to the neutral money axiom, Keynes threw out two additional restrictive classical axioms, namely:

1. *the gross substitution axiom,* and
2. *the ergodic axiom.*

IV. The gross substitution axiom

The axiom of gross substitution asserts that everything is a good substitute for everything else. The existence of gross substitutes means that any change in the relative prices of a specific good and/or service will induce buyers to purchase more of the item(s) that has become relatively cheaper and less of the now more expensive good while spending the same amount of income. For example, if tea and coffee are gross substitutes, when the price of tea rises, people will buy less tea and more coffee. Ubiquitous application of the gross substitution axiom therefore assures that if all market prices are perfectly flexible, then in any market, when at the current market price not all of the items offered on the market are sold, sellers can always sell all of the unsold inventories by merely lowering the market price relative to all other prices. By analogy, it follows that if at any given wage rate there are any unemployed workers, then, given the gross substitution axiom, all workers will be hired only if the market wage rate is reduced.

When all the items offered for sale in a market can be sold at the going market price, the economist says that the market "clears". Full employment occurs when the labor market clears, i.e., when everyone who wants to work at the market wage rate has a job; there is no involuntary unemployment.

Arrow and Hahn (1971, pp. 15, 127, 215, 305) have demonstrated, however, that if gross substitution is removed as an axiom universally applicable to all markets, then all mathematical proofs of the existence of a general equilibrium solution, where all market – including the labor market – clears are jeopardized. In other words, if the axiom of gross substitution is not initially imposed as a foundation of a theory, then the theory cannot demonstrate that all markets (including the labor market) will clear simultaneously even if all prices are instantaneously flexible. In the absence of gross substitution, full employment of all resources cannot be demonstrated to be an automatic and inevitable outcome of a system of freely competitive markets with flexible wages and prices.

As we will explain in chapter 7, Keynes (1936a, ch. 17) rejected the gross substitution axiom in his discussion of liquidity and "the essential properties of interest and money".

V. Uncertainty and the ergodic axiom

What is this ergodic axiom? If one conceives of the path of an economy over time and into the future as governed by what statisticians call a stochastic (probability) process, then the future outcome of any current decision is determined via a probability distribution. Logically speaking to make statistically reliable forecasts about any future economic outcome or event, the decision maker should obtain and analyze sample data from the future to calculate a statistically reliable estimate of the future market value or outcome. Since it is impossible to obtain a sample from the future, the assumption that the economy is determined by an ergodic stochastic process permits the analyst to assert that samples drawn from past and current data are equivalent to drawing a sample from the future. In other words, the ergodic axiom implies that the outcome at any future date is the statistical shadow of past and current market data.

To explain this, "statistical shadow" argument requires us to develop the concept of ergodicity using some technical jargon. A realization of a stochastic process is defined as a sample value of a multidimensiona variable over a period of time, i.e., a single time series of recorded outcomes.

A stochastic process provides a universe of such time series. *Time statistics* refer to statistical averages (e.g., the mean, the standard deviation, etc.) calculated from a singular realization over a period of calendar time *Space statistics*, on the other hand, refer to statistical averages calculated at a fixed point of time and are formed over the universe of realizations i.e., space statistics (e.g., the arithmetic mean or average, the standard deviation, etc.) are calculated from cross-sectional data, that is, data collected from individual participants at a single point of time.

If, and only if, the stochastic process is ergodic, then for an infinitely large realization the time statistics and the space statistics will coincide. For finite realizations of ergodic processes, time and space statistics coincide except for random errors. In other words, calculated time and space statistics tend to converge (with the probability of unity) as the number of observations increase. Consequently, if the ergodic axiom is applicable, statistics calculated from either past time series or cross-sectional data are statistically reliable estimates of the space statistics that will occur at any future date.

The ergodic axiom therefore assures that the outcome associated with any future date can be reliably predicted by a statistical analysis of already-existing data obtained either from time series or cross-sectional data. The future is therefore never uncertain. The future can always be reliably predicted (actuarially known) by a sufficient statistical analysis of already existing data. Future outcomes, in an ergodic system, are probabilistically risky but reliably predictable.

In nonprobabilistic (deterministic) classical economic models, the ordering axiom of classical theory plays the same role as the ergodic axiom. The ordering axiom assumes that at any point of time people "know" all the possible future outcomes of any action taken today and can correctly order these possible outcomes associated with various choices in a list from most preferable to least desirable prospect. In deterministic models, true uncertainty occurs whenever an individual cannot specify and/or order a complete set of prospects regarding the future, either because: (i) the decision maker cannot conceive of a complete list of consequences that will occur in the future; or, (ii) the decision maker cannot assign preferability weights to all consequences because "the evidence is insufficient", so that possible consequences "are not even orderable" (Hicks, 1979, p. 113, 115). In cases of true uncertainty, therefore, neither the ergodic nor the ordering axioms are applicable.

In essence, the ergodic axiom asserts that the future can always be statistically reliably predicted by calculating probabilities from past and present market data, and applying these probabilities to possible future outcomes. In other words, the ergodic axiom presumes that the future outcome of any decision made today can be predicted with a high degree of statistical accuracy. Rejecting the ergodic axiom means that the future is uncertain in the sense that it cannot be reliably predicted by examining existing market data. Or as Nobel Prize winner Sir John Hicks[6] (1977, p. vii) stated, "economic models should be built where people in the model do not know what is going to happen and know they do not know what is going to happen. As in history!"

By contrast, it should be noted that one of the founders of the rational expectations hypothesis and New Classical Economics has noted that, by imputing the ergodic axiom, "Rational expectations ... imputes to the people inside the model much *more* knowledge about the system they are operating in than is available to the economist or econometrician who is using the model to try and understand behavior" (Sargent, 1993, p. 23). In other words, new classical theory assumes people already know more about the future than the economists who are assuming such clairvoyant inhabitants.

Since the terminology of the ergodic axiom was explicitly developed by the Moscow mathematical school of probability, in 1935, and did not become popular in Western Europe and the United States until well after World War II, and Keynes's death, Keynes never knew of this ergodic terminology and hence did not use the expression "ergodic axiom" in his emphasis on the importance of uncertainty and the demand for liquidity in his 1936 book or any other writings. Nevertheless, the idea of the inapplicability of the ergodic axiom to the economic system in which we live is embedded not only in Keynes's writings on uncertainty, but also in his famous criticism of Professor Tinbergen's econometric methodology[7] (Keynes, 1939a, p. 308).

Keynes (1936a, p. 161) wrote that at any point of time, when entrepreneurs consider today's alternative investment opportunities, they recognize that the future is uncertain in the sense that for each investment project, any actuarial estimate of future profits that is a reliable statistical assessment of potential gain, calculated in accordance with existing probabilities, cannot be obtained from any existing data set. Keynes emphasized the difference between his "general theory" and classical orthodoxy, where,

> [f]acts and expectations were assumed to be given in a definite form; and risks ... were supposed to be capable of an exact actuarial computation. The calculus of probability ... was supposed capable of reducing uncertainty to the same calculable state as that of certainty

> itself. ... I accuse the classical economic theory of being itself one of these pretty, polite techniques which tries to deal with the present by abstracting from the fact that we know very little about the future. ... [Every classical economist] has overlooked the precise nature of the difference which his abstraction makes between theory and practice, and the character of the fallacies into which he is likely to be led.
>
> (Keynes, 1938, pp.var 112–5)

Keynes's rejection of the ergodic axiom meant that realistic theories cannot demonstrate that unregulated financial markets can optimally allocate investment funds into those projects that in the future will earn the greatest returns. In nonergodic circumstances it can be demonstrated that the primary function of financial markets is to provide liquidity and not to optimally allocate capital as classical theory contends.

In the following chapters, we will explain how Keynes's emphasis on uncertainty (nonergodic circumstances) led him to argue that a decision of income recipients not to spend a portion of their current income on the products of industry (i.e., to save) then required savers to make a second decision regarding in what liquid financial market assets these savers would store their savings. These savings and liquidity-preference choice decisions by income recipients, according to Keynes, are not linked in the way classical theory presumed to the decision of entrepreneurs on current investment spending.

In the 19th-century classical theory, the possibility of an uncertain future was ignored by the classical postulate that economic decision makers possessed perfectly reliable foreknowledge of the future. In the early 20th-century classical theory it was assumed that even if decision makers did not possess perfect knowledge about the future, the future could be actuarially predicted based on previous market data. In the New Classical theory that came to prominence in the late 20th century, the ergodic axiom is specifically assumed as a necessary condition for agents to form rational expectations about a statistically reliable predictable future. In New Classical theory, it is explicitly asserted that all decision makers in the economic system, by analyzing past and present market prices possess "rational expectations" that are the equivalent of actuarially certain forecasts. For developing this theory of rational expectations, Professor Robert Lucas won the Nobel Prize in Economics in 1995.

The reader may be surprised to learn that although Lucas has admitted that the axioms required for his New Classical analysis are "artificial, abstract, patently unreal"(Lucas, 1981, p. 563), Lucas argues that the unreality of his axioms is a decided advantage for his New Classical theory.

Lucas insists that invoking these artificial and unreal postulates is the *only* scientific method of doing economics for these classical axioms that permit the development of logical conclusions that are independent of real world political and economic institutions. The resulting immutable and infallible economic "laws" developed by classical theory, Lucas alleges, are the social science equivalent of the unchanging scientific principles established by the "hard" sciences.[8] Lucas's designation of what is the only scientific approach to economics means that Keynes's rejection of some classical axioms can be dismissed as "unscientific" and not worthy of serious study.[9] Lucas (1977, p. 15) stated that "in conditions of uncertainty, economic reasoning will be of no value". No wonder Keynes's analytical system is currently ignored in mainstream academic papers and textbooks.

When the three restrictive classical axioms of neutral money, gross substitution, and ergodicity are removed from the classical theorist's black hat economic theory, then the classical theorist-magician can no longer pull the rabbit of flexible wages and prices out of the hat to demonstrate that liberalizing labor and product markets produce the price flexibility that is *the* cure for unemployment.

In the following chapters we shall explain specifically how these overthrown classical axioms produce important differences between classical theory and Keynes's *General Theory*. We will also indicate why the use of the three aforementioned axioms by classical theory produces characteristics that have no analog in the world of experience, while Keynes's analysis produces an economic system which matches everyday life experiences.

VI. Aborting Keynes's revolutionary analysis

In *The General Theory* Keynes did not specifically name the three restrictive classical axioms that were equivalent to the Euclidean axiom of parallels that his analysis of a general theory of employment, interest, and money required be overthrown. Primarily this was because, in 1936, the rigorous axiomatic foundations of classical theory had not been fully and explicitly specified and consequently could not be quickly identified by Keynes. It is not surprising, therefore, that at that time many readers of *The General Theory* were not clear either as to what were the specific classical axioms Keynes rejected in developing his "nonEuclidean" general economic theory, or why Keynes rejected these particular classical axioms. Of course, as the earlier quote demonstrated, Keynes did specifically state that in his new "monetary theory of production" the neutral money axiom was not applicable to the operation of a monetary, entrepreneurial economy in either the short run or the long run. Still the gross substitution axiom and the ergodic axiom are not explicitly identified in *The General Theory* as axioms to be rejected in Keynes's general theory.

Many of the cleverest young economists who were entering the economics profession in the United States and England in the 1930s (e.g., Paul Samuelson, James Tobin, J.R. Hicks, James Meade) recognized that the unemployment problem was too deep and persistent to be sloughed off as merely a temporary aberration or friction that a self-adjusting market could cure in the long run. Common sense told them that the invisible hand might not be able to resurrect a prosperous economy over any reasonable period of calendar time. These "young Turks" were too impatient to wait for the long-run revival that was promised by classical theory.

Yet these young economists of the 1930s had been trained in the classical economics tradition. Consequently, their heads were "already so filled with contrary notions" that they could "not catch the clues" to his thought that Keynes's was throwing to them. They did not find Keynes's essay in persuasion an easy one to understand as to why we needed to throw out some classical axioms. As classically trained economists, these "young Turks" were unwilling to dispense with any of the implicit fundamental axioms required by the classical theory of demand. Moreover, as we shall see in chapter 12, political forces in the United States after World War II made the retention of these classical axioms a necessary prerequisite for sales of economics textbooks and retention of academic appointments.

For those disciplined to believe in the beneficence of the invisible hand, all classical axioms are, by definition, universal truths. After working so hard to earn a Ph.D. in economics and earn the respect of their classical theory professors that was necessary to obtain a tenured academic appointment in an economics department of a prestigious university, it would be a Herculean task for these young economists of the 1930s and 1940s to question what one had been trained to believe in as self-evident verities. The economists of this generation were unwilling, or unable, to free their formal models of these classical restrictive axioms underlying demand conditions. Their minds were so filled with "Euclidean" classical theory notions that they could not catch the "non-Euclidean" analytical insights that Keynes was throwing at them.

Instead, this younger generation of professional economists tried to translate Keynes's conclusions into formalizations of the evolving mathematical classical theory that was coming into vogue during this period as a result of the work of Hicks, Meade, Samuelson, Debreu and others. Unable to decipher Keynes's "NonEuclidean" message, they tried to develop his unemployment results by introducing *ad hoc* supply constraints (e.g., the fixed money wages and fixprice models) to the classical theory upon which they had been brought up.

Today, most economists are even more rigorously trained in the mathematical formalisms where the restrictive classical axioms are buried beneath the debris of a mountain of mathematical formulations. Consequently, most of today's mainstream economists are not even aware of the axioms of classical analysis that they are wedded to when developing interpretations of their complex mathematical models. Nevertheless, today's conventional macroeconomic models that are used to justify "independent" central bank policy decisions and fiscally conservative governmental economic policy decisions are still founded on the three classical axioms that Keynes overthrew. The resulting policy implications of these mathematical models in use today are, as Keynes noted, "misleading and dangerous" if applied to the real world in which we live, especially in the globalized economy of the 21st century. A result of applying the highly formal mathematical version of classical theory to policy decisions has been stagnation or slow growth of economies in most of the developed nations of the world, especially in the European Union, where the European Central Bank model assumes that all unemployment tends to be frictional.

5
The Conceptual Difference between Keynes's General Theory and Classical Theory – Savings and Liquidity

I. What is a classic book?

A sage once said that the definition of a "classic" is a book that everyone cites but no one reads. Since it was published in 1936, John Maynard Keynes's book *The General Theory of Employment, Interest and Money* is a classic in the sense that economics professors at some of the most prestigious universities, particularly in the United States, have not read Keynes's book. In fact, ever since World War II, in highly regarded universities' economics departments, students are told that *The General Theory of Employment, Interest and Money* is so obscure and confusing that they need not (and should not) read it. For example, a founder of the so-called New Keynesian theory, Harvard Professor N. Greg Mankiw (1992, p. 561) has written that

> The *General Theory* is an obscure book ... [it] is an outdated book. ... We are in a much better position than Keynes was to figure out how the economy works. ... Few macro economists take such a dim view of classical economics [as Keynes did] ... Classical economics is right in the long run. Moreover, economists today are more interested in the long-run equilibrium. ... [There is] widespread acceptance of classical economics.

For more than 70 years, students of economics at these respected universities have been taught something which these learned professors call "Keynesian" economics although it has no connection with Keynes's revolutionary analysis. As already noted, Keynes's biographer, Skidelsky (1992, p. 512) recognized the disconnect between what is called the Keynesian theory at most universities and Keynes's *General Theory* when he wrote that "mainstream economists after World War II treated Keynes's theory as a 'special case' of the classical theory, applicable to conditions where money wages ... were 'sticky'. Thus his [Keynes's] theory was robbed of its theoretical bite, while allowed to retain its relevance for policy". In the following chapters we will try to restore the "theoretical bite" of Keynes's analysis as public information.

If, in 1936, Keynes was merely arguing that unemployment was the result of price and wage rigidities, as mainstream Keynesian economists have claimed (and still do), then Keynes was not providing a revolutionary theory for analyzing the major macroeconomic problems that plague modern market-oriented, money-using economies. Even in the 19th century, classical economists had argued that the lack of flexible wages and prices was *the* cause of unemployment. It is, therefore, incomprehensible that anyone could claim Keynes's general theory was revolutionary if its teaching was merely to reiterate that rigidities in wages and /or prices cause persistent unemployment in the world in which we live.

In *The General Theory* Keynes explicitly denied that the fundamental cause of unemployment is the existence of wage and/or price rigidities. Keynes (1936a, p. 257) wrote: "the Classical Theory has been accustomed to rest the supposedly self-adjusting character of the economic system on an assumed fluidity of money wages; and when there is a rigidity, to lay on this rigidity the blame of maladjustment [i.e., unemployment]. ... My difference from this theory is primarily a difference of analysis."

Even more directly in his published response to Dunlop and Tarshis, Keynes (1939b) had already responded in the negative to this question of whether his analysis of underemployment equilibrium required imperfect competition, administered prices, and/or rigid wages. Dunlop and Tarshis had argued that the purely competitive model was not empirically justified, therefore it were monopolistic and administered pricing and wage fixities that was the basis of Keynes's unemployment equilibrium. Keynes reply was simply: "I complain a little that I in particular should be criticised for conceding a little to the other view" (Keynes, 1939b, p. 411). In chapters 17–19 of his *General Theory*, Keynes explicitly demonstrated that even if a competitive economy with perfectly flexible money wages and prices existed ("conceding a little to the other view"), there was no automatic market mechanism that could restore the full-employment level of effective demand. In other words, Keynes's general theory could show that, as a matter of logic, less than full-employment equilibrium could exist in a purely competitive economy with freely flexible wages and prices.

Given these clear statements by Keynes that his explanation of unemployment does not require any wage (or price) rigidities, it should be obvious that those mainstream economists who today call themselves "Keynesians" – and yet attribute unemployment to wage, price, or interest-rate stickiness – must think of Keynes's *General Theory* as a literary classic that they can cite to justify their arguments without bothering to read or understand.

Instead, students are educated to believe that the hi-tech mathematical model known as the Walras-Arrow-Debreu general equilibrium system is the basic general theory for providing an explanation of how our economic system functions. This general equilibrium analysis teaches students that the cause of unemployment is supply-side price imperfections (rigidities), especially in the labor market of the last half a century, where the "welfare" state has coddled workers.

In contrast to this general equilibrium view, we will explain why Keynes's analysis demonstrated that price and/or wage rigidities, or even a sticky minimum rate of interest,[1] are neither necessary nor sufficient conditions for explaining the existence of persistent unemployment in a money-using, market-oriented, entrepreneurial economy. Rather, the cause of unemployment is nested in the peculiar properties possessed by money and other liquid assets and the desire of people to save income in the form of these liquid assets. To understand the difference between Keynes and mainstream economic theory we begin with a discussion of a fundamental aspect of classical theory, Say's Law. For, as Keynes argued, all of classical theory is based on the assumed validity of Say's Law (Skidelsky, 1992, p. 511).

II. Say's Law

The 19th-century economic proposition known as Say's Law is the foundation of the classical argument that a competitive market with flexible wages and prices is the mechanism that ensures that market forces will inevitably bring the economy to a situation where all available resources are fully employed. Say's Law evolved from the writings of a French economist, Jean Baptiste Say, who in 1803 stated that "products always exchange for products". In 1808, the English economist James Mill translated Say's French language dictum as "supply creates its own demand". Mill's phraseology has since been established in economics as Say's Law.

A simple illustration of Say's Law is as follows:

The sole explanation of why people produce, that is, work to supply things to the market, is to earn income. Working and engaging in income-earning productive activities is presumed to be disagreeable. On the other hand, people obtain pleasure (utility) solely from the purchase and consumption of producible goods and services. People, therefore, will be willing to work only if they can earn sufficient income for each unit of work effort to buy enough products of industry to provide the buyers sufficient pleasure to more than offset the unpleasantness of their income-earning efforts.

In other words, all income-earning workers would not be maximizing their individual economic welfare if they engaged in the disagreeable act of contributing to the production process in order to earn income if these income earners did not intend to spend every penny that they earned on pleasure yielding goods and services produced by industry. Say's Law presumes that if people have their own self-interest in mind and wish to maximize the utility or happiness they obtain from their economic endeavors, then all income earned in the market from the production and sales of goods and services will be spent to buy (demand) things produced by industry. There is never a lack of effective demand for all the products that an economy can produce when it fully employs its resources.

Keynes (1936a, p. 26) declared that Say's Law "is not the true law relating the aggregate demand [for goods and services] and supply [of produced goods and services] functions. If, however, this is not the true law, there is a vitally important chapter of economic theory that remains to be written and without which all discussions concerning the volume of aggregate employment are futile".

With this declaration that the Say's Law homily that everything supplied in an economy creates its own demand was not a "true law", Keynes threw down the gauntlet to classical economists. Keynes was arguing that the Say's Law basis of classical theory is not applicable to the economic world of experience. Instead, Keynes suggested that he would provide the vitally important chapter of a general theory of employment where an increase in supply (produced by industry) did not create automatically an equivalent increase in demand for the products of industry.

Keynes's argument was that if one accepted the fundamental axioms underlying classical theory, then Say's Law was not formally (logically) wrong. Indeed Say's Law is a logically consistent "special case" that could be obtained from Keynes's *General Theory* by adding the three restrictive axioms: (1) the neutral money axiom, (2) the gross substitution axiom, and (3) the ergodic axiom. These three classical theory axioms, however, are not applicable to a monetary economy where entrepreneurs organize the production process. Consequently, Say's Law was not applicable to an entrepreneurial economy, and therefore classical theory is a special case whose "teaching is misleading and disastrous if we attempt to apply it to the facts of experience" (Keynes, 1936a, p. 3).

One example of a misleading and potentially socially disastrous teaching of classical theory involves government regulation of the workplace environment and conditions of employment. Since classical theory teaches us that unregulated competitive markets promote efficiency and prosperity, it logically follows that legislation to set minimum wages, and to promote occupational safety rules, and to restrict the use of child labor interferes with normal market forces and thereby prevent the economy from achieving a prosperous and efficient full-employment equilibrium. If, therefore, classical theory was applicable to our economic system, then good economic policy should advocate the repeal of all such legislation. Surely, the reader would find the repeal of such regulatory labor market legislation to be of doubtful desirability if not calamitous to the establishment of a civilized economic society.

In *The General Theory* (1936a), Keynes set himself the task to explain why supply did not create its own demand even in a hypothetical, purely competitive economy with instantaneously flexible wages and prices of the products of industry. Keynes, therefore, had to explain why utility-maximizing households would engage in the unpleasant activity of working or otherwise contributing to the production process to earn income, if they planned to save a portion of their income, where Keynes defined savings as refraining from spending all of one's hard earned current income on utility-providing producible goods.

In developing his general theory analysis, it became obvious to Keynes that the classical concept of savings was a vague notion that often meant different things in different contexts. Under the influence of G. E. Moore's *Principia Ethica*, Keynes realized that to understand the unemployment problem it was necessary to develop a precise taxonomy regarding classes of expenditure and savings. By developing a new classification system Keynes could ask exacting questions to explain why Say's Law was a special case whose teachings would be calamitous if made the foundation of economic policies.

Nevertheless, to communicate and convince his classical theory-oriented professional colleagues, Keynes tried to salvage as much of the tools of classical economic theory as possible. To understand the basis of Keynes's argument against the applicability of Say's Law, therefore, we must introduce a bit of economist jargon and technical tools.

When Keynes was an undergraduate, the discipline of economics at Cambridge University was dominated by the great economist Alfred Marshall (Harrod, 1951, p. 142). In his *Principles of Economics* (1890), Marshall developed an analytical framework that divided all economic forces operating in the marketplace into two categories: demand and supply. Marshall's supply and demand functions were specifically constructed to capture the different factors affecting seller and buyer behavior in individual markets. Marshall's demand function related to the quantity of a specific good that buyers would be willing to purchase at alternative market prices. Marshall's supply function related to the quantity of goods that profit-maximizing sellers would be willing to produce and sell at alternative market prices. In equilibrium, the market price and sales (equal to purchases) would be established at the intersection of these Marshallian demand and supply functions, i.e., where the quantity demanded at a given market price just equaled the quantity supplied at that market price.

In his *The General Theory of Employment, Interest and Money* (1936a), Keynes attempted to utilize these Marshallian micro-demand and supply function concepts to develop (for the total economy) an aggregate supply function and an aggregate demand function. Keynes called the intersection of these aggregate demand and supply functions as the point of effective demand.[2] This effective demand point, Keynes argued, was the aggregate equivalent of Marshall's micro-equilibrium solution. The point of effective demand indicated the equilibrium level of aggregate employment and output where buyers would purchase just enough output from business enterprises at profitable prices to justify hiring the specific number of workers necessary to produce the volume of output being purchased.

It was Keynes's contention that in a monetary economy, this point of effective demand need not coincide with the full employment of all workers in the economy. If the point of effective demand was at less than full employment, then even if the existence of flexible wages and prices was built in to the aggregate supply function, Keynes argued, the point of effective demand would not move toward the full-employment level unless the wage and price (supply) flexibility automatically generated additional market demands to be added onto the initial aggregate demand function. Consequently, Keynes argued it was the analysis of the components of an independent aggregate demand function that had been ignored by classical theorists in their belief that aggregate supply automatically creates an equivalent amount of aggregate demand. Consequently, Keynes believed that the aggregate demand function required further study after one has developed the aggregate supply function that displays the relationship between entrepreneurial expectations of sales and the employment they will offer workers.

III. The aggregate supply function

Keynes's (1936a, pp. 44–5) aggregate supply function relates the aggregate number of workers (*N*) that profit-maximizing entrepreneurs would want to hire for all possible alternative levels of expected aggregate sales proceeds (*Z*), given the money wage rate, technology, and the average degree of competition (or monopoly) in the economy (cf. Keynes, 1936a, p. 245). Each point on an aggregate supply function indicated the total sales proceeds that profit-maximizing entrepreneurs would expect to receive to be sufficiently profitable to justify a given level of employment hiring. Obviously, if, at any point of time, entrepreneurs decided to hire additional workers, then entrepreneurs must expect buyers to be willing to spend sufficient additional sums of money to make it profitable for entrepreneurs to expand production. In other words, aggregate supply or expected sales receipts (*Z*) is an increasing function of employment (*N*).

Keynes did not believe this aggregate supply concept was new or novel. In a letter to D. H. Robertson, Keynes (1935b, p. 513) indicated that his aggregate supply function was "simply the age-old supply function" and that this aggregate supply function could be readily derived from ordinary Marshallian micro-supply functions (Keynes, 1936a, pp. 44–5). Hence, the properties of this aggregate supply function "involved few considerations which are not already familiar" (Keynes, 1936a, p. 89). Keynes briefly described the aggregate supply function (1936, pp. 25, 44–5) and its inverse, the employment function (1936a, pp. 89, 280–1). (The technical derivation of the aggregate supply function from Marshall's micro-supply analysis of business firm behavior is given in the appendix to chapter 6.)

IV. The aggregate demand function

The bulk of *The General Theory* is devoted to developing the distinctive components of the aggregate demand function. The components of the aggregate demand function have some distinguishing characteristics and properties that are not identical with those associated with the aggregate supply function. One cannot, therefore, be assured that supply will always create its own demand.

If, on the other hand, Say's Law was true and applicable so that aggregate supply always created its own demand at each and every level of employment, then the aggregate demand function would have the same value as the value of aggregate supply function at each level of employment, i.e., the aggregate supply function and the aggregate demand function would be identical for all possible levels of employment (Keynes, 1936a, pp. 25–6). But, Keynes (1936a, p. 21) warned that this assumption of equality of aggregate demand and supply at all possible employment levels was necessary to support traditional claims regarding the economy reaching a full-employment equilibrium and "the unqualified advantages of *laissez-faire* in respect of foreign trade and much else we shall have to question".

Keynes's revolutionary analysis therefore stems from his belief that, in a monetary economy, the aggregate demand function differed from, and was *not* coincident with, the aggregate supply function over all levels of possible employment. Consequently, the aggregate demand function had to be analyzed as a function independent of the characteristics and properties of the classical aggregate supply function.

Let us illustrate this view by utilizing chapter 4's analogy of theorists as the equivalent of professional magicians. The backstage rabbits that are put in the hat of classical theory model builders represent the presumption that the only source of utility is producible goods. Accordingly, in the black hat of classical theory's utility maximizing decision makers, all income earned will be immediately spent only on producible goods. If it is assumed that only the products of industry provide utility to income earners, and this utility-maximizing behavior "rabbit" is unquestioningly accepted as *the* microfoundation of aggregate demand, then the aggregation of all market micro-demands (for producibles) must always be equal to all income earned and spent on the products of industry.

Why would any utility maximizer engage in the unpleasant task of working to earn income, if all of his/her income was not to be spent on the only things that are assumed to provide utility, namely, the products of industry? Keynes's answer was that, in our world, the purchase of certain nonproducible things could also provide utility. We shall explain what nonproducible things Keynes was referring to *infra*. In classical theory, however, only producibles provide utility. Consequently, classical theory argues that any additional supply of the products of industry must increase people's income *pari passu*, and therefore every increase in supply must create an exact equivalent additional total demand for the products of industry[3] by utility-maximizing buyers. Classical economic theory must assume that the aggregate supply and demand functions are identical and that Say's Law prevails.

However, as Keynes claimed, if Say's Law is not applicable to the real world, then "it was the part played by the aggregate demand function which has been overlooked" (Keynes, 1936a, p. 89) by classical theorists in their acceptance of the rabbit that only producible goods provide utility for income earners. Keynes's aggregate demand function (*D*) indicates what the total of all buyers of the products of industry plan to spend on producibles at every alternative possible level of employment (*N*). Most importantly, Keynes's analysis indicates that income earners "know" that they do not know what will happen in the future (cf. Hicks, 1977, p. vii). If income recipients fear the possibility of adverse conditions in the uncertain future, then income recipients can obtain utility by saving a portion of their income – where by "savings" Keynes meant spending a portion of their income on the purchase of money and other liquid assets. These liquid assets, though *not* the products of industry, provide the utility of security for income earners in that with sufficient liquidity they can meet any unforeseen substantial contractual obligations in the uncertain future.

It is in the discussion of aggregate demand and its components that Keynes's taxonomy differs significantly from the classical view of spending and saving out of income. In the classical view, the only reason an income earner would save a portion of today's income is because he/she knows *with certainty* that he/she will want to purchase some specific producibles at a specific price and at a specific future date. And at that future date, today's saver knows that he/she will not have sufficient income on that specific date to make all of their planned purchases. In other words, classical theory claimed that utility-maximizing income earners saved only to fill in the periods where their known income receipts would be less than their "known" future consumption expenditure plans. In the long run, the total income earned by a household would be entirely spent on the products of industry.

Let us illustrate this point with an overly simple, and ridiculous, example, but an example that is implicit in classical theory's analysis of savings. Assume someone who earns $1000 per week plans to take on additional future spending, such as a one week's skiing vacation (beginning on the second Sunday next February). Assume that the income earner knows that the cost of this one-week vacation next February will be exactly $2000. The classical economist would argue that this vacation-desirous household would forgo some consumption spending each week, perhaps savings $100 out of each week's

$1000 of income for a period of 20 weeks before the skiing trip in February. In essence, the saver would merely be substituting additional consumption-demand of $2000 for the week beginning the second Sunday in February for the forgone consumption-demand of $100 a week for the 20 weeks leading up to the vacation period.

In classical theory, the saver would, via the loan market, lend his weekly savings out during the weeks before the vacation. The borrower of the saver's funds could be a hotel owner (perhaps one with a rental ski shop on the premises) who by studying past market data would "know" in advance that this vacationer's demand for hotel rooms, skis, meals, etc. for a week beginning the second Sunday in February would be in addition to the normal demand for facilities at his hotel in the second week of February. The hotel owner could use the borrowed funds to invest additional resources and facilities, to meet the additional demand for ski vacations next February.

Accordingly, classical theory argues the $1000 income earned each week by the ski vacation planner during the 20 weeks before the February vacation would be spent as follows: (1) by the income-earning vacation planner, $900 worth of consumption goods per week and $100 savings, while (2) the $100 per week savings would be borrowed and spent by the hotel owner on investment in additional facilities. Consequently, in this over-simplified example even the weekly planned savings of the vacationer would automatically be spent each week by the investing entrepreneur on producibles necessary for building up additional resources for his hotel. All income earned each week would be spent on producibles each week, while over 21 weeks the vacationer would spend all his income for the 21 weeks (including the savings of the previous 20 weeks). Thus even while the skier was saving out of each week's income, in this hypothesized classical theory world, the hotel owner was spending in excess of his income each week before the second Sunday in February to make sure he had sufficient facilities available on that February week when the skier would spend his savings to buy things from the hotel owner.

By contrast, Keynes (1936a, p. 210) argued, "An act of individual saving means – so to speak – a decision not to have dinner today. But it does *not* necessitate a decision to have a dinner or to buy a pair of boots a week or a year hence or to consume any specified thing at any specified date. Thus, it depresses the business of preparing today's dinner without stimulating the business of making ready for some future act of consumption. It is not a substitution of future consumption-demand for present consumption-demand – it is a net diminution of such demand".

Keynes rejected the classical concept of saving out of income where the saver knows precisely at what future dates consumption plans will exceed income, and so additional purchasing power (obtained by spending past savings at the future date) will be needed to complete specific future purchase plans. Instead, Keynes argued savings occurred because the future was uncertain and the saver wanted to protect himself/herself from being unable to meet unforeseen needed future purchases (or other contractual commitments) if either his income should decline and/or his consumption need should suddenly be in excess of his incoming income. Or as it is often said in the vernacular, income earners are putting away some of today's income in the form of savings for the proverbial uncertain future rainy day.

Keynes defined the decision to save out of income merely as a decision *not* to spend today's income on today's products of industry. In Keynes's taxonomic system, the decision to save is not a simultaneous decision to order a specific producible good or service at a specific future date. The next question then became, "If a household saved by not consuming all of current income on today's products of industry, what did the household do with this fund of savings?"

To respond to this query, Keynes defined a two-stage spending decision-making process for those who save out of current income (see Figure 5.1). At the first stage the income earner decides how much of current income will be spent *today* on produced goods and how much of current income will *not* be spent on currently produced goods and services, i.e., how much of current income will be saved. Classical economists call this first stage of the spending decision process the *time preference decision,* for today's savings supposedly reflect how much consumers *prefer* to substitute spending on specific producible goods at a specific future *time* (date) rather than spend today's savings on today's products of industry.

Keynes theory differed from the classical theory with regard to the motivation for savings. In order to highlight this difference, Keynes called this first stage of the spending decision process, which involved deciding what proportion of current income to spend immediately on newly produced consumer goods, the *propensity to consume* rather than the time preference decision. This propensity to consume labeling does not infer any desire to necessarily spend today's savings on any producible goods and services at any specific date in the future. In Keynes's taxonomic view of this consumption-savings decision process, he who hesitates (to spend today) saves and can therefore make a decision to buy goods or services at any other (unspecified) future day. Accordingly, Keynes's propensity to

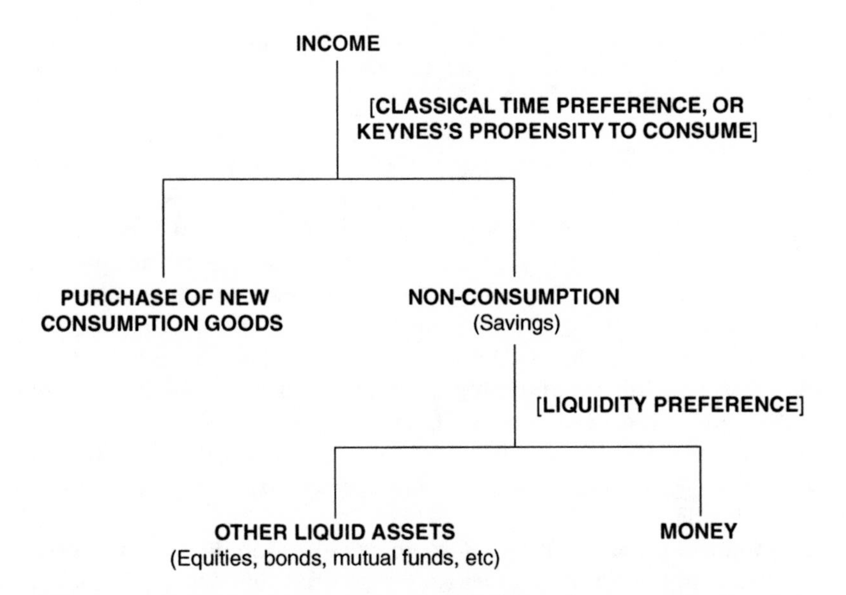

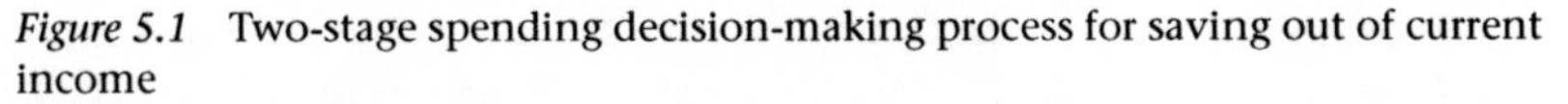
Figure 5.1 Two-stage spending decision-making process for saving out of current income

consume dichotomization of income earned into consumption purchases of producible goods versus savings via liquid assets provides a stark contrast to classical theory's view of this spending-saving decision process, which merely reflects a specified exact time preference for spending all income on the products of industry by income earners committing their current saving to specific consumption purchases at specific future dates.

In Keynes's analysis, once the propensity to consume decision is made to save a portion of current income, savers are required to make a second decision – the *liquidity preference* decision. To carry their saved (unused) spending power of current income forward in time, savers have to decide on one or more vehicles (time machines) for moving this unspent purchasing power into the indefinite future. If the future is uncertain and cannot be reliably predicted, then savers can never be sure when, if ever, they shall want to utilize the spending power of these savings to make purchases at any future specific date(s). Consequently, savers will look for time machines to transport the spending power of their savings to the future. In order to minimize the real cost of utilizing these time machines, these savings vehicles must be durables that exist for a considerable length of time without deterioration. These durables will require a zero or minimum carrying cost (e.g., maintenance, repair, insurance, and warehousing costs) for the period of time that these savings are held and not spent.

In a monetary economy, we should recognize that "goods sell for money and money sells for goods, but goods do not sell for goods" (Clower, 1967, pp. 208–9). Consequently, if a saver decides to use his/her savings to purchase some products of industry at some future date, and if the saver has not stored his/her saving in the form of money, then at some future date the saver will have to sell his/her time machine vehicle for money in order to finance the purchase of the producible good at that future date. Thus, savers will search for time machines that incur a minimum not only of carrying costs but also of transactions costs, the costs of buying the time vehicles and later reselling these time machines when they are, if ever, sold to obtain money to be used in a specific future goods purchase or other contractual obligation settlement.

In sum, in a money-using, entrepreneurial economic system, savers will use as liquid time machines (to transfer the contractual settlement power of their current savings to the indefinite future) only those things that have small or negligible carrying costs *and* small or negligible transactions costs of buying and reselling. *Liquid assets* can be defined as durable assets that have minimal carrying costs and that can be readily resold for money (liquidated) while incurring small or negligible transactions costs for purchase and resale.

Consequently, in an economic environment where income earners "know" that they cannot reliably predict the future, then in that first-stage spending-saving decision process that Keynes called the propensity to consume, people decide on how much of current income is to be spent on consumer goods and how much is to be saved, i.e., not to be spent today on producible goods. In the second stage of the decision process – the liquidity preference decision – savers decide how to allocate their savings among alternative liquid assets that are available to them as vehicles for storing and moving savings to the future.

Anything that is, by definition, durable, can be carried into the future. Durable real assets such as plant and equipment, consumer durables, etc., however, have very high carrying costs. Moreover, although the transactions costs of purchasing new real durables may, or may not, be very large, the costs of reselling these durables at future dates can be very large, if these durables can be sold at all in second-hand markets. Durable goods that cannot be readily resold are called *illiquid assets*. Most real durable products of industry are illiquid assets and therefore are not useful time machines for moving saved purchasing power into the indefinite future. Accordingly, given Keynes's definition of savings, illiquid assets, including producible durables (e.g., investment goods) are not vehicles used to move savings to the future.

In an economy with a developed financial system, there are many possible time machine vehicles available to savers where both the transactions and carrying costs of holding are relatively small or negligible. Liquid financial assets such as money, equities traded on organized security markets, negotiable bonds, shares of mutual funds, etc., are among the most obvious time machines. Keynes's liquidity preference decision stage indicates that each saver will decide how to allocate unspent income (savings) among alternative *time machines* (liquid stores of value) that can transport generalized purchasing power from today to the indefinite future.

Keynes developed this theory of liquidity preference late in his evolving general theory analysis when he recognized that to explain the existence of involuntary unemployment required specifying "The [Two] Essential Properties of Interest and Money" (Keynes, 1936a, ch. 17). These "essential properties" clearly differentiate Keynes's general theory from classical theory. Keynes (1936a, pp. 230–3) specified these essential properties as

1. the elasticity of production associated with all liquid assets including money is zero or negligible,[4] and
2. the elasticity of substitution between liquid assets (including money) and reproducible goods is zero or negligible.[5]

The zero elasticity of production means that when some portion of income is "saved", these savings will be used to purchase things that are not producible by the use of labor in the private sector, especially since durable producibles are typically associated with large carrying and transactions costs.

What is the implication for employment of the availability of liquid assets with these essential elasticity properties? The following hypothetical example may help the reader to understand the importance of these essential properties. Suppose a significant number of people suddenly decided to buy fewer space vehicles (automobiles) and use this unspent income (savings) to buy additional time vehicles (liquid assets) instead. As a result, sales, and therefore employment, in the automobile industry would decline, while, all other things being equal, there would be no increase in private sector employment to produce additional time vehicles (liquid assets).

A zero elasticity of production means that *money* (or any other liquid asset) *does not grow on trees*. Consequently, private sector entrepreneurs cannot employ workers to pluck more money from the money trees whenever the demand for money (liquidity) increases as aggregate savings occur. Or as Keynes wrote: "money ... cannot be readily reproduced; labour cannot be turned on at will by entrepreneurs to produce money in increasing quantities as its price rises" (Keynes, 1936a, p. 230).

In other words, current resources are never used (employed, consumed) to satisfy this liquidity demand by savers reducing their demand for producibles. In Keynes's lexicon, in a money-using entrepreneurial economy, a decision to save out of current income involves a decision to save in the form of nonproducible money or other liquid assets. Given the zero elasticity of production of money and all other liquid assets, a decision to save out of current income implies a reduced demand for the products of industry while liquid assets have a zero elasticity of production, and so saving does not create a demand for more workers to be hired to produce additional money or other liquid assets. Contrary to Benjamin Franklin's adage, a penny saved is a penny not earned.

All other things being equal, any reallocation away from the spending on the products of industry toward increasing one's savings increases the demand for liquid assets, but workers cannot be hired in the private sector to produce more liquid assets in response to the hypothesized increase in demand. In a money-using economy, the decision to save a portion of one's income in terms of nonproducible liquid time machines (financial assets) involves what Hahn (1977, p. 39) has labeled "a non-employment inducing demand" – a type of demand that is incompatible with Say's Law.

But why was it necessary for Keynes to identify a second essential property of money and all other liquid assets, namely that the elasticity of substitution between liquid assets and producible goods is zero or negligible? When savings out of current income occur, the demand for liquid assets increases. If liquid assets are nonproducibles, then their supply cannot increase, and hence the price of liquid assets must rise with any increase in demand for liquid assets. If the durable products of industry were good substitutes (had a high elasticity of substitution) for liquid assets as a store of value, then the rising price of liquid assets would reallocate the demand for liquidity toward producibles, and therefore employment would increase in the industries producing substitutes for liquid assets. But as we have already noted, the high transactions and carrying costs mean that durable producibles can never be a good substitute for liquid assets as liquidity time machines, hence, the zero elasticity of substitution.

This zero elasticity of substitution between liquid assets, which savers use as time machines, and reproducible durables ensures that that portion of income that is not spent on by the products of industry, i.e., savings, will find, in Hahn's (1977, p. 31) terminology, "resting places" in the demand for nonproducibles. Some 40 years after Keynes, Hahn rediscovered Keynes's point that a stable involuntary unemployment equilibrium could exist *even in a classical general equilibrium (Walrasian) system with flexible wages and prices* whenever there are "resting places for savings in other than reproducible assets"(Hahn, 1977, p. 31).

Hahn rigorously demonstrated what was logically intuitive to Keynes. Hahn (1977, p. 37) showed that the view that with "flexible money wages there would be no unemployment has no convincing argument to recommend it. ... Even in a pure tatonnement in traditional [classical] models convergence to [a general] equilibrium cannot be generally proved" if savings are held in the form of nonproducibles. Hahn (1977, p. 39) argued that "any non-reproducible asset allows for a choice between employment inducing and non-employment inducing demand". The existence of a demand for money and other liquid nonreproducible assets (that are *not* gross substitutes for the products of the capital goods-producing industries) as a store of "savings" means that all income earned by households engaging in the production of goods is not, in the short or the long run, necessarily spent on the products of industry. Households who want to store that portion of their income that they do not consume (i.e., that they do not spend on the products of industry) in the form of liquid assets are choosing, in Hahn's words, "a non-employment inducing demand" for their savings.

Just as in non-Euclidean geometry, lines that are apparently parallel often crash into each other, in the Keynes/Post Keynesian non-Euclidean economic world, an increased demand for "savings" even if it raises the relative price of nonproducibles, will not spill over automatically into a demand for producible goods. Consequently when households save a portion of their income they have made a choice for "non-employment inducing demand" that is incompatible with Say's Law.

Keynes (1936a, p. 241) argued that the "attribute of 'liquidity' is by no means independent of these two [elasticity] characteristics". Thus, as long as wealth owners demand any liquid asset that has "low elasticities of production and substitution and low carrying costs"(Keynes, 1936a, p. 238) as a resting place (store of value) for their savings out of current income, then (involuntary) unemployment equilibrium is possible even in the long run. In a money-using, entrepreneurial economy, earned income is saved in the form of nonproducible financial assets rather than spent on the products of industry.

Classical theory, on the other hand, assumes that *only* producible goods and services provide utility. Why then would any rational human being engage in unpleasant income-earning activities only to store that portion of their income that they save in the form of nonproducible liquid assets which, classical theorists insist, provide no utility to the saver? In the classical long run of Professor Mankiw, only an irrational lunatic would behave this way and make a fetish over the liquidity of one's portfolio. Yet, in the world of experience, sensible people do store their savings in nonproducibles such as currency, bank deposits, and a plethora of other liquid financial assets traded on well-organized, orderly, financial markets.

In a world where the ergodic axiom is not applicable, people recognize that they do not "know" and cannot know the future in a statistically reliable sense. Decision makers may fear a future that they "know" that they cannot know. It is, therefore, sensible for decision makers to store some portion of their income in money and other nonproducible liquid assets that can be readily converted into money, as long as future liabilities can be expected to be legally discharged by the tendering of money. Sensible behavior of savers implies that they do not use all their earned claims on industry's products and resources today. The more liquid the asset used to store savings today, the more readily it can be used another day to command resources in the future.

If, as Keats wrote, "A thing of beauty is a joy forever", then one can never have too many of beautiful things. Similarly, if liquidity is a cushion against an uncertain economic future, then in a world of uncertainty, one can never have too much of liquidity. Holding nonproducible liquid assets provides a utility security blanket that can be used to meet unforeseen future contractual commitments. Purchasing illiquid producibles, however, means spending income today for something that cannot be used to meet any future contingencies.

The existence of savings in the form of money and other liquid assets breaks the Say's Law proposition that supply must create its own demand. The reason why savings are stored in these non-employment-inducing demand for liquid assets is, according to Keynes, the recognition by income recipients that the future is uncertain and that one must protect oneself against unforeseen and unforeseeable future contractual commitments and eventualities by storing savings that possess zero or relatively negligible carrying costs and transactions costs.

The existence of money and other liquid assets that have the essential elasticity properties identified by Keynes provides savers with the privilege of not having to spend all their income immediately on goods and services if they do not want to do so. Keynes's analysis will be rendered even more intelligible, when we delve further, in chapter 7, into the role of money and money contracts in our economy. But before engaging in that task we will, in the next chapter, further differentiate Keynes's aggregate demand function from the classical demand function by analyzing the other components of aggregate demand that are completely independent of aggregate supply.

V. A note on Friedman's alternative definition of saving

Using classical theory's association of utility solely with the consumption (or using up) of the products of industry, Nobel Prize winner Milton Friedman developed his *permanent income theory of consumption,* which appears to reach conclusions completely opposite to those of Keynes's general theory. This difference, however, is primarily due to the fact that Friedman uses definitions for consumption and savings that, though they are compatible with those of classical theory, are different from Keynes's definitions – and will, we shall see, strike the reader as very peculiar and in conflict with usual meanings.

In Friedman's lexicon, income received today is divided into two components: transitory (or windfall) income and permanent income. Transitory income is associated with one-shot, non-repeatable changes in current income, e.g., winning the lottery, or receiving a one-time bonus at work. Permanent income is defined by Friedman in terms of long-term income (utility) flows that every forward-looking consumer can expect to receive each future period throughout his/her life. Friedman argued that any change in permanent income would primarily affect one's consumption purchases in every period of the remainder of one's life, while changes in transitory income would have little or no effect on consumption, but instead would be almost entirely saved. Technically, this implies that the marginal propensity to consume out of permanent income is close, if not exactly equal, to unity. The marginal propensity to consume out of temporary income, on the other hand, is approximately zero, as all transitory income increments are saved. Based on these definitions of income, consumption, and savings, Friedman developed empirical evidence that he claims supports his permanent income hypothesis, but these "facts" are incompatible with Keynes's measured current income theory of consumption (Friedman, 1957).

In developing his theoretical framework, Friedman uses the terms consumption and savings in a way that not only differs from Keynes's definitions, but in a way that would also appear strange to the ordinary layperson not educated in the lexicon of classical economics. Friedman defines consumption as "the value of services [flow of utility] consumed" during any specific time period, e.g., the total utility obtained by the consumer from consuming products of industry in a specified time period such as a given year. Producible durables, however, by definition last more than a year and therefore provide a flow of utility to their owners over their useful multi-year life. Accordingly, Friedman defines consumption of durables as equal to the amount of depreciation of durables during a given year.

Friedman's definition of savings involves any portion of durables – those that already exist plus durables that are produced during the current year – that are not consumed (depreciated or used up) during this year. Consequently, Friedman's measure of total consumption in any year is equal to the depreciation (or wearing out) during the year of *all* existing durables owned by the consumers plus consumers' purchases of all nondurables and services that, by definition, must yield their total utility during the year (Friedman, 1957, p. 11).

To a layperson it might be a shock to discover that under Friedman's definition of savings, the purchase of a new gas-guzzling $45,000 Hummer automobile that is expected to last many years is a form of private savings. Only that portion of the utility value of the Hummer auto that depreciates during the current accounting period is classified as consumption. So unless the consumer totally wrecks his new Hummer driving out of the showroom, most of the purchase price of the Hummer will be recorded as savings in Friedman's accounting scheme. If the car is purchased just before midnight on December 31, then, Friedman will record in his database the total purchase price of $45,000 as savings.

Friedman prides himself on *not* defining consumption as the purchase of currently produced durables such as ostentatious sports cars, mink coats, yachts, jewelry, etc. Indeed, Friedman boasts that his taxonomy is superior to others such as Keynes's definitions because "much that one classified as consumption is reclassified as savings" (Friedman, 1957, p. 28). When transitory (windfall) income, e.g., lottery winnings, is received, Friedman (1957, p. 28) states, "Is not the windfall likely to be used for the purchase of durable goods?" If windfall income is spent primarily on durable producible goods, then, by definition, Friedman has validated his hypothesis that transitory incomes will (almost) always be "saved" and not consumed in the year that this "transitory" income is received. After all, if a household suddenly received a large one-time windfall of, say, $10 million, how many additional nondurables could the household purchase out of this windfall *in the current accounting period*?

The average layperson would be surprised to learn that if she won a $10 million lottery and spent the receipts on newly produced yachts, jewelry, a jet plane, etc., then these purchases are *not* classified as conspicuous consumption by a Nobel Prize–winning economist, but are instead defined as savings. Such uncommon use of common language can be highly misleading. Even though the average person would associate his/her saving out of current income with *not* spending income on the products of industry, Friedman's use of language encourages politicians to believe that saving creates jobs just as much as consumption spending on nondurables does. Moreover, under Friedman's definition, saving is even better than consumption for society as saving creates utility for many future periods, while the utility associated with Friedman's definition of consumption is dissipated immediately.[6] Of course, purchases of yachts and jewelry creates jobs today in these durable goods–producing industries. These purchases are consumption in Keynes's lexicon. They are primarily savings in Friedman's. But to paraphrase Shakespeare's Juliet – "What's in a name? That which we call a rose by any other name would smell as sweet" – so current spending on the durable products of industry would, were it called savings instead, still retain that dear perfection of creating jobs.

What Keynes's taxonomy does is, without engaging in semantic obfuscation, recognize that savings mean the purchase of a liquid asset that is not the current product of industry. Can Friedman's or any other classical economist's lexicon be so clear?

6
Further Differentiating Keynes's Aggregate Demand Function

I. Two aggregate demand components

To differentiate Keynes's general theory from classical theory's "special case" and to explain why the aggregate demand function is not identical to the aggregate supply function, Keynes developed a new and expanded taxonomy for the components of the aggregate demand function.

Under Say's Law, the aggregate market demand for all the products of industry are grouped into a single category that can be labeled D_1. This D_1 spending represents all expenditures on producibles where the amount spent is related to the income earned (aggregate supply). Given all the restrictive axioms underlying the classical special case of Say's Law, D_1 is not only a function of the income earned, but is also exactly equal to the income earned (aggregate supply) at any given level of employment.

Keynes's new taxonomy (1936a, pp. 28–30) differed from the classical categorization because Keynes split aggregate demand expenditures into two demand categories, D_1 and D_2. The D_1 spending category includes *all* expenditures on products of industry that "depend on the level of aggregate income and, therefore, on the level of employment N" (Keynes, 1936a, p. 28). Keynes's D_1 category, therefore, is similar (but not identical) to the single D_1 category of classical theory. Unlike the D_1 category of Say's Law, Keynes's D_1 spending is only a function of, and is not necessarily equal to, aggregate income (supply) at every possible alternative level of income and employment.

Keynes called the relationship between D_1 expenditures and the aggregate income level the propensity to consume function. Keynes's argument was that not all income received currently would be spent on the products of industry. That portion of income that was not spent on the products of industry is "saved" in the form of purchases of nonproducible liquid assets, including money. Consequently, as long as there is a propensity to save out of current income, D_1 expenditures would not be equal to income earned at every possible level of income.

Keynes defined D_2 spending as representing *all* expenditures that are *not* related to current aggregate income and employment. D_1 plus D_2 expenditures, therefore, make up an exhaustive categorization of all possible demands for the products of industry. What types of expenditures can be identified as not necessarily dependent on current income?

Examples of D_2 expenditures that need not be related to current aggregate income include:

1. investment expenditures by entrepreneurs (I),
2. government purchases of goods and services (G) that are not explicitly tied to government tax revenues when the latter are related to aggregate income and
3. in an open economy, i.e., an economy that trades with other nations, foreigners' purchases of export products from domestic industries (X).

Keynes initially dealt with the most simple model of the economy where there are no government taxes or expenditures and no trade with foreigners, so both G and X will be equal to zero. If, even in such a simple economic system, it were possible for Keynes to explain why Say's Law was not applicable, then, clearly, classical theory would not be applicable to the more complex real-world economies where government spending and foreign trade also affect the level of domestic employment.

In the simple economy system, where there is no government spending or foreign trade, D_2 spending represents the private sector's investment expenditures. Since all income earned goes either to planned consumption or planned savings, if, as classical theory presumes, investment expenditure is equal to the planned savings at any level of income and employment,[1] then investment spending would be included under the D_1 category, and Say's Law would be resurrected. As we already noted, in classical theory it is presumed that entrepreneurs already "know" the growth of market demand at specific dates in the future (where this growth is presumed to be equal to current savings). Consequently, current investment spending is assumed to be just sufficient to equal the savings propensity of households as the savers are merely showing a time preference for some specific future output. Consequently, investment expenditure is just another form of D_1 in the classical Say's Law theory.

II. Investment spending

To explain why investment spending is *not* equal to a planned savings at every possible level of income, and is therefore not included in D_1, Keynes invoked the concept of true uncertainty regarding the future. If the future is uncertain, according to Keynes, then future possible revenues that today's investment expenditures might be expected to earn are not foreseeable and therefore cannot be reliably predicted by using past or current market data. As Keynes noted (1936a, pp. 149–50)

> The outstanding fact is the extreme precariousness of the basis of knowledge on which our estimates of the prospective yield [of any investment] have to be made. Our knowledge of the factors that will govern the yield of an investment some years hence is usually very slight and often negligible. If we speak frankly, we have to admit that our basis of knowledge for estimating the yield ten years hence of a railway, a copper mine, a textile factory, the goodwill of a patent medicine, an Atlantic liner, a building in the City of London amounts to little and sometimes nothing; or even five years hence.

In technical terms, the type of uncertain environment that Keynes was describing in this explanation of the basis for estimating the future yield of any investment is one where the classical ergodic axiom – like the axiom of parallels in a non-Euclidean world – is not applicable.

In Keynes's theory, although investment spending depends on expectations regarding future market demand, and the resulting profitability accruing to the future output of today's investment projects, entrepreneurs recognize that this future market demand cannot be reliably predicted. Consequently, investment spending by entrepreneurs is more the result of what Keynes called "animal spirits" and other autonomous forces motivating entrepreneurs, than some actuarial estimate of future profits. Since the animal spirits of entrepreneurs can differ from the propensity to save, therefore today's investment spending by entrepreneurs is not directly related to the current planned aggregate savings propensity of the community. At any point of time, what entrepreneurs desire to spend on investment may be more than, less than, or equal to planned saving at any specific level of income and employment. In other words, once the classical ergodic axiom is thrown over and true uncertainty is recognized as an important force determining entrepreneurial investment planning, the D_2 expenditures component of the aggregate demand function can be considered to be determined independent of the value of aggregate supply at any level of income and employment.

The Nobel Prize winner and self-proclaimed Keynesian economist Paul A. Samuelson (1969, p. 182), however, has insisted that economists must impose the ergodic axiom if "we theorists" hope to remove economics from the "realm of history" and move it into "the realm of science". In other words, Samuelson has made the acceptance of the ergodic axiom the *sine qua non* for the scientific method in economics. When recipients of the Nobel Prize make such statements, it should not surprise the reader that Keynes's revolutionary argument that Say's Law is not applicable to our economic system because the aggregate demand function is not identical to the aggregate supply function has been ignored by mainstream economic theorists since World War II. (See chapter 12 for a further discussion of how Keynes's revolutionary theory was aborted.)

Samuelson's invoking of the ergodic axiom permits his scientific methodological approach to economic theory to presume that all future events can be actuarially determined by analyzing existing market (price) data. Consequently, in an analysis of an economic system based on the ergodic axiom, when people earn income today they can accurately forecast when, and for what, every dollar of savings will be spent at each and every future possible date. Entrepreneurs can also reliably estimate when this future spending on the products of industry will occur, and therefore install sufficient plant and equipment today to meet this future demand efficiently. Accordingly, logical consistency in Samuelson's ergodic axiom analysis would require that income earned at any employment level today will be entirely spent: (i) either on produced goods for today's consumption or (ii) on buying investment goods that will be used to produce specific goods for the (actuarially known) future consumption spending pattern of today's savers.

The ergodic axiom, therefore, is a fundamental building block underlying classical theory's presumption that all income is always immediately spent on producibles so that there is never a lack of effective demand for things that industry can produce and Say's Law is applicable. In this ergodic economic world, the proportion of income that households save does not affect total (aggregate) demand for producibles; it only affects the composition of demand (and production) between consumption and investment goods, or in Friedman's permanent income system, between the production of durables and nondurables. Thus, savings creates jobs in the capital goods-producing industries (or, for Friedman, in the durable-goods producing industries) just as much as consumption spending creates jobs in the consumer goods producing industries. Accordingly, it should not be surprising to hear mainstream economic "experts", whether they claim to be classical theorists or Samuelson-type "Keynesians", argue that the government ought to promote policies that increase the propensity to save as a sure way to stimulate economic growth and investment in productive durables.

In Keynes's theory, as opposed to the classical theory and the "scientific" approach of Professor Samuelson, people recognize that their economic future is uncertain (nonergodic) and cannot be reliably predicted from existing market information. Consequently, investment expenditures on production facilities and people's desire to save are typically based on differing expectations of an unknowable, uncertain future. If income earners' fear of the future increases, then income earners will try to save more out of current income. Hence the greater the fear of an unknown future, the lesser employment entrepreneurs will offer workers, as income earners spend less on the products of industry in an attempt to save more for the uncertain rainy days that may lie ahead.

On the other hand, the brighter the entrepreneurial expectations of future sales and profits, the greater their "animal spirits", and therefore, all other things being equal, the more would entrepreneurs desire to spend on investments in plant and equipment today. Since the purchase of large durable investment projects involve spending more funds than most entrepreneurs have in current income and/or savings, any investment expenditures must be funded via borrowing and/or selling equity securities on a financial market. If entrepreneurs can sort the expected profitability of various investment projects in terms of expected declining rates of profitability, then the lower the interest rate necessary to borrow money, the more investment projects and spending is likely to be undertaken. Alternatively, the more entrepreneurs fear the future, the less willing they will be to invest. So if fear of the future is rampant, entrepreneurs may not be willing to invest very much in plant and equipment even in the face of very low interest rates.

What can create entrepreneurial optimism, or fear of the uncertain future? Keynes (1936a, p. 162–3) noted:

> It is safe to say that enterprise which depends on hopes stretching into the future benefits the community as a whole. But individual initiative will only be adequate when reasonable calculation is supplemented and supported by animal spirits so that the thought of

> ultimate loss ... is put aside as a healthy man puts aside the expectation of death.
>
> "This means, unfortunately ... that economic prosperity is excessively dependent on a political and social atmosphere which is congenial to the average business man. If the fear of a Labour Government or a New Deal depresses enterprise, this need not be the result either of a reasonable calculation or of a plot with political intent; – it is the mere consequence of upsetting the delicate balance of spontaneous optimism. In estimating the prospects of investment, we must have regard, therefore, to the nerves and hysteria and even digestions and reactions to the weather of those upon whose spontaneous [investment] activity it largely depends ... We should not conclude from this that everything depends on waves of irrational psychology. ... We are merely reminding ourselves that human decisions affecting the future, whether personal or political or economic, cannot depend on strict mathematical expectations [of future profits], since the basis for making such calculations does not exist; and that it is our innate urge for activity which makes the wheels go round.

In a world of nonergodic uncertainty, future profits, the classical theory's rational basis for current D_2 investment spending, can neither be reliably forecasted from existing market information, nor endogenously determined via today's planned saving propensity of income earners. Instead, the expected profitability or yield of today's investment expenditures (D_2) depends ultimately on the optimism or pessimism of entrepreneurs and their ability to obtain funding for their investment projects. Or as Keynes (1936a, p. 212) noted, "prospective yield wholly depends on the expectations of future effective demand in relation to future conditions of supply". The effective demand at any future date, however, depends at least partly on D_2 at that future date. But that future date's D_2 level of investment spending depends on the entrepreneurial expectations of aggregate demand and supply conditions even further in the future. Thus, unless one assumes that entrepreneurs can accurately predict the future from here to eternity, current expectations of prospective yield must depend on the animal optimism or pessimism of entrepreneurs and their ability to raise money in the financial markets to fund the purchase of today's investment purchase commitments.

> "Our decisions to do something positive, the full consequence of which will be drawn out over many days to come, can only be taken

> as a result of animal spirits – of a spontaneous urge to action rather than inaction, and not as the outcome of a weighted average of quantitative benefits multiplied by quantitative probabilities. Enterprise only pretends to itself to be mainly actuated by the statements in its own prospectus, however, candid and sincere. … If the animal spirits are dimmed and the spontaneous optimism falters … enterprise will fade and die; – though fears of loss may have a basis no more reasonable than hopes of profit had before"
>
> (Keynes, 1936a, pp. 161–2).

In sum, once uncertainty about future economic aggregate demand and supply conditions is recognized by economic theorists, then the investment component (D_2) of aggregate demand cannot be assumed to be a function of current income and employment. Once we accept Keynes's general theory's rejection of axioms that are fundament building blocks of classical theory's assertion that decision makers can "know" the future – at least in an actuarial sense – then it follows that the aggregate demand function must be composed of two classes of expenditures, D_1 and D_2, neither of which have the identical behavior characteristics of the D_1 category in a Say's Law classical system. In sum, if the future is uncertain (nonergodic), then the general theory form of the aggregate demand function is not identical with the aggregate supply function at each level of income and employment. Or as Keynes (1936a, p. 21) described the classical Say's Law special case as "the assumption of equality between the [aggregate] demand … [for] output as a whole and its [aggregate] supply … which is to be regarded as the classical theory's 'axiom of parallels'". Instead, there is the possibility of a unique level of income and employment where the independent aggregate demand and aggregate supply curve have equal values at only a unique level of employment and income that need not be full employment. Keynes (1936a, p. 55) called this unique point of equality between aggregate demand and supply the point of effective demand.

III. What about other components of D_2?

So far we have discussed the aggregate economic system that would be applicable if the only form of D_2 spending was the private sector expenditures of entrepreneurs on investment goods. Thus, our discussion of Keynes's analysis until now has presumed certain conditions that typically underlie a simple classical theory model of the economy. These conditions are (1) there is a *laissez-faire* system so that the economy operates without any government interference via taxes and government expenditures to alter the private sector's aggregate demand for goods and services, and (2) the economy is a closed economy, i.e., there are no transactions between residents of this nation with residents of other nations. Even in such a simplistic economy, Keynes's analysis of an aggregate demand function that is independent of aggregate supply because of entrepreneurial behavior toward investment spending demonstrates that even in the absence of additional complications involving the government and foreign sectors, there is no automatic market mechanism in the private sector of a *laissez-faire* closed economy that assures full employment of all available resources in either the short run or the long run.

Let us now briefly explore how governments can affect employment and output in Keynes's general theory. The discussion of the effects of foreign trade on employment and production will be discussed in chapters 8 through 10.

IV. Government taxes and spending

A nation's government can affect output and employment through its fiscal policy, i.e., through decisions regarding the levying of taxes, and government expenditures on goods and services. At this stage of our discussion, we are only interested in how government taxes and spending affect employment levels and aggregate income, and not in how government fiscal policy affects the composition of aggregate output.

Any increase in government expenditures on goods and services produced by the private sector, *ceteris paribus*, will increase sales of industries, thereby, encouraging entrepreneurs to increase employment especially in the industries from which the government directly purchase, e.g., military hardware.[2] To the extent government levies taxes on the private sector, all other things being equal, these taxes reduce the after-tax income of the community available for consumption expenditures at any level of income and employment and hence lowers the propensity to consume out of gross (before-tax) income.

Since there is no automatic mechanism that ensures that private spending on consumption will be just sufficient to assure full employment, it is the hope of those who favor government taking a positive role in assuring full employment that the government will decide on its level of spending and taxation, running deficits or surpluses or a balanced budget, with the primary aim of keeping "the total rate of spending in the country on goods and services, neither greater nor less than the rate which ... would buy all the goods it is possible to produce"(A. P. Lerner, 1955, p. 469). Lerner called this view of the role of government fiscal policy "functional finance", by which he meant that government fiscal policy is conceived as the balancing wheel, exogenously increasing aggregate demand whenever private sector spending falls short of a full-employment level of output and reducing demand if aggregate demand exceeds the full-employment level.

The acceptability of using governmental functional finance fiscal policy opens the possibility of several alternative routes for achieving full employment. There are three ways that fiscal policy can affect the level of effective demand. These are (1) a change in tax receipts with no change in government spending; (2) a change in government spending with no change in tax receipts; and (3) simultaneous changes in taxes and spending. Of course, decisions on whose taxes to raise or lower will affect demand for specific products, while decisions on what specific government purchases should be made or cut will affect the output and employment of specific industries.

The choice among these alternatives should rest on a national discussion similar to what Galbraith tried to start in his book *The Affluent Society* (1957). This national discussion should weigh the relative merits or demerits of creating jobs through additional government spending on education, maintenance or improvement of the health of the population, infrastructure spending, etc., versus encouraging additional consumption (conspicuous or otherwise) by households or military defense, pork barrel projects in home districts of powerful elective officials, etc.[3] In any case, if we accept the functional finance role for fiscal policy, then whenever aggregate demand is insufficient to create employment opportunities for all who are willing to work at the going wage, then the government has a responsibility to induce an increase in aggregate demand in order to assure sufficient sales and profit opportunities for our private sector entrepreneurs for them to hire enough workers to achieve full employment.

To the extent that the public fears the size of the public debt *per se*, while it still recognizes the desirability of government providing additional services such as education, health facilities, infrastructure, etc, then the government should opt for an incremental increase in a balanced budget – i.e., a dollar increase in government taxes for every dollar increase in these socially desirable government spending projects without increasing total government debt. Since every dollar of increase in taxes will tend to reduce private consumption by less than one dollar as households strive to maintain their consumption habits, while every dollar of increased government spending on goods and services will increase someone's gross income by one dollar, the result will be a net addition to aggregate income demand and employment whenever there is a lack of effective demand. If fear of larger government absorption of total output is an overriding constraint, then a tax cut alternative can be pursued. If fear of too much "wasteful" consumption of an affluent society vis-à-vis public squalor ranks high in the public mind, then a modest increase in government spending financed by an equal increase in the deficit might be the alternative choice. None of the aforementioned fears should encourage the government to do "nothing" in the hope that a free market economy will soon right itself. This is the basic message of Keynes's analysis for his

> theory is moderately conservative in its implications. For whilst it indicates the vital importance of establishing certain central controls in matters which are now left in the main to individual initiative, there are wide fields of activity which are unaffected. The State will have to exercise a guiding influence on the propensity to consume partly through its scheme of taxation, partly by fixing the rate of interest, and in other ways. Furthermore, it seems unlikely that the influence of banking policy on the rate of interest will be sufficient by itself to determine an optimum rate of investment. I conceive, therefore, that a somewhat comprehensive socialisation of investment will prove the only means of securing an approximation to full employment: though this need not exclude all manner of compromises and devices by which the public authority will co-operate with private initiative. But beyond this no obvious case is made out for a system of State Socialism which would embrace most of the economic life of the community. It is not the ownership of the instruments of production which it is important for the State to assume. If the State is able to determine the aggregate amount of resources to augment the instruments and the basic reward to those who own them, it will have accomplished all that is necessary.
>
> (Keynes, 1936a, pp. 377–8)

While imploring government decision makers to actively use fiscal policy to achieve full employment,

> there will still remain a wide field for the exercise of private initiative and responsibility. Within this field the traditional advantages of individualism will still hold good ... above all, individualism ... is the

> best safeguard of personal liberty ... it greatly widens the field for the exercise of personal choice. It is also the best safeguard of the variety of life, which emerges precisely from this extended field of personal choice, and the loss of which is the greatest of all the losses of the homogeneous or totalitarian state. For this variety ... being the handmaid of experience as well as of tradition and of fancy, is the most powerful instrument to better the future.
>
> (Keynes, 1936a, p. 380)

Appendix to chapter 6: deriving the aggregate supply and aggregate demand functions

Keynes argued (1936, p. 41) that money values and quantities of employment are the only two homogeneous "fundamental units of quantity" that can be added together to provide meaningful aggregates for the economy as a whole. Accordingly, to develop an aggregate supply function, Keynes argued that entrepreneurs' aggregate expected sales proceeds associated with alternative levels of employment hiring should be specified (1) either in money terms (Z) or (2) in Keynes's wage unit terms (Z_w), where the aggregate expected money sales proceeds, Z, is divided by the money wage rate (w). Hence, Keynes's aggregate supply function is an increasing function of employment specified as either:

$$Z = f_1(N) \tag{6.1}$$

or

$$Z_w = Z/w = [f_1(N)/w] = f_2(N) \tag{6.2}$$

The Marshallian supply curve for a single firm (s_f) relates the profit-maximizing output possibilities for alternative expected market prices. The supply-price function (s_f) of any profit-maximizing firm depends on the degree of competition (or monopoly) of the firm (k_f) and its marginal production costs (MC_f). In the simplest case where labor is the only variable factor of production, $MC_f = w/MPL_f$ where w is the wage rate and MPL_f is the marginal product of labor. Accordingly, the Marshallian micro supply-price function is specified as

$$s_f = f_3(k_f, MC_f) = f_3(k_f, [w/MPL_f]) \tag{6.3}$$

Lerner's (1933–4) measure of the degree of monopoly (k_f) is $[1\text{-}1/E_{df}]$ where E_{df} is the absolute value of the price elasticity of demand for the output produced by the firm for any given level of effective demand. For a perfectly competitive firm, $k_f = 0$ and only marginal costs affect the position and shape of Marshall's supply-price function for a given firm.

The Marshallian industry supply-price function can be obtained by the usual lateral summation of the individual firm's supply curves:

$$s = f_4\ (k, \text{mc}) = f_4(k, w/\text{mpl}) \tag{6.4}$$

where the symbols without subscripts are the industry's average equivalent to the aforementioned firm's variables.

Although output across firms in the same industry may be homogeneous and therefore can be aggregated to obtain Marshall's industry supply quantities [as in equation (6.4)]; this homogeneity of output assumption cannot be accepted as the basis for summing output across industries to obtain the aggregate supply-price function (Keynes, 1936a, Ch. 4). Since every point on the Marshallian industry supply function, s, is associated with a unique profit-maximizing price, p, and quantity, q, combination whose multiple equals total industry expected sales proceeds, z, [i.e., $p \times q = z$], and since every industry output level (q) can be associated with a unique industry hiring level, n [i.e., $q = f(n)$], then every point of equation (6.4) of the s-curve in p versus q space can be transformed to a point on a z-curve in z versus n space to obtain, for any industry,

$$z = f_5\ (n) \tag{6.5}$$

Keynes aggregated these equation (6.5) industry supply functions to obtain the aggregate supply-price function in terms of aggregate money proceeds (Z) and the aggregate quantity of employment units (N) as specified in equation (6.1). To achieve a unique aggregation Keynes assumed that corresponding to any given point of aggregate supply price there is a unique distribution of employment between the different industries in the economy (Keynes, 1936a, p. 282).

Given the discussion of the aggregate demand categories D_1 and D_2 in this chapter, the aggregate demand curve relating money expenditures to employment levels will be upward sloping, i.e., the greater the level of employment, the larger aggregate demand in money terms. If the money aggregate demand is deflated (divided by) the money wage unit (the average money wage rate) then the aggregate demand function in wage units will also be upward sloping for any given wage rate. Given that investment expenditures are independent of each possible level of aggregate income and employment, the slope of the aggregate demand

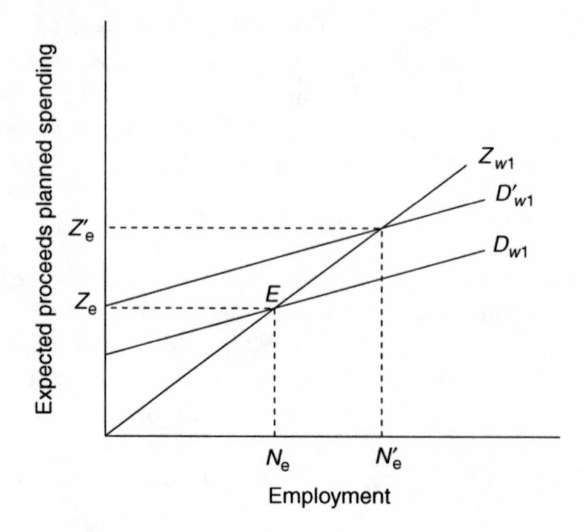

Figure 6.1 Aggregate demand and supply

curve will depend on the marginal propensities to consume of the various income recipients.

For any given wage rate (w_1), the aggregate supply function in wage units can be represented as Z_{w1} in Figure 6.1, while the aggregate demand curve in wage units is represented by the upward sloping D_{w1} in Figure 6.1. The point of effective demand, *E*, is given by the intersection of the aggregate demand curve $D_{w1,}$ and aggregate supply curve Z_{w1}. The equilibrium level of employment and the value of GNP is N_e and Z_e in Figure 6.1.

If, *ceteris paribus*, there is an exogenous increase in D_2 spending the aggregate demand curve will shift from D_{w1} to D'_{w1} in Figure 6.1. Employment will rise from N_e to N'_e and GNP will increase from Z_e to Z'_e.

The Multiplier. Figure 6.1 indicates that the increase in total income (and employment) exceeds the total increase in D_2 expenditures. This larger increase in income than the increase in spending on investment is called the "multiplier". This larger increase in income is due to the assumption that when more workers are employed in the investment goods industries, total income in the investment goods industries rise. This income increase induces those employed in these investment goods-producing industries to spend a portion of the increase in income on additional consumption, thereby increasing the income of workers and entrepreneurs in the consumer goods industries and, as a result, total income increases by more than the initial increase in investment expenditure.

Some economists have claimed that the miraculous multiplier effect of creating more jobs and income than in the initial increase in exogenous investment spending is the revolutionary aspect of Keynes's analysis. Actually, however, the multiplier is not revolutionary; it is merely a mechanical outcome of presuming that one portion of spending is endogenously related to income while another potion is exogenous.

How should we interpret the multiplier effect for different values of the exogenous investment variable? Since economists try to portray themselves as "scientists", their models are supposed to depict the symbolic equivalent of the controlled experiment in the "hard sciences". In a "hard science" controlled experimental environment, the investigator chooses two like populations of subjects – one is designated the control group, the other the experimental group. The investigator designs the experiment so that the values of all possible variables are initially the same for the two groups. Then the value of only one variable for the experimental group is altered and any significant differences that occur between the two groups are recorded.

For example, suppose a scientist wishes to investigate whether the absence of vitamin C in the diet will "cause" the disease known as Scurvy. Rats whose genetic makeup is as similar as possible are obtained. The rats are randomly sorted into two cages, an experimental cage and a control cage. The rats are fed identical diets except that the food of the experimental group will have all the vitamin C removed. The investigator records how many animals in each group develop Scurvy over a period of time.

This experiment is designed to disprove the null hypothesis that the absence of vitamin C does *not* cause Scurvy to develop. Given certain conventionally acceptable rules regarding statistical significance, if a statistically significantly larger number of rats in the experimental group develop scurvy compared to the control group, the investigator can reject the null hypothesis and, in the absence of any further evidence, the investigator tentatively accept the alternative hypothesis that a lack of vitamin C is associated with the contracting of Scurvy. This leads to the conclusion that taking vitamin C will prevent the onset of Scurvy.

In a similar manner, economists should interpret multiplier data as follows: Suppose we have two economies, A and B. Both A and B are characterized by the same propensity to consume and aggregate supply function. Assume the control economy A is exposed to exogenous investment spending of $1000, while the experimental economy B receives $1500 worth of exogenous investment spending. Let us assume that the resulting level of aggregate income in A is $7000, while it is $9500 for economy B. If these results are from a controlled experiment environment, then the economist can accept the argument that the GNP in B is $2500 larger than in A because exogenous investment spending in B is $500 higher than in A.

Of course, no real-world controlled experiment was done to generate our numerical results. Only a conceptual one was undertaken. Consequently, using a multiplier model to predict a future level of aggregate income resulting from a change in exogenous spending can be quite misleading. A more cautious but accurate statement would be:

> If an economy experiences more exogenous spending, say an additional $500, next period than it would otherwise in the next period, and if the aggregate supply function and the propensity to consume function correctly characterize the economy's structure *in the next period*, then the resulting aggregate income will be a multiple of the $500 greater exogenous spending than aggregate income would be if this additional exogenous spending did not take place.

Unfortunately such cautious but accurate statements are unlikely to please real-world politicians and entrepreneurs who have to make decisions today and who do not want such waffling conditional forecasts regarding future outcomes.

Deriving The Consumption Function (Propensity to Consume) from Marshallian Micro-Demand Curves. The propensity to consume suggests that as aggregate income (Y) rises, total consumption expenditures (C) increase, i.e., C is an increasing function of Y. Unlike this upward-sloping aggregate consumption demand curve, the Marshallian micro-demand curve facing an industry is normally downward sloping in price versus quantity space. Despite these different slopes, the aggregate consumption demand curve can be derived from a Marshallian micro-demand and supply analysis.

A Marshallian demand curve is based on the assumptions of given tastes, given other industry demand and supply conditions, and *given the aggregate effective demand*. As Keynes (1936a, p. 259) noted, the Marshallian micro-demand schedule for this industry "can only be constructed on some fixed assumption as to the nature of demand and supply in other industries and as to the amount of the aggregate effective demand". In Figure 6.2, the upward-sloping Marshallian industry supply curve, s_a, is drawn. At an expected price of p_1, entrepreneurs in

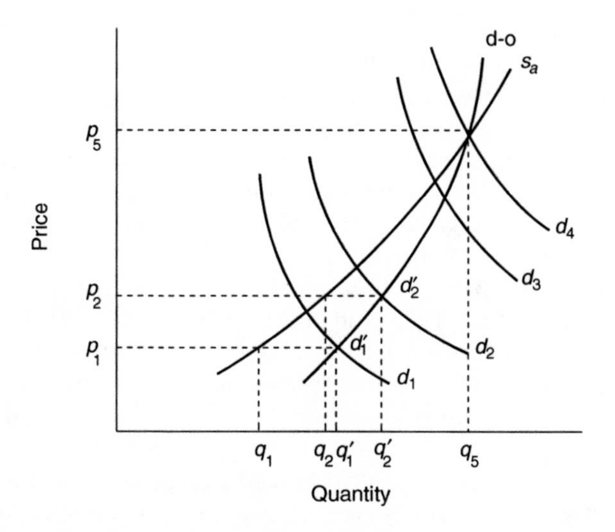

Figure 6.2 Deriving the demand-outlay curve

industry a will produce q_1 output, will hire n_1 workers, and expect a total revenue of z_1 (= p_1q_1). If entrepreneurs in industry *a* expect p_1 choose to produce q_1 there must be implied concomitant prices and outputs of all other industries that will generate a level of aggregate income such that the demand curve facing industry *a* will be d_1 in Figure 6.2.

At the supply price of p_1 in Figure 6.2, the quantity buyers demand would be q_1'. Buyers's intended demand-outlay is d_1'(= p_1q_1'). As drawn in Figure 6.2, at the supply price of p_1, intended demand-outlay exceeds expected sales ($d_1 > z_1$). The supply price p_1 is less than the equilibrium price, given the implicit assumption regarding demand and supply in other industries and the level of effective demand this assumption entails.

At an alternative expected supply price of p_2, entrepreneurs in representative industry *a* expect to sell q_2 output for a total revenue of z_2 (= p_2q_2) and will hire n_2 workers. This increased output and employment in representative industry *a* will be associated with similar increases in all other industries. The result will be larger factor incomes throughout the economy associated with supply price p_2 compared to supply price p_1. The larger aggregate factor payments mean more total consumption of goods in the market place and therefore imply that a new, higher Marshallian demand curve, d_2 in Figure 6.2, is the relevant demand curve facing industry *a*. At the supply of p_2, consumers intend to purchases q_2' output and intended demand-outlay is d_2'(= p_2q_2'). Intended spending still exceeds expected sales revenue ($d_2' > z_2$).

In this way, an intended demand-outlay can be developed from a family of Marshallian demand curves for each supply price in Figure 6.2. Connecting the relevant demand-outlay points at alternative supply prices, the demand-outlay curve d-o in Figure 6.2 is obtained. This upward-sloping demand-outlay function is the industry analogue of Keynes's aggregate consumption demand curve. At any level of aggregate employment, aggregate demand is the summation of intended demand outlays over all industries.

Implicit in this analysis that any other expenditures (D_2) other than consumption are a fixed sum and do not change with income. Thus the Marshallian demand curves facing firms producing output for D_2 spending remains unchanged while all the Marshallian demand curves representing D_1 markets are rising as employment and output expands in each industry, then aggregate factor incomes rise and the quantity of aggregate consumption demand plus D_2 demand increases. Every movement up the given aggregate consumption demand curve associated with an alternative higher level of employment and output generates a higher member of the Marshallian family of industry demand curves. As long as the marginal propensity to consume is less than one, the increase in aggregate demand-outlay (including the fixed spending on D_2) will rise slower than the increase in aggregate factor incomes. At some supply price (p_5 in Figure 6.2), the Marshallian demand-outlay function intersects the industry supply curve in each market and intended outlay just equals expected sales. This point of intersection is the industry analogue to the point of effective demand (where the aggregate demand curve intersects the aggregate supply curve) for the economy as a whole.

7
The Importance of Money, Contracts, and Liquid Financial Markets

> ... in the *General Theory* ... injustice becomes a matter of uncertainty, justice a matter of contractual predictability.
> —Skidelsky (1992, p. 223)

> The terms in which contracts are made matter. In particular, if money is the good in terms of which contracts are made, then the prices of goods in terms of money are of special significance. This is not the case if we consider an economy without a past or future. ... *If a serious monetary theory* comes to be written, the fact that contracts are made in terms of money will be of considerable importance.
> —Arrow and Hahn (1971, pp. 356–7, emphasis added)

> In the first place, the fact that contracts are fixed ... in terms of money unquestionably plays a large part.
> —Keynes (1936a, p. 236)

I. The reality of money contracts

The neutral money axiom is an essential building block not only of 19th-century classical theory, but as the previously cited quote from Professor Blanchard indicated, it is also a matter of faith underlying the conventional wisdom of today's mainstream macroeconomic models of the economy. Since in classical theory producible goods and services exchange for other producible goods and services and the supply of producibles always equals the demand for producibles (Say's Law), then there is no need for money, except as a counting device – a *numeraire* – in the production and exchange processes.

The conventional wisdom of mainstream economic models implies that in essence the economy deals only with barter transactions. A barter transaction occurs when the seller of commodity A exchanges a specific quantity of A for a specific quantity of commodity B that the buyer of A is willing to give up to receive the specific quantity of A. Since in any economy there are a multitude of people and firms trying to exchange a legion of producible products and services for numerous other producibles, finding buyers and sellers who possess the specific commodities wanted in any specific barter transaction would be extremely difficult. Accordingly, in classical theory money is merely something that facilitates the accounting for these otherwise cumbersome barter exchanges.

Keynes, on the other hand, recognized that he had to throw over the classical neutral money axiom to explain the existence of unemployment. As Keynes (1933a, pp. 408–9) stated:

> The theory which I desiderate would deal, in contradistinction to this [classical theory], with an economy in which money plays a part of its own and affects motives and decisions and is, in short, one of the operative factors in the situation, so that the course of events cannot be predicted either in the long period or in the short, without a knowledge of the behavior of money between the first state and the last. And it is this which we ought to mean when we speak of *a monetary economy*. ... Booms and depressions are peculiar to an economy in which ... *money is not neutral.*

In removing the neutral money axiom from his general theory, Keynes was denying that barter transactions are the essence of our economic system. Instead, Keynes was assigning an important role for the human institutions that we call money and contracts, and Keynes's general theory would capture some essential characteristics of this real world in which we live. These include:

1. Money matters in both the long and short run. Money and the possession of liquidity affects decision making that impact on employment and output outcomes. (How many of the readers of this book would make a decision to buy an expensive durable such as a house, or an automobile, or even everyday purchases at the grocery store, without first looking at their wallet, or checkbook, or securing a bank

loan commitment, or confirming they had a sufficient line of credit on their credit card to be sure they had access to a sufficient sum of money to pay for the purchase? Although most readers of this book face liquidity and finance questions over and above the size of today's pay check in making the significant purchases with money and/or credit card purchases, in classical theory these liquidity issues have no role to play.)

2. The economic system is moving through calendar time from an irrevocable past to an uncertain and statistically unpredictable future. In the world of experience everyone recognizes that the economic and political future is uncertain and therefore cannot be reliably predicted from the analysis of existing market data. Even if we did not realize how uncertain the future is, the law requires, for example, mutual fund managers to warn potential purchasers that past market performance does not necessarily provide any reliable information regarding future earnings of the mutual fund. In the technical jargon of statisticians the existence of such an unpredictable future means that past market price and output data are *not* generated by a stochastic ergodic process.
3. In a money-using market system, all legal economic transactions require a money contractual commitment made on either a spot market or a forward market. A *spot market* is any market where buyers and sellers contract for immediate payment and delivery at the moment of contractual agreement. A *forward* market is any market where the buyer and seller enter into a contractual agreement today for payment and delivery at a specific date(s) in the future.[1]

A *contract* is a legal agreement between the parties to perform specific actions at a specified time. In our entrepreneurial, market oriented economic system, money contracts are used ubiquitously to organize production and exchange transactions. Money contracts are a human institution that have been developed to help transactors deal with an uncertain future while engaging in complex, time consuming production and exchange transactions. In our world, entrepreneurs of business enterprises are continually making production, hiring, marketing and sales decisions that require them to enter into monetary contractual commitments. The use of such contracts provides some legal assurance to the contracting parties as to their future cash inflows and outflows.

The sanctity of money contracts is the essence of the entrepreneurial system. If either party to a legal contract reneges on its commitment, under the civil law of contracts, the aggrieved party can request that the State enforce the contract. Enforcement will require the other party to honor its contractual commitments or else pay a sum of money sufficient to compensate the aggrieved party for any pecuniary damages suffered. In other words, the State can always require the defaulting party to discharge its contractual obligation by the payment of a sum of money.

Accordingly, money is defined as that thing that the State decrees, under the civil law of contracts, which will always discharge any and all legal contractual obligations. This approach of linking State enforcement of contracts with the definition of money is known as *Chartalism*. In his *Treatise on Money*, Keynes (1930, 1, p. 4) noted that "Today all civilised money is, beyond the possibility of dispute, Chartalist".

As long as all future contractual liabilities are expected to be expressed in terms of a specific money, then money will also function as a store of value that permits the movement of purchasing (contractual settlement) power from the present to the indefinite future where it can be used to discharge future contractual obligations. Thus, money and liquid assets (where the latter are defined as assets that are readily convertible into money by being sold in an organized, orderly market) can be envisioned as *liquidity time machines* that permit the contractual settlement power of income earned today to be carried forward into the future when a saver may want to make a total sum of purchases that exceed his/her future income at any future point of time.

The civil law of contracts has evolved to help humans organize time consuming production and exchange processes in a world of uncertainty where the ergodic axiom is not applicable. In any money-using entrepreneurial economy, entrepreneurs' decisions regarding the volume of production and the contractual hiring of labor and material inputs depend on entrepreneurs' uncertain expectations of receiving future money sales revenues (cash inflows) in excess of the contractual money costs of production (cash outflows) of items produced for sale. "The firm is dealing throughout in terms of money. It has no object in the world except to end up with more money than it started with. *That is the essential characteristic of an entrepreneur economy*" (Keynes, 1933b, p. 89).

II. Contracts, markets, and the security blanket of liquidity

In a money-contracting economic system, one is said to possess sufficient *liquidity* if one possesses (or can obtain either by borrowing cash or by readily selling a liquid asset for cash) a sufficient quantity of money to meet all future monetary contractual obligations as they come due. Faced with an uncertain future and hence the possibility that at some point one might find oneself unable to meet a future contractual obligation, it is quite sensible for people to demand and hold an excess of money and other liquid assets (readily resalable for money) over and above the amount of already existing future contractual obligations. The holding of money and liquid assets acts as a security blanket protecting the holder from unpredictable changes that might occur in the person's future cash flow position.

The more uncertain the future appears to any individual, the more liquidity that person is likely to want to possess. In a classical theory system, on the other hand, where all currently produced goods essentially exchange for currently produced goods, and future purchase commitments and earnings are always known with statistical predictably, there is no rational need to hold money over any period of calendar time for liquidity purposes.

Unemployment, rather than full employment, is a normal outcome in any competitive market-oriented, money-contract using entrepreneurial system operating in a *laissez-faire* environment where households and enterprises value highly the "fetish of liquidity, the doctrine that it is a positive virtue on the part of investment institutions to concentrate their resources upon the holding of 'liquid securities'" (Keynes, 1936a, 155). In this age of mutual funds, hedge funds, and irrational exuberance in financial markets, can anyone doubt that the fetish of liquidity is an important aspect of developed modern economies?

Yet today's basic mainstream economic theory presumes that a liquidity fetish plays no part in determining the aggregate level of employment and output of an economy. If something that is called money exists in orthodox theory, that thing called money is assumed to be just another producible commodity, like peanuts, that is used merely as a counting device to measure relative prices. Consequently, whether people spend their income purchasing consumption goods or save some of their income by holding their savings in the form of the peanut commodity money of classical theory, all income earned in the production of goods and services will be spent on producible goods and services – including peanuts. In such a classical theory world, Say's Law is being met whether people consume their entire income or save some of their income in the form of the peanut commodity money. Full employment is the long-run inevitable outcome of a market economy as long as the only things that people spend their entire current income on is the current products of industry. As long as one assumes that money is a readily producible product of industry, then all income earned today represents a demand for today's products of industry.

An *elemental contract* is one where the date of payment and date of delivery is the same specified date. There are only two types of elemental contracts: (1) an elemental spot contract, when both payment and delivery are specified to be carried out at the instant of contractual agreement, and (2) an elemental forward contract, when a specific future date is the time where both delivery and payment will be made.

Actual real-world money contracts are often more complex than these elemental ones but any complex contract can always be analyzed as a combination of elemental contracts. Thus, if deliveries (and/or payments) are to be made at a specified sequence of dates in a real world contract, this can be analyzed as a series of elemental forward contracts each of which calls for delivery (and/or payment) at a different specified date. If the date of payment is later in calendar time than the date of delivery, this difference between date of payment and date of delivery can be explained by recognizing that the actual sales contract included an elemental loan contract where the seller (or as third party intermediary such as a credit card company) is furnishing a loan to the buyer for the period between the delivery date and the payment date.

In classical economic theory textbooks, it is typically assumed that entrepreneurs solely "produce to spot market", i.e., firms produce goods but do not maintain order books involving any forward money-contractual sales orders from buyers. In classical economic theory, when production is complete, entrepreneurs bring the products to market to sell them at whatever spot market price clears the market that particular day.

This "produce to spot market" notion can be categorized as "produce to speculation" behavior since, in this case, when the seller brings the finished products to the spot market, he/she does not know what price he/she will obtain in the spot market place. Moreover, in classical theory, the product brought to the market by entrepreneurs is implicitly treated as a non-durable and therefore must be sold immediately at whatever is the market clearing price. At the end of the market day, it is implicitly assumed that if the product is not sold, it will "spoil" and therefore cannot be held in inventory to be sold another day.

In the real world, most retail establishments are entrepreneurial firms that produce to market in the sense that they order goods from manufacturers before they have orders from retail buyers to purchase the products. If the product is durable, however, the retailer-seller can always hold the product in inventory (at some carrying cost) if today no buyer will pay the seller's asking price. At the end of a "season", however, retailers often have liquidation sales where asking prices are often 40 percent or more off the original asking price.

Most non-retail enterprises do not produce to market. Rather these business firms typically "produce to contract", i.e., these firms undertake the hiring of inputs and the supervision of the production process only after they receive forward contractual orders specifying quantity, a delivery date, and a purchase price. Accordingly, in real world capitalist economies, most entrepreneurial firms "produce to contract".

Time is a device that prevents everything from happening at once. Production takes time. The production period was defined by Keynes (1933b, p. 89) as the calendar "time which elapses between the decision to employ labor in conjunction with capital equipment to produce output and output being 'finished'".[2] If a production period spans any significant length of calendar time, then it would be foolish for any entrepreneur to undertake the daily hiring of workers and purchase of other inputs necessary to organize the production process unless the firm has some significant method of maintaining (1) cost controls over these inputs during the entire production period and (2) the liquidity to meet these money input cost commitments. These money cost controls are achieved by entrepreneurs executing forward money contracts (at the beginning of the production period) with workers and other suppliers of inputs to provide services and goods at specific dates during the production period. With the abolition of slavery, the labor-hiring money-wage forward contract has become one of the most universally used contracts for production cost control purposes.[3]

If a firm is willing to enter into these employment hiring and purchase of other input forward money contractual commitments, then the entrepreneur "must have enough command over money to pay the wages of the workers and to purchase those goods which it has to purchase from other firms during the period which must elapse before the output can be, conveniently and economically sold for money" (Keynes, 1933b, p. 64).

Spot purchases and delivery of all needed raw and intermediary materials at the initial start-up day of any long duration production process would be cost inefficient, for it would involve incurring warehousing and other carrying costs for many material inputs that are not needed until well into the production period. If, on the other hand, the producer waited and entered a spot market for the purchase of material inputs or labor on the actual day when such inputs were required in the production process, then from the very beginning the entrepreneur would have given up all control over labor and material costs during the entire production process since the spot price at any specific future date cannot be known with certainty today. Thus, the institution of forward money contracts is a *sine qua non* for cost efficient entrepreneurial firms involved in long-duration production processes.[4] The success of the Toyota motor car company, for example, was initially associated with its innovative "just in time" method of inventory control. In this method, Toyota used forward contracting to assure that suppliers' delivery is efficiently timed to Toyota's production process schedule so that Toyota did not need to carry a large inventory of component parts during the assembly process of its automobiles.

There are some products of industry that may be sold on both spot and forward markets. For example, retail sales of newspapers and magazines at the newsstand involve a spot market transaction, while subscriptions to such publications involve a forward contract for delivery in combination with a spot contract for payment at the signing of the subscription contract – and, hence, an implicit interest free loan from the buyer to the publisher. In the newsstand spot market for newspapers and magazines, however, the publisher normally "makes" the spot market price by being willing to credit the retail newsdealer for the return of all unsold publications, i.e., the publisher repurchases all unsold newspapers. This contractual repurchase agreement prevents a fall in the retail spot price to clear the market at the end of the day if there are still unsold newspapers and thereby avoids "spoiling the spot market" for today's and tomorrow's newspapers and magazines sales.

That thing we call money is defined in terms of its primary function as the means of contractual settlement. In an uncertain economic environment where contractual obligations are enforceable in terms of money, possessing sufficient *liquidity*, i.e., the ability to meet all one's money contractual obligations as they come due becomes a major economic problem for most decision makers. In an entrepreneurial system where unforeseeable future monetary contractual obligations may come due, a primary consideration in the plans of all participants in the system is the need to possess liquidity. This demand for liquidity would be unimportant if one lived in a classical theory economy where it is assumed, as in Walrasian general equilibrium theory, that *all* contracts require spot payments at the initial instant of analysis even if delivery of the product by the seller is specified contractually for some date in the future.

In the entrepreneur economy in which we live, workers and other participants in the economy willingly and freely enter into forward money contracts where a future money payment date is specified. As long as these people are law-abiding, the civil law of contracts will be the legal institution for enforcing these production and exchange forward contractual agreements. Hence, money will be the thing in which future liabilities (e.g. the money cost of future production, the future cost of living, etc.) will fall due.

As the legal enforcer of the civil law of contracts, the State determines that thing that will legally discharge contract and therefore specifies exactly what is the thing we call money in any nation's economy. The State typically designates currency as the *legal tender* for settling all public and private contracts. Accordingly, legal tender will be one portion of the economic system's money. Anything other than legal tender that the State and/or the Central Bank of the nation undertakes to accept from the public in payment of tax obligations or in exchange at a fixed rate of exchange for legal tender currency will also be part of the money supply of the economy. Since the central bank stands ready to instantly convert the public's checking deposit accounts at banking institutions into currency, therefore bank deposits that can be drawn upon via checks, although not legal tender, have become a major portion of the money of most nations.

As long as the system maintains its money contracting institutions to organize production and exchange transactions, then whatever the State designates as money possesses the capability of acting as a vehicle for moving generalized purchasing (contractual settlement) power for goods and services from the present to the future; i.e., money is a one-way time vehicle or *time machine* for store of value purposes. Today's money can always be held to be used to pay for future contractual purchases, as long as the carrying cost in the shape of storage, wastage, etc. of today's money is lower than any other thing that possesses this attribute of liquidity. Money is, as far as the private sector is concerned, a liquidity time machine *par excellence*.

In sum, money serves two specific functions: (1) money is the means of contractual settlement and (2) money is a store of value, i.e., a liquidity time machine for moving purchasing power to the future. Given the importance of money contracts in organizing production and exchange activities, the possession of money always gives one the ability to purchase anything that is available for sale in the market.

By definition, any durable besides money cannot legally settle a contract. Nevertheless, the second function of money – the liquidity function – can be possessed in various degrees by some, but not all, durables other than money. As long as claims on the economy's resources are exercised primarily through the use of money contracts, however, any durables, with negligible holding (carrying) costs, can possess some degree of liquidity if this durable can promptly and easily be resold (convertible into money) in an *organized and orderly spot market.* For example, financial assets such as equities, debt obligations, derivatives, options, etc., that can readily be resold on orderly, well-organized markets will also possess some degree of liquidity.

For any spot market to be well organized and orderly, there must be a "market maker" whose primary function is to assure the public that the actual market price will, at most, change from moment to moment according to well publicized rules that determine the orderliness of price changes in the market. The market maker provides this function by intervening in the market to buy or sell[5] whenever market forces threaten to move the market price rapidly in a disorderly manner either upward or downward. The market maker must be ready (1) to sell the asset whenever those who want to buy (the "bulls") are overwhelming those who want to sell (the "bears") the asset or (2) to buy when the bears are overwhelming the bulls. Durables with low to negligible carrying costs that are traded in such organized, orderly markets are called *liquid assets*.

A *fully liquid asset* is defined as any durable other than money that is traded in a well-organized market where the market participants "know" that the market price in terms of money will not change for the foreseeable future. There must therefore be a market maker who can guarantee that the price of the asset will not change over time even if circumstances change. An example of a fully liquid asset occurs when a foreign currency's value in terms of domestic money, i.e., the foreign exchange rate, is fixed by the domestic central bank of the nation. As long as the central bank has sufficient foreign exchange reserves it can, if it wishes, guarantee a "fixed" exchange rate. (This fixity versus flexibility of exchange rates is discussed in more detail in chapters 8 and 9 *infra*.)

A *liquid asset* is any durable with low carrying costs that is readily resalable in an organized, orderly market where the market maker does not guarantee an unchanging price. The market maker only guarantees that the market price will change in an orderly manner according to explicit, known rules under which the market maker operates. For any liquid asset, the next moment's market price is never known with certainty. What is known is that the next moment's market price will not differ in a disorderly way from this moment's price, as long as the market maker has a sufficient inventory of the asset and liquidity to back his/her assurance of maintaining orderliness in the market price.

Illiquid assets, by definition, are durables for which there is no well organized and orderly spot market available for resale of the assets.

Consequently, illiquid durable assets cannot be easily, if at all, converted into money. By definition, illiquid assets cannot provide a liquidity time machine function for savers.

The saver's choice of which of the myriad of available liquidity time machines to use to transport purchasing power to the future is limited to a choice between liquid assets, fully liquid assets, and money itself.

Keynes conclusion that planned saving is a demand for a liquid asset store of value and not a demand for illiquid real investment goods such as plant and equipment is in stark contrast to classical economists' belief that any increase in the propensity of households to save out of current income is equivalent to an expansion of entrepreneurial demand for newly produced investment goods. If the classical view were applicable to the real world, then any policy that increases household savings out of each level of income automatically and instantaneously increases the demand for real investment. When, on television and other mass media, one sees or reads that economic "experts" claim that the economy, although not at full employment, is not growing rapidly because there are not enough savings being done by the nation's population, one should recognize that these "experts" are espousing classical theory and not Keynes's analysis of the operation of a monetary economy. Misled by these classical theory economic advisors, politicians often propose special tax incentives to encourage people to save more and consume less in the mistaken belief that if people attempt to save more, then this increased propensity to save out of any income level will automatically translate into more investment in productive plant and equipment.

If Keynes's liquidity preference view of savings is applicable to our economic system, then a policy to increase saving and reduce the propensity to consume will, *all other things being equal*, reduce today's effective demand for the products of industry and therefore depress real economic activity and reduce employment. As long as the economy is at less than full employment, any increase in the propensity to consume will increase total employment and output and thereby improve the economic performance of the nation's economy.

Thus, for example, in the United States, the initial recovery from the recession of 2001 was accompanied by a very large tax rate reduction that induced an increase in consumption expenditures by United States households. These tax cuts were followed by a large increase in military expenditures starting in 2003 with the invasion of Iraq. By the year 2005, United States personal savings were actually negative (−0.5 percent) indicating that, by borrowing from foreigners and/or drawing down previous savings stored in liquid assets, United States households were on average consuming more than their income. Nevertheless, the result was that, in 2005, the United States experienced a healthy 3.6 percent rate of economic growth, while China, whose major market is United States consumers, showed a growth rate of almost 10 percent. As we will explain in the following chapters, the higher growth rate of China was due to the growth in demand for Chinese exports by the growth of United States household spending (faster than the growth of United States household income) on consumption goods made in China.

Keynes's anti-classical perspective where savers were people who spent a portion of their current income on the purchase of nonproducible liquid financial assets (including money) means that our entrepreneur-directed, market-oriented, monetary economy is fundamentally different from a classical theory world. In the latter, liquidity is irrelevant and a larger savings propensity implies a demand for more investment goods and therefore full employment today, and increased productivity and more rapid economic growth in the future.

Keynes (1933b, p. 85) noted: " It is the essence of an entrepreneur economy that the thing ... [money] in terms of which the factors of production are rewarded can be spent on something which is not current output". In contrast, the classical Say's Law theory presumes that the thing that rewards the factors of production will always be spent entirely on the current products of industry.

Recognizing the use of nonproducible money and liquid financial assets as stores of value, Keynes's liquidity theory can explain the implications for the real economy of the development of financial markets with financial intermediaries who "make" the financial markets. Only under this Keynes/Post Keynesian conceptual approach to the relationship between savings and financial markets can we understand why

1. money is demanded both as a means of contractual settlement and as a liquid store of value, i.e., a vehicle for transferring savings (generalized purchasing – contractual settlement – power) over time;
2. titles to capital goods (equity securities), debt contracts, and other liquid financial assets, with negligible carrying costs, that are traded on the spot in organized and orderly resale markets are demanded primarily as liquid stores of value, rather than to gain control of the management of any underlying real durables capital goods. Most owners of widely held "blue chip" equity securities are at best dimly aware of the products and sales plans of the companies they own.

Accordingly, in any entrepreneurial economy with developed markets for financial assets there will be an institutional separation of ownership from control of real-capital facilities;[6]

3. plant and equipment (capital goods) are illiquid assets that will be demanded by entrepreneurs primarily as an input to produce a flow of goods and services that are expected to be sold and thereby expected to yield a stream of cash inflows where these inflows are associated with specific future dates. Producible durable goods are not demanded as a store of value of generalized purchasing power in an economy with developed financial markets where people have confidence in the State and its chartalist money.

In an uncertain (nonergodic) world money and all other liquid assets possess Keynes's specified essential properties of zero or negligible elasticities of production and substitution. If savers hold their "saving" in the form of money or other liquid assets, this demand for liquidity does not use up any real resources. Holders of these liquid assets obtain satisfaction (utility) by knowing that the possession of liquid assets reduces the fear of risking insolvency or bankruptcy by not being able to meet future contractual obligations as they come due.

As long as producible goods are not gross substitutes for holding nonproducible liquid assets (including money) for liquidity purposes, no change in relative prices can induce income earners to buy producibles with that portion of income they wish to use to obtain additional liquidity for security purposes. Or as Hahn (1977, p. 31) put it: "there are in this economy resting places for savings other than reproducible assets".

In sum, the demand for liquidity is the fundamental cause of the existence of involuntary unemployment. The possible lack of perfect competition, the existence of labor unions, the existence of minimum wage legislation, etc., are neither necessary nor sufficient conditions for explaining the failure of a money-using, entrepreneurial economy from achieving a full-employment prosperity. The existence of a desire to save in the form of money and other liquid assets is a necessary and sufficient condition for indicating the possibility of involuntary unemployment, even in a freely competitive economy with fully flexible prices.[7]

III. Liquidity and contracts

Nevertheless, the question may remain, "Does applying Keynes's smaller axiomatic base make any difference to our understanding of the real world in which we live vis-à-vis applying classical theory's wider axiomatic foundation? The answer is definitely yes because only if we overthrow these three classical axioms can the concept of liquidity play an important role in our analysis – as it does in our lives.

Important decisions involving production, investment, and consumption activities are often taken in an uncertain (nonergodic) environment. Hiring inputs and buying products using forward contracts in money terms are a human institution developed to efficiently organize time-consuming production and exchange processes. Unemployment, rather than full employment, is a common *laissez-faire* outcome in such a market-oriented, monetary production economy.

The economy in which we live utilizes money contracts – not barter contracts – to seal production and exchange agreements among self-interested individuals. The ubiquitous use of money contracts is an essential element of all real world entrepreneurial economies. Moreover, *recontracting without income penalty* (an essential characteristic of the Walrasian general equilibrium system) whenever parties have entered into a contract at a price other than the implicit full-employment general equilibrium price *is never permitted under the civil law of contracts.* Why, one might ask, do economies continue to organize production and exchange on the basis of money contracts if such use interferes with the rapid achievement of a socially optimum situation that is always attained in an economy operating as an Arrow-Debreu-Walrasian general equilibrium system?

The use of money contracts has always presented a dilemma to classical theorists. Logically consistent classical theorists must view the universal use of money contracts by modern economies as irrational, since such agreements fixing payments over time in nominal terms can impede the self-interest optimizing pursuit of real incomes by economic decision makers. Mainstream economists tend to explain the existence of money contracts by using noneconomic reasons such as social customs, invisible handshakes, etc., – societal institutional constraints which limit price signaling and hence limit adjustments for the optimal use of resources to the long run.

For Keynes and Post Keynesians, on the other hand, *binding* nominal contractual commitments are a sensible method for dealing with true uncertainty regarding future outcomes whenever economic activities span a long duration of calendar time. In organizing production and exchange on a money contractual basis, buyers need not be as worried about what events happen in the uncertain future as long as they have, or can obtain, enough liquidity to meet their contractual commitments as they come due. Thus, liquidity means survival in a money-using, contractual, entrepreneurial-directed market economy. Bankruptcy, on the other hand, occurs when significant contractual monetary obligations cannot be met. Bankruptcy is the equivalent of a walk to the economic gallows.

Keynes's general theory's emphasis on money and liquidity implies that agents who planned to spend in the current period need not have earned income currently, or previously, in order to exercise this demand in an entrepreneur system. All these buying agents' need is the liquidity to meet money contractual obligations as they come due. This means that investment spending, which we normally associate with the demand for reproducible fixed and working capital goods, is not constrained by either actual current income or inherited endowments – as long as there are unemployed resources available. Investment can be a form of exogenous spending flow that is constrained, in a money-creating banking system, solely by the expected future *monetary* (not real) cash inflow (Keynes, 1936a, Ch. 17) upon which banks are willing to make additional working capital loans to entrepreneurs to provide the latter with sufficient liquidity, so that they can meet their hiring and material-purchase contractual commitments during the production process of capital goods.

In a world where money is created primarily only if someone increases their indebtedness to banks in order to purchase newly produced goods, real investment spending will be undertaken as long as the purchase of newly produced capital goods are expected to generate a future of dated cash inflows (net of operating expenses) whose discounted present value equals or exceeds the money cash outflow (the supply price currently needed to purchase the capital good).

For any component of aggregate demand not to be constrained by actual income, therefore, agents must either have previously stored savings in the form of liquid assets and/or have the ability to finance purchases by borrowing from a banking system that can create money. This Post Keynesian financing mechanism where increases in the nominal quantity of money are used to finance increased demand for producible goods results in increasing employment levels. Money, therefore, cannot be neutral and can be endogenous.

To reject the neutrality axiom does not require assuming that agents suffer from a money illusion. It only means that "money is not neutral" (Keynes, 1935c, p. 411) in the sense that money (and liquidity) matters in both the short run and the long run affect the equilibrium level of employment and real output. If it weren't for orthodox theorists' insistence on neutral money as a foundation for all economic theory, economists might have recognized that in a money-using entrepreneurial economy that organizes production and exchange with the use of spot and forward money contracts, money is a real phenomenon. Accordingly, the neutral money axiom must be rejected.

To repeat, Arrow and Hahn (1971, pp. 356–7) implicitly recognized this necessity of overthrowing the neutral money axiom when they insisted that "if money is the good in terms of which contracts are made, then the prices of goods in terms of money are of special significance. This is not the case if we consider an economy without a past or future. ... *If a serious monetary theory* comes to be written, the fact that contracts are made in terms of money will be of considerable importance" (italics added).

Moreover, Arrow and Hahn demonstrate (1971, p. 361) that if production and exchange contracts are made in terms of money (so that money affects real decisions) in an economy moving along in calendar time with a past and a future, then *all general equilibrium existence theorems are jeopardized.* The existence of money contracts – a characteristic of the world in which we live – implies that there need never exist, in the long run or the short run, any rational expectations equilibrium or any general equilibrium market clearing price vector. New Classical theory and Walrasian general equilibrium theories are not reliable basis for analyzing real world economies that use money and money contracts to organize economic activities.

IV. The role of financial markets

How one interprets financial market activity and chooses a policy stance regarding the regulation of such markets depends on the underlying economic theory that one explicitly, or implicitly, utilizes to explain the role of financial markets in an entrepreneurial economy. There are two major alternative theories of financial markets: (1) the Classical Efficient Market Theory (hereafter CEMT) and (2) Keynes's Liquidity Preference Theory (hereafter LPT). Each theory produces a different set of policy prescriptions.

CEMT is the backbone of conventional economic wisdom. The mantra of CEMT is "the market knows best" how to optimally allocate scarce real-capital resources and promote maximum economic growth. The classical ergodic axiom based analysis assumes that there exists today "economic fundamentals" data that contains all the information necessary for deriving correct ("rational") expectations regarding future demand and supplies of the assets trading in all domestic and international financial markets. Given the availability of this correct information about the future, rational decision makers, acting in their own self-interest, will force the market to establish the "correct" long-run equilibrium price or exchange rate in international markets to assure that the economic system operates at an efficient full-employment prosperity path over time. Any observed variations (often called "white noise" by econometricians) around this optimum economic path is attributed to "random shocks" to the system. These shock-induced variations from optimality are assumed to be quickly dampened down by the alert action of the informed rational market participants.

This "white noise" explanation of observed price and output (employment) volatility around the presumed optimum trend over time implicitly assumes that the dispersion of output (and/or prices) around a calculated moving average (equilibrium?) price does not affect future trends by causing a significant volume of false trades, bankruptcies, and other events that can rewrite the future path of the economy. This CEMT view was succinctly epitomized in the following statement by economist and former United States Secretary of the Treasury, Lawrence Summers: "the ultimate social functions [of financial markets are] spreading risks, guiding the investment of scarce capital, and processing and disseminating the information possessed by diverse traders ... prices will always reflect fundamental values. ... The logic of efficient markets is compelling" (Summers and Summers, 1989, p. 166).

The widespread acceptance of the efficient market hypothesis by mainstream economists prevented Keynes's psychological liquidity preference theory of financial markets from being applied to explain the role of both domestic financial markets and the international exchange rate markets in the economic system. This is true despite the mounting empirical evidence that, both in the short run and long run, market participant behavior in real world financial markets is incompatible with the efficient market theory. For example, Shiller (1981) examined the long-run relationship between real stock prices and real dividends in the United States from 1889 to 1981 and concluded that "the volatility of stock market price indices appears to be too high to accord with the efficient market model". In the decades that have followed, Shiller's analysis has never been credibly challenged by mainstream economists (see Shiller, 2000).

In the 1990's Federal Reserve Chairman Alan Greenspan's comment on the "irrational exuberance" of the bull equities market in the United States during the Clinton presidential years became a hackneyed phrase after the United States stock market collapsed in 2001. Since then, the continuing discussion of financial "bubbles" by talking heads on TV, in the printed financial media such as the Wall Street Journal, as well as academic discussions in professional economic journals suggests a schizophrenia in the conventional wisdom of mainstream economic theorists regarding the operation of domestic and international financial markets. Apparently, many mainstream economists are willing to admit that, in the short run, financial markets can be racked with irrational bubbles while believing, as an act of faith, that all markets are efficient in the long run.

Speculative bubble theories attempt to explain the "excessive" financial spot market price volatility often observed in the real world within the context of a predetermined external reality that imparts fundamental values to all economic assets. If the bubble is "rational" in the classical theory sense, decision makers believe that there is a probability of a positive deviation from the "intrinsic" value (i.e., the "real" value inherent in an asset derived from the fundamentals based on the programmed immutable real deep parameters of the system) in next period's financial spot market price. This probability will not only already be expressed in today's spot price, but it will also represent the prospect of an even larger deviation in each future period *ad infinitum*.

As long as the theorists assume that the economic model is open-ended, the deviation of market values from their fundamentals based values can increase without limit. Although this "bubble" analysis appears to utilize a rational expectations equilibrium framework, it is fundamentally inconsistent with the logical foundation of rational expectations where subjective evaluations (in probability terms) equal the objective probability distributions of intrinsic objective fundamental valuation. If people had rational expectations, then today's spot market price would always be a statistically reliably reflection of the intrinsic value (objective reality) of each asset. Moreover, in rational expectations equilibrium, current expectations are backward (rather than forward) based in the sense that past data provide the reliable information upon which today's expectations are founded.

The term "bubble", on the other hand, suggests that sooner or later, before the long run, the bubble valuations will burst. The deviation from the intrinsic fundamental value will not go on to infinity, but rather in the long run, the intrinsic value will prevail in the market.

Glickman (1994) has argued that the attempt to obtain theoretical consistency between the bubble literature and the CEMT view leaves the bubble theory devoid of any explanation of "why future deviations occur or why agents should expect that they will do so ... the argument is therefore no more than a neoclassical abstraction which shuffles off into a mysterious and indefinite remote future the problem of what is happening today". Speculative bubble theory permits exuberant but false forecasts of intrinsic value to persist indefinitely only by postponing the long-run day of reckoning to the infinite horizon. No one, however, has yet satisfactorily explained how a series of short-run bubbles can result in the existence of ubiquitous efficient financial markets in the long run.

If Keynes's argument that the economic future is uncertain and unknowable (nonergodic) is accepted as applicable to the world of experience, then the CEMT cannot be applicable to real world financial markets. In Keynes's liquidity preference theory of financial markets, flexible price movements in domestic and international financial markets can generate their own (irrational?) momentum, while the institution of a market maker merely attempts to maintain orderliness (stability) in the movement in market prices. The bursting of the bubble usually implies the market maker cannot stop the flood of bear sellers of the asset, and the market price declines in a disorderly manner.

Unlike speculative bubble theorists, Keynes reminded his readers that "we must not conclude from this that everything depends on waves of irrational psychology. ... We are merely reminding ourselves that *human decisions affecting the future*, whether personal or economic, cannot depend on strict mathematical expectation, since the basis for making such calculations does not exist" (Keynes, 1936a, pp. 162–3).

The logic of Keynes's *LPT* indicates that the primary function of financial markets is to provided liquidity not efficiency. A liquid market requires *orderliness*. If the market maker does not possess a sufficient inventory of the asset being traded and money supply to maintain orderliness and the bubble threatens to burst, then there is a significant decline in the liquidity of the asset. Often, in well organized financial markets when the market maker cannot stem the flood of sell orders and the price starts to decline in a disorderly manner, then trading is suspended in this asset. This suspension is often referred to as a "circuit breaker". During the suspension, the asset has lost its liquidity, while the suspension gives the market maker time to rally sufficient resources to restore orderliness when the market reopens.

If Keynes's LPT of orderly financial markets is relevant, then the world's national and international capital markets can never deliver, in either the short run or the long run, the efficiency results claimed by CEMT.

Peter L. Bernstein is the author of the best-selling book entitled *Against the Gods* (1996) a treatise on risk management, probability theory and financial markets. Bernstein argues that the LPT and not CEMT is the relevant theory for the financial markets of the world in which we live. Bernstein states "The fatal flaw in the efficient market hypothesis is *that there is no such thing as an [efficient] equilibrium price* ... [and] a market can never be efficient unless equilibrium prices exist and are known"(1998b, p. 132, emphasis in original; also see Bernstein, 1998a). In other words, in Bernstein's view, CEMT is not applicable to real world financial markets.

In the absence of liquid financial markets, however, "[t]here is no object in frequently attempting to revalue an investment to which we are committed" (Keynes, 1936a, p. 151) for there can be no fast exit strategy. If capital markets were completely illiquid then there would be no separation of ownership and control. Once some volume of real capital was committed, the owners of these illiquid assets would have an incentive to search for the best possible use of the existing real-capital facilities no matter what unforeseen circumstances might arise. Perhaps then capital markets might behave more like the efficient markets of mainstream theory.

If CEMT theory is not applicable to the real world of liquid financial markets, then there can be an important role for governments to maintain stability of domestic and international financial markets. Bernstein's (1998a, p. 23) homily that "an efficient market is a market without liquidity" is a lesson that policy makers must be taught. Judicious use of capital flow controls for funds moving into or out of specific markets can promote efficiency by constraining any sudden change in the demand for liquidity that would adversely affect the real economy.

Since the 1970s, however, Summers's "compelling" efficient market logic has provided the justification for nations to dismantle most of the ubiquitous postwar capital regulations of financial markets. The argument for this "liberalization" of financial markets was that it would properly allocate capital to promote efficiency by producing lower real costs of capital and higher output and productivity growth rates compared to the growth rates experienced between World War II and 1973 when international capital flow controls were practiced by most countries of the world, including the United States.[8]

What are the facts and do they support this CEMT argument for financial liberalization? In the late 1990s when the Asian tigers' currencies collapsed, the Russian bear defaulted on its debt, and the fear of the Brazilian "real" reeling menaced our global economy. We were haunted by the question "Can 'it' happen again?" Can we have another Great Depression at the end of the 20th century?

Keynes (1936a, p. 159) noted, "It is enterprise which builds and improves the world's possessions. ... Speculators may do no harm as bubbles on the steady stream of enterprise. But the position is serious when enterprise becomes the bubble on a whirlpool of speculation". Comparing the pre-1973 and post-1973 United States record indicates that, since 1973, enterprise has slowly become enmeshed in an ever-increasing whirlpool of speculation.

For almost a quarter of a century after the Great Depression and World War II, governments actively pursued the types of economic policies that established regulations for domestic financial markets. In 1944, at Bretton Woods, nations agreed to create an institution, the International Monetary Fund, whose function it would be to maintain stability in international exchange rate markets. Moreover, when it was deemed necessary, most nations instituted international capital controls to limit the flow of funds between nations.

The result of deliberate government activities, especially in international financial markets was to encourage per capita economic growth in the capitalist nations to proceed at a rate that has never been reached in the past nor rarely matched since[9] (see Table 7.1). Adelman (1991) has characterized this postwar "Keynesian" era of unsurpassed economic global prosperity performance as a "Golden Age of Economic Development ... an era of unprecedented sustained economic growth in both developed and developing countries". The *average* annual per capita economic growth rate of OECD nations from 1950 till 1973 was "almost precisely double the previous *peak* growth rate of the industrial revolution period. Productivity growth in OECD countries was more than triple (3.75 times) that of the industrial revolution era" (Adelman, 1991, p. 15).

The resulting prosperity of the industrialized world was transmitted to the less developed nations through world trade, aid, and direct foreign investment. As Table 7.1 indicates, from 1950–73, average per capita economic growth for all less developed countries (LDCs) was 3.3 percent, almost triple the average growth rate experienced by the industrializing nations during the industrial revolution. Aggregate economic growth of the LDCs increased at almost the same rate as that of the developed nations, 5.5 percent and 5.9 percent respectively. The higher population growth of the LDCs caused the lower per capita income growth.

By 1973, however, Keynes's analytical vision of how to improve the operation of a market-oriented, entrpreneurial system had been lost by politicians, their economic advisers and most academic economists.

Table 7.1 Real GDP (annualized growth rate)

		Real GDP per capita	
Years	**World**	**OECD nations**	**Developing nations**
1700–1820	na	0.2%	na
1820–1913	na	1.2%	na
1919–1940	na	1.9%	na
1950–1973	na	4.9%	3.3%
1973–1981	na	1.3%	na
1981–1990	1.2%	2.2%	1.2%
1991–1993	-0.4%	0.6%	2.6%
1993–2002	2.7%	2.0%	3.0%
1998–2005	2.8%	1.9%	4.2%

		Total Real GDP	
Years	**World**	**Industrial nations**	**Developing nations**
1950–1973	na	5.9%	5.5%
1966–1973	5.1%	4.8%	6.9%
1974–1980	3.4%	2.9%	5.0%
1981–1990	2.8%	2.9%	2.4%
1991–1997	2.2%	1.9%	5.0%
1998–2005	3.9%	2.5%	5.0%

Note: na = not available.
Sources: Adelman (1991), IMF, *World Economic Outlook* (1999, 2002, 2006).

As a result, Keynes's policy prescriptions fell from grace. As Table 7.1 demonstrates, in the 25 years after 1973, the economic performance of capitalist economies was much more dismal than it was during the quarter century after World War II. The annual growth rate in investment in plant and equipment in OECD nations fell from 6 percent (before 1973) to less than 3 percent (since 1973). Less investment growth meant a slower economic growth rate in OECD nations (from 5.9 percent to 2.5 percent) while labor productivity growth declined dramatically (from 4.6 percent to 1.6 percent).

V. Financial markets and Keynes's liquidity theory

In the world of experience, market participants believe that financial markets will always be able to provide liquidity as long as financial assets can be easily and quickly sold. In a world where the economic future is uncertain, financial market prices tend to be stable as long as market participants accept the convention "that the existing state of affairs will continue indefinitely, except as we have specific reasons to expect a change" (Keynes, 1936a, p. 152). Accordingly, "a practical theory of the future ... is based on a flimsy foundation, it is subject to sudden and violent changes. The practice of calmness and immobility, of certainty and security, suddenly breaks down. New fears and hopes will, without warning, take charge of human conduct. The forces of disillusion may suddenly impose a new conventional basis of valuation"(Keynes, 1937, pp. 114–5).

In the real world, protecting the monetary value of one's portfolio of liquid (resalable) financial assets against unforeseen and unforeseeable volatile (especially downward) changes in financial market values becomes an important economic activity. As long as financial markets are orderly, every holder of assets traded on such markets can have a *fast exit strategy* where they believe they can sell their holdings of liquid assets (i.e., their position) at a price not significantly different from the last quoted market price as soon as they perceive the market is adopting a new conventional basis of valuation other than the one they had expected.

In our world with instant global communications, every portfolio fund manager must, in an instant, conjecture how other market players will interpret a news event occurring anywhere in the world. Any event occurring in the world can set off rapid changes in subjective evaluation of the market value of one's portfolio. Speculation about the psychology of other market players can result in lemming-like behavior which can become self-reinforcing and self-justifying. In a nonergodic system, if enough agents possess the same "incorrect" expectations (to use a Stiglitz [1989] phrase), the result can be that these faulty expectations induce almost all market participants to try to execute a fast exit strategy that can overwhelm any private market maker institution and thereby actually create future volatile outcomes (cf. Arestis and Sawyer, 1998, pp. 188–9). The first "irrational" lemmings to hit the ocean of liquidity may not drown. They may survive to make more mistakes and lead more leaps into an ocean of liquidity in the future.

VI. The need for market orderliness

Financial markets furnish liquidity only by providing an orderly, well-organized environment where financial assets can be readily resold for cash. Orderly liquid financial markets, however, encourage investors to believe they can have a fast "*exit strategy for the moments when they are dissatisfied with the way matters are developing*. Without liquidity, the risk of making an investment as a minority owner would be intolerable"(Bernstein, 1998a, p. 18).

All liquid assets provide the liquidity time machine store-of-value function for savers wanting to move resource claims into the uncertain future. Since the liquid asset must be resold for money at a future date when the holder wishes to make a purchase, therefore any liquid asset has a lower degree of liquidity than money itself. Accordingly, if a saver gives up money to purchase a liquid asset it must be because the saver believes that the value of the asset in terms of interest and/or dividends earned, and/or the possible capital gain if the market price rises during the period the liquid asset is held, is sufficient compensation for giving up the liquidity of money. Moreover, if the holder of any liquid asset believes the market price will decline significantly but in an orderly fashion over a period of time, then the holder of such a liquid asset also believes he/she always has available a fast exit strategy available for selling the asset at a price that will not be significantly different from the last quoted market price. This fast exit strategy comforts the saver with the belief that if his/her expectations regarding the value of the asset appears to be wrong, the saver can quickly "cut one's losses" without incurring a major capital loss.

VII. Booms and busts

If financial markets are primarily organized to provide liquidity, then when bullish sentiment about the uncertain future dominates financial markets, rising capital market prices encourage savers to readily provide the funding that induces entrepreneurial-investors to spend sums on new investment projects that (i) far exceed their current incomes and (ii) induce exuberant expectations of future returns. The result is an investment boom. If some time in the future, doubts suddenly arise concerning the reliability of these euphoric expectations, then bearish sentiment will come to the fore and the investment boom will turn into a bust.

When the bearish view of the future becomes overriding, an excessive demand for liquidity can develop that will impede the production of new investment capital even when real resources are idle and therefore readily available to produce new real-capital goods. The basic message of the Keynes's *General Theory* is that too great a demand for liquidity can prevent "saved"(i.e., unutilized) real resources from being employed in the production of investment goods. These resources will be involuntarily unemployed.

New Keynesians such as Joseph Stiglitz (1989) and Lawrence Summers (Summers and Summers, 1989), following the lead of Old Keynesian

James Tobin (1974; also Eichengreen, Tobin, and Wyplosz [hereafter ETW], 1995), have argued that an *ad valorem* tax on financial market transactions, that is a tax equal to a fixed percentage of market value, is socially desirable in that it will reduce the observed volatility in our "super-efficient financial markets". In 1995, for example, ETW (1995, p. 164) recognized and forcefully argued that short-term volatility in foreign exchange markets due to speculation can have "real economic consequences devastating for particular sectors and whole economies". To limit this speculative behavior, ETW proposed a global transaction tax to discourage short-term speculative movements of funds. This transaction tax put "grains of sand" into the operation of what ETW (1995, p. 164) called the "super-*efficient* financial markets" of our global financial system.

Unlike Old and New Keynesians, Keynes explicitly recognized that the introduction of sand in the wheels of liquidity-providing financial markets via a transactions tax can create a quandary. Keynes (1936a, p. 160) noted that a financial transactions tax "brings us up against a dilemma, and shows us how the liquidity of investment markets often facilitates, though it sometimes impedes, the course of new investment".

In the absence of concerted intervention by a market maker, what market conditions will create nonvolatile movements of prices in real world financial markets? "It is interesting that the stability of the [financial] system and its sensitiveness ... should be so dependent on the existence of a variety of opinion about what is uncertain. Best of all that we should know the future. But if not, then, if we are to control the activity of the economic system ... it is important that opinions differ" (Keynes, 1936a, p. 172).

In other words, an ergodic system would provide the "best of all" possible worlds for financial market stability. Then the future can be reduced to actuarial certainty, i.e., "we should know the future". Market efficiency would be assured as long as agents operated in their actuarially known self-interest. There would be no need for a fast exit strategy in this hypothetical classical theory world.

If the system is nonergodic, however, then actuarial certainty and the possibility of rational probabilistic risk spreading – which, according to Summers, is an essential function of efficient markets – is impossible. Consequently, a second best solution is to encourage substantial numbers of market participants to hold continuously differing expectations about the future so that any small upward change in the market price brings about a significant bear reaction, while any slight downturn induces a bullish reaction. The result will be to maintain spot financial market (resale) price orderliness over time and therefore a high degree of liquidity[10] without substantial intervention by the market maker.

If there is a sudden shift in the private-sector's bull-bear disposition, what can be called a bandwagon effect, then price stability requires regulations constraining capital flows into and/or out of the market to prevent the bears from liquidating their position too quickly (or the bulls from rushing in) and overcoming any single agent (private or public) who has taken on the responsible task of market maker to promote "orderliness". Capital controls serve the same function as laws that make it a crime to yell fire in a crowded theater. In the absence of such social constraints on free speech, the resulting rush to the exit may inflict more damage than any potential fire.

Despite their willingness to accept the "compelling logic" of CEMT, the common sense of Tobin and his New Keynesian followers regarding real-world financial markets cannot help but break into their logical models – with injury to their logical consistency. Thus to solve today's international monetary problems, some "Keynesians" advocate a Tobin tax. Tobin (1974) warned that free international financial markets with flexible exchange rates create volatile international financial markets that can have a"devastating impact on specific industries and whole economies". Tobin advocates that governments limit market volatility by increasing the transactions costs on all international payments via a small "Tobin tax". Unfortunately, though Tobin's assessment of the problem is correct, the empirical evidence is that any increase in the transactions costs significantly increases rather than decreases measured market volatility (Davidson, 1997). Moreover, a Tobin tax does not create a greater disincentive for short-term speculators as Tobin has claimed (Davidson, 1997). Hence, the "Tobin tax" solution is the wrong tool to solve the growing international financial speculative market problem.

(In the following chapters we will discuss Keynes's proposal for stabilizing international financial markets, but first let us delve further into what is implied in different theoretical approaches to the concept of the existence of certainty or uncertainty regarding the external reality of our economic future.)

VIII. Is reality predetermined, immutable and ergodically knowable or nonergodic, unknowable and transmutable?

Economic theories can be classified as to how they attempt to deal with knowledge regarding the economic future. Table 7.2 classifies various theories according to whether they assume the future is immutable or

Table 7.2 Concepts of external economic reality

A. Immutable reality

Type 1. In both the short run and the long run, the future is known or at least knowable. Examples are:

(a) Classical perfect certainty theory including Walrasian general equilibrium.
(b) Actuarial certainty equivalents, and New Classical rational expectations theory.
(c) Some New Keynesian theories that incorporate rational expectations.

Type 2. In the short run, the future is not completely known due to some limitation in human information processing and computing power. Examples are:

(a) Bounded rationality theory
(b) Knight's theory of uncertainty
(c) Savage's expected utility theory
(d) Some Austrian theories
(e) Some New Keynesian models (e.g. coordination failure theories)
(f) Chaos, sunspot, and bubble theories
(g) Post-Walrasian theories

B. Transmutable or creative reality

The future is ontologically uncertain. Some aspects of the economic future will be created by human action today and/or in the future. Examples of theories are:

(a) Keynes's *General Theory* and Post Keynesian monetary theory.
(b) Post-1974 writings of Sir John Hicks.
(c) G. L. S. Shackle's crucial experiment analysis.

mutable and changeable due to human action. Immutable theories are subdivided into type 1 immutable theories where the people in the theory "know" the economic future and type 2 immutable theories where, although the future is preprogrammed, the people in the theory suffer from some form of epistemological uncertainty.

By assuming that economic agents operate in a world of perfect certainty, 19th-century classical economists presumed that agents had *full knowledge* of a *pre-programmed external economic reality* that governed all past, present, and future economic outcomes. The external economic environment was *immutable* in that it was not susceptible to change induced by human action. The path of the economy, like the path of the planets under Newton's classical mechanics, was determined by timeless, immutable natural laws.

While rejecting the perfect certainty model, most mainstream economists today, following the lead of Samuelson and Lucas, have accepted as a universal truth the existence of a predetermined reality that can be fully described by either an unchanging objective conditional probability functions or a deterministic future spelled out by the existence of a complete set of spot and forward markets.[11] These Nobel Prize–winning economists are presuming, without proof, an immutable future path of the economy where the future consequences of all possible choices are predetermined (i.e., programmed by natural laws). This does not preclude an economy that is moving or changing over time. It does mean that all future movements and changes are already predetermined by the fundamental real (deep) parameters of the system that, in the long run, cannot be changed by human action. In such a setting, to paraphrase Shakespeare, all the economic world's a stage and all the men and women merely players who are reading the lines already programmed into the script for them by the immutable economic system.

Unlike the old classical economists, rational expectations theorists do not claim that the agents in their models obtain *complete* knowledge of reality. Rational expectations models only require agents to use existing market price signals to calculate subjective probabilities that are statistically reliable estimates of the "true" objective probability function that governs future events. Subjective probabilities calculated from current and/or past market data can provide these statistically reliable estimates if, *and only if*, the economic system is *ergodic*. Hence, all rational expectations models are based on the ergodic axiom.

In a wider sense, however, ergodicity means the presumption of a preprogrammed stable, conservative system where the past, present, and future reality are predetermined whether the system is stochastic or not (See Davidson, 1991). A consistent general equilibrium (Walrasian) theory that recognizes there is an economic past, present, and future must presume the existence of a multi-period relative price vector that allows agents to maximize their welfare over a multi-period future.[12] Nobel Prize winner Milton Friedman would argue that even if agents do not or cannot calculate probabilities about future outcomes, those decisions-makers who have make choices that prove to be economically successful have acted "as if" they had estimated the true probabilities about the future, that is "as if" they had drawn reliable sample information from the future.[13]

If reality is that the economic future is immutable, then society cannot enact laws (policies) to alter the inevitable predetermined future outcomes any more than a legislature can overturn Nature's "law of gravity" or the probability distribution associated with a fair game of roulette. In this ergodic conception of reality, humans have no freedom to alter their long-run economic future (See Lawson, 1988). Moreover the State cannot have any more "information" about the future than individuals in a free market can obtain. The ergodic presumption provides the rationalization for the Ronald Reagan-type rhetorical question: "How can bureaucrats in Washington know better how to spend your money than you do?"

The only issues for immutable reality theorists are:

(1) How, and at what cost, do humans obtain reliable information to learn about the future from existing market signals?
(2) If each agent's computing ability is not sufficient to calculate statistically reliable conditional probabilities (or decision weights), i.e., if each agent is assumed to face an epistemological uncertain future, then does a nonhuman *deus ex machina* exist that will process the data and provide the relevant probabilities and predictions that are, in principle, computable in an ergodic system?
(3) In the absence of such a god-like machine, how do people make decisions with either little or no information about the preprogrammed future, at least in the short run? (In the long run, those who make incorrect guesses about the programmed future are doomed to fail in a market environment. Consequently, in an inevitably social Darwinist fashion, only those whose guesses turn out to be compatible with the preprogrammed future will survive.)

In responding to these queries, orthodox economists have developed a number of variants of two basic types of immutable reality models (see Table 7.2). An epistemological assumption regarding how much, if any, reliable information about the immutable reality can be obtained and processed by agents in the short run distinguishes type 1 from type 2 immutable theories.

Type 1 immutable reality theories presume that at the initial instant knowledge regarding future outcomes is either perfect or, at least, statistically reliable. Decision makers, therefore, can do the necessary calculations to make "efficient" and "rational" choices. Type 1 models include old classical perfect certainty models including Walrasian general equilibrium systems, New Classical and all New Keynesian models that assume that agents possess rational expectations, and any other models where in the short run, agents are presumed to already "know" actuarial certainty equivalents of future outcomes.

Type 2 immutable reality theories assume that, in the short run, agents's knowledge regarding reality is severely incomplete, or even completely unknown, as some limitation on human ability (i.e., a constraint on human's computing power) prevents agents from using (collecting and analyzing) historical time series data (information) to obtain short-run reliable knowledge regarding *all* future economic variables. Colander (2006a, p. 2), who believes that post-Walrasian theories are the wave of future developments in economic theory, has written that "Post-Walrasians assume low-level information processing capabilities and a poor information set". Under this definition, post-Walrasian theories are forms of type 2 immutable reality theory. Human ignorance about some aspect(s) of the presumed immutable reality is the hallmark of all type 2 theories.

The long run is conventionally defined as that point of time when all agents' plans are being met and no forecasting errors occur. Or as Friedman (1974, p. 150) states: "The long-run equilibrium in which, as I put it, 'all anticipations are realized' and that is determined by 'the earlier quantity theory plus the Walrasian equations of general equilibrium' ... is a logical construct that defines the trend to which it [the actual world] is tending to return". In this long run, all immutable reality models presume that reality is somehow revealed to all successful market participants, or, at least, successful agents behave "as if" they know this reality.

If reality is really immutable, then it is easy to understand Mankiw's (1992, p. 561) earlier cited comment that "classical economics is right in the long run. Moreover, economists today are more interested in long-run equilibrium".

Friedman and some other mainstream economists conceptualize long-run equilibrium as a "center of gravity" towards which the system is being attracted, but which it may never reach. As a logical construct, however, the long run *must* be ultimately realized unless (a) either the analyst postulates continuous additional exogenous "shocks" to the system, or (b) the analyst deals only with an open-ended model where the long run is never reached within the time confines of the model.

Type 2 immutable reality models typically employ a subjectivist short-run orientation. Agents may form subjective probabilistic expectations. In the short run, these subjective probabilistic expectations need not coincide with the presumed immutable objective probabilities. Today's decision makers, therefore, can make short-run errors regarding the uncertain (i.e., probabilistic risky) future. Agents, however, should "learn" from these short-run mistakes so that subjective probabilities or decision weights tend to converge to an accurate description of the programmed external reality. (This is a form of what is called Bayesian probability analysis.) Grandmont and Malgrange (1986, p. 9) have characterized this learning process as follows:

> Individual traders are bound to make significant forecasting errors ... while they are learning the [ergodic] dynamical laws of their environment, during the period of transition of the economy towards an hypothetical long run equilibrium – if it ever reaches one along which all forecasting errors vanish eventually.

Those agents whose subjective probabilities do not converge on the objective probabilities will make persistent systematic forecasting errors. The market embodies some form of a Darwinian process of natural selection that weeds out the persistent error-makers who make inefficient choices until, in the long run, only agents who do not make systematic errors remain.

Theories that claim that free markets are efficient are usually based on some variant of this Darwinian story where the long-run *intrinsic real value* of all economic assets is determined by the programmed real (deep) parameters of the system *that cannot be changed by any deliberate human action*. In the long run, rational agents make efficient choices as subjective expectations adapt to the predetermined and immutable reality, even if, in the short run, successful agents do not "know" they are making optimal choices.

Old and New Classical theorists, many Austrian theorists, Old (neoclassical synthesis) Keynesian and New Keynesian theorists, as well as Walrasian and post-Walrasian theorists, either explicitly or implicitly share the fundamental belief in a predetermined reality. Whether the theories explicitly adopt a probabilistic lexicon or not, this shared presumption of a preprogrammed reality can be labeled the ergodic axiom of classical economics (Davidson, 1984, 1994).

Agents in type 2 models suffer from some form of epistemological uncertainty. An originator of the type 1 rational expectations theory approach, Sargent (1993, pp. 3–4) has switched his approach to type 2 models of "bounded rationality" where agents are

> attempting to learn about probability distributions which, under rational expectations, they already know ... [and] the choices that we the researchers, as the 'gods' or creators of these artificial people, have in informing (or 'hard wiring') them about their environments before we turn them loose.

Frank Knight, an economist in the early 20th century, was one of the first to recognize the possibility of epistemological uncertainty for certain economic processes. Knight explicitly distinguished between quantifiable risks and uncertainties. Knight wrote that

> the practical difference between the two categories, risk and uncertainty, is that in the former the distribution of the outcome in a group of instances is known (either through calculation *a priori* or from the statistics of past experience), while in the case of uncertainty, this is not true, the reason being in general that it is impossible to form a group of instances, because the situation dealt with is in a high degree unique.
>
> (Knight, 1921, p. 233)

In an ergodic universe, however, any single event will appear to be unique to the observer only if she does not have a sufficient *a priori* or statistical knowledge of reality to properly classify this event with a group of similar conditional events. Knight (1921, p. 198) explains that uncertainty involving "unique events" occurs only when agents possess "partial knowledge" of the cosmos.[14] As such, Knight appears to be a precursor for what Colander calls the post-Walrasian theorists of today. Knight's reflections on the immutability of the economic cosmos are, like the post-Walrasians, somewhat ambiguous. Knight appears to argue that as a stylized fact uncertainty is an epistemological factor in an ontological immutable reality when he wrote (Knight, 1921, p. 210) that the

> universe may not be knowable ... [but] objective phenomenon [reality] ... is certainly knowable to a degree so far beyond our actual powers ... [and therefore] any limitation of knowledge due to lack of real consistency [i.e., ergodicity] in the cosmos may be ignored.

In other words, Knight suggests that any lack of knowledge about external reality that might be attributed to a lack of real consistency over time in the cosmos is insignificant and may be ignored when compared to humans' cognitive failures to identify the predetermined external reality. Knight (1921, p. 198) suggests, rather than dogmatically claims, that it "is *conceivable* that all changes might take place in accordance with known laws". Though Knight left the theoretical door slightly ajar, it does appear that his analysis is primarily based on the concept of a predetermined immutable cosmos. The primary difference between risk and uncertainty for Knight is that uncertainty exists only because of the failure of human's "actual powers" to process the information "knowable" about the programmed economic cosmos.

Since probabilistic risks can be quantified by human computing power, Knight argued that the future is insurable against risky occurrences. The cost of insurance, or self-insurance, will be taken into account in all entrepreneurial marginal cost calculations (or by contingency contracts in a complete Arrow-Debreu general equilibrium system). This insurance process permits entrepreneurs to make profit-maximizing rational production and investment choices even in the short run.

The existence of what appears to be uncertain or "unique" events, on the other hand, arises because humans do not have sufficient cognitive powers to group correctly these uncertain outcomes by their common characteristics. Hence for Knight agents cannot capture the insurance costs of these "uncertain" events in their marginal cost computations.

If we accept Knight's position that we can ignore the possibility of a "lack or real consistency in the cosmos", then the objective probabilities associated with what Knight labels "uncertain" events are already programmed into the consistent cosmos. In the long run, those entrepreneurs who in their price-marginal cost calculations include these insurance costs "as if" they knew the objective probabilities implicit in Knight's unchanging reality will make the efficient decision and will, in Knight's system, earn profits.

Chaos theory. The short-run emphasis of type 2 theories on the limitations of human computing power may explain the popularity of complex mathematical models such as "Chaos Theory" and other nonlinear mathematical models to analyze economic fluctuations – especially those in the financial markets.

> Chaos theory shows that a simple relationship that is *deterministic* but *nonlinear.* can yield a complex time path. ... When chaos occurs economic forecasting becomes extremely difficult ... basic forecasting devices become questionable.
>
> (Baumol and Benhabib, 1989, p. 79)

This *determinate* theory of chaos claims that the fluttering of a butterfly's wings[15] in China will, through a complex but completely determinate system of nonlinear difference equations "cause" a hurricane in the Atlantic Ocean. For an omnipotent Mother Nature, there is no uncertainty about butterfly-induced hurricanes in a structure described by such a programmed (time immutable) nonlinear equation system. The problem is that the structure is *so complex* that unless humans already know it or have some *deus ex machina* to describe it, it is extremely difficult to discover the future before the hurricane hits.

Austrian theory. Modern-day Austrian economic theorists such as O'Driscoll and Rizzo (1985) believe in an economic world where there is an immutable external reality similar to the way 19th-century physicists viewed the operations of the physical world. In their emphasis on uncertainty, however, these Austrians differ from mainstream Old and New Classical theorists. Many Austrians believe that the external reality may be predetermined by Mother Nature but this reality is too complicated for any single human being *ever* to process the information being sent out by market signals. The free market is the Austrians' *deus ex machina* that provides the (in principle calculable) relevant probabilities and reliable predictions to coordinate plans and outcomes via a Darwinian process[16] in a world of epistemological uncertainty and a programmed external reality.

Expected utility theory. Savage's expected utility theory (EUT) specifies the existence of economic relationships solely as an axiomatic based theoretical system. EUT is the basis of all demand theories espoused by mainstream economists whether they be Old or New Classical theorists, Old or New Keynesians, Walrasian or post-Walrasian theorists. In developing EUT, Savage presumes that a decision maker examines and evaluates all possible future outcomes of all possible alternative choices. Savage (1954, p. 16) characterizes this evaluation process as "Look before you leap". Underlying Savage's "look before you leap" EUT framework is the *ordering axiom*, i.e., the presumption that there exists a finite set of acts and outcomes and that each agent can make a *complete* and transitive preference *ordering* of all possible alternative choices (Savage, 1954, pp. 17–9).

Savage (1954, p. 15) recognizes that his "Look before you leap" analysis is *not* a general theory of decision making for it does not explicitly deal with uncertainty *per se*. Savage (1954, p. 15) admits that "a person may not know [all] the consequences of the acts open to him in each state of the world. He might be ... ignorant" and hence might want to leave his options open. This leaving options open that Savage (1954, p. 15) characterized as "You can cross that bridge when you come to it" is, Savage admits, often a more accurate description of human behavior than "look before you leap". In fact, the "look before you leap" approach "[c]arried to its logical extreme ... is utterly ridiculous ... because the task implied is not even remotely resembled by human possibility" (Savage, 1954, pp. 15–6). There is, therefore, a "practical necessity of confining attention to, or isolating, relatively simple situations in almost all applications of the theory of decision [EUT] developed in this book"[17] (Savage, 1954, pp. 82–3).

Savage's ordering axiom implies that the EUT is useful only when one "attack[s] relatively simple problems of decision by artificially confining attention to so small a world that the 'Look before you leap' principle can be applied" (Savage 1954, p. 16). EUT is "practical [only] in suitably limited domains. ... At the same time, the behavior of people is often at variance with the theory. The departure is sometimes flagrant" (Savage, 1954, p. 20). If, in some areas of economic activity, the assumption that humans can form a complete preference ordering is "preposterous" (Savage, 1954, pp. 15–6), then EUT cannot provide a useful explanation of the behavior of decision makers in these areas. Here, Keynes's association of uncertainty with the demand for liquidity becomes paramount in order to defer indefinitely resource using decisions.

The ordering axiom is violated whenever agents are unable to "look before they leap". In these cases, agents will prefer to leave their options open ("Cross that bridge when they come to it") rather than attempt to make, at the initial instant, the "rational" decisions described by EUT. The existence of money and other liquid assets permits income earners to leave their options open as to what producible goods they will buy with their earnings.

If the future is uncertain in an ontological sense, then sensible decision makers "know" it will always be impossible to possess at any future date a complete list prospects for any specific scenario. In this case of ontological uncertainty, the future is transmutable, and economic theorists should recognize that (1) Savage's ordering axiom is violated even in the long run, and (2) there will exist a positive long-run demand for liquidity.

Nobel Prize winner J. R. Hicks (1979, p. 113) has associated the violation of the "ordering axiom" with Keynes's *long-term* "liquidity" concept. Keynes (1936a, pp. 94, 145n, 148n, 168, 182, 216–8; 1937) emphasized relating nonprobabilistic uncertainty with liquidity preference and the nonneutrality of money in both the short and long run. EUT, therefore, is not a logical ubiquitous explanation of decision making in Keynes's general theory of a money-using economy.

For Keynes and the Post Keynesians, long-run uncertainty is associated with a nonergodic and transmutable reality concept. A fundamental tenet of Keynes's Revolution (e.g., 1936a, Ch. 12) is that probabilistic risks must be distinguished from uncertainty where, for the latter, probabilities calculated from historical data are not reliable guides to future performance.

Probabilistic risk may characterize routine, repeatable economic decisions where it is reasonable to presume an immutable (ergodic) reality. Keynes (1936, pp. 147–8), however, rejected the ergodic axiom as applicable to all economic expectations when he insisted that the "state of long term expectations" involving nonroutine matters that are "very uncertain" form the basis for important economic decisions involving investment, the accumulation of wealth, and finance. In these areas, agents "know" they are dealing with an uncertain, nonprobabilistic *creative economic external reality*.[18]

Can the advocates of mainstream economics justify their restrictive ergodic or ordering axioms as a better description of the economic world in which we live? The empirical evidence (see Christiano and Eichengreen, 1991) indicates that many macroeconomic time series have unit roots and are therefore nonstationary, and nonstationary is a sufficient condition for nonergodicity. Indeed Keynes's (1973, p. 308) criticism of Tinbergen's econometric methodology was that economic time series are not stationary for "the economic environment is not homogeneous over a period of time (perhaps because nonstatistical factors are relevant)". Since ergodicity is a necessary and sufficient condition for a predetermined immutable external reality, it would appear that the empirical evidence conflicts with the fundamental ergodic axiom of mainstream macroeconomic theory.

Nobel Prize laureate Robert Solow (1985) has argued that the economy is a nonstationary process moving through historical time. Solow states that there is an interaction of historical-societal circumstances and economic events. In describing "the sort of discipline economics *ought* to be", Solow (1985, p. 328) has written: "Unfortunately, economics is a social science. To express the point more formally, much of what we observe cannot be treated as the realization of a stationary stochastic process without straining credulity ... the end product of economic analysis is ... contingent on society's circumstances – on historical context. ... For better or worse, however, economics has gone down a different path". Had the Keynes/Post Keynesian discussion on uncertainty and a transmutable reality been more widely understood by economists, then the discipline Solow thinks economics "ought" to be would have been the discipline that developed in the last half century.

If agents "know" that the economic process is not stationary, decision makers should know that if objective probability distribution functions exist they are "subject to sudden [i.e., unpredictable] changes" (Keynes, 1973, p. 119) and the economy is ontologically uncertain.

Some theorists, however, prefer to have it both ways, namely recognizing nonergodicity in the short run, while presuming immutable fundamentals (or what they sometimes call unchanging "deep" parameters") in the long run. In these theories the decision makers believes their own (or others) subjective expectations are liable to changes induced by some noneconomic factor such as sun spot activity, while in the long run time immutable objective probabilities exist. This latter case of nonstationary subjective expectations (a case of short-run epistemological uncertainty) appears in modern "sunspot theories" of the business cycle where "prices change simply because they are expected to" (Azariadis, 1981).

Sunspot theory. Sunspot theorists often appear to claim compatibility "to earlier Keynesian macromodels" (Grandmont and Malgrange, 1986, p. 10) involving "animal spirits" (Cass and Shell, 1983, p. 193). Sunspot theorists attempt to marry the rational expectations hypothesis with the view that the subjective probability distributions need not, in the short run, match the objective (and assumed ergodic) probability functions governing real production and exchange processes.[19] In such systems, only in the "hypothetical long run" will "forecasting errors vanish" (Grandmont and Lagrange, 1986, p. 10).

Such models of "self-fulfilling" forecasts seem to permit mainstream economists to salvage a more sophisticated longer run form of what Samuelson has called the "ergodic hypothesis" (and thus meet Samuelson's criterion for economist-cum-hard scientist) while providing models that possess, at least in the long *short run*, a real world business cycle.

Sunspots represent extrinsic uncertainty, that is a random phenomenon that *does not affect "tastes, endowments, or production possibilities ... [t]he basic [deep] parameters defining an economy ... the fundamentals of that economy"* (Cass and Shell, 1983, p. 194–6 italics added). These fundamental forces of tastes, endowments, and productive technology predetermine the economic reality environment and produce the programmed long-run center of gravity or long-run equilibrium towards which the endogenous forces in the economy are always pushing. Only continuous demand and/or supply shocks[20] creating incessant new exogenous "extrinsic" uncertainty can prevent the system from settling down to this long-run equilibrium position. This extrinsic or "extraneous uncertainty", however, always "disappears in the long run – or in a stationary state, or when enough contingent claims markets exist to cover all probabilities" (Azariadis, 1981, p. 380), i.e., when probabilities associated with the presumed immutable reality are calculated by a *deus ex machina* marketplace.

Sunspot theorists only permit "temporary" departures from the long-run equilibrium determined by immutable real economic "fundamentals" in the system. In the long run, though we may all be dead, the ergodic economic process involving the real deep parameters defining the economic system will persist and determine the final solution to the economic problem. Since all "the basic parameters defining an economy" listed by Cass and Shell (1983, p. 196) are nonpecuniary, then all sunspot theorist must accept as a "matter of faith"[21] that in the long run money is neutral.

Despite claims of comparability to Keynes by demonstrating the possibility of short-run "Keynes-type" unemployment, sunspot theories, like Post-Walrasian theories, are *not* compatible with Keynes's "animal spirits" analysis where (1) money is nonneutral in both the short and the long run and (2) *crucial decisions* by humans (under uncertainty) alter the fundamental real forces of the economic system as decision makers create (and therefore affect) the future.

IX. Crucial decisions and Schumpeterian entrepreneurship

Shackle has developed the concept of crucial choice, i.e., a situation where a decision is made that changes forever the economic environment so that the identical decision conditions are "never to be repeated" (Shackle, 1955, p. 7). The future is transmutable in that it is created by crucial choice decisions[22] although *the future that is created is often not precisely what anyone intended.* The future is not discovered through the Bayes-LaPlace theorem regarding relative frequencies or any error-learning model.[23] This principle of cruciality ties Shackle's LSE-Austrian background with Schumpeter's theory of the entrepreneur.

Crucial decisions and the entrepreneurial function. If entrepreneurs have any important function in the real world, it is to make crucial decisions. Entrepreneurship, which is but one facet of human creativity, by its very nature, involves cruciality. To restrict entrepreneurship to robot decision making through ergodic calculations in an ergodic stochastic world, as Lucas and Sargent [hereafter L-S] explicitly do (see L-S, 1981, p. xii), ignores the role of the Schumpeterian entrepreneur – the creator of technological revolutions that bring about future changes that are often inconceivable even to the innovative entrepreneur. Exogenous expectations are a necessary condition for assuming human free will in important economic matters.

Ergodic probability models are a beguiling representation of decision making only in a world where routine decisions are made by L-S's

(1981, p. xii) "robot decision maker" entrepreneur. Since crucial decisions are never made by entrepreneurs in L-S's world, these models cannot explain the essential creative function of entrepreneurial behavior in a Keynes-Schumpeter world, where the reality is transmutable.

The possible existence of crucial decisions and their resulting nonergodic world has implicitly been recognized and summarily rejected by mainstream theorists in their desire to be seen as "hard-headed" scientists. For example, L-S indicate that they desire to draw conditional inferences about human behavior from observed economic times series:

> we observe an agent, or a collection of agents behaving through time; we wish to use these observations to infer how this behavior *would have* differed had the agent's environment been altered in some specified way. Stated so generally, it is clear that some inferences of this type will be impossible to draw. (How would one's life have been different had one married someone else?) The belief in the possibility of a non-experimental empirical economics is, however, equivalent to the belief that inferences of this kind can be made, under *some* circumstances.
>
> (L-S, 1981, pp. xi–xii)

Unlike Shackle, whose principle of cruciality defines a sufficient condition for the existence of nonergodic worlds, L-S provide neither necessary nor sufficient conditions when "*some* circumstances" will prevail. If L-S are correct and only in "some circumstances" can statistical inferences based on a realization be drawn, then an immutable (ergodic) reality cannot be ubiquitous in economics. Necessarily, there must be *other* circumstances where nonergodic circumstances pertain, and in such instances probability theory and the rational expectations hypothesis can be a seriously misleading analogy.[24]

If the relatively innocuous (and replicative?) choice of spouse is admitted by L-S to be so crucial that despite the large number of marriages recorded over time, statistical inferences about conditional probabilities regarding happy marriages cannot be drawn, then should not decisions "marrying" entrepreneurs to plant and equipment, or to production runs, or even decisions marrying the economy to money supply policies, or to specific banking institutions, etc., also be classified as crucial choices?

Crucial choices are more common than one might expect. Whenever there are significant transactions costs: no decision is fully reversible.[25] Mainstream micro- as well as macro-theorists ignore this element of cruciality in almost all decisions. (Walrasian theorists assume the ability to recontract without costs if one does not initially trade at the generasl equilibrium prices that embody the objective reality governed by the real parameters of a predetermined economic system.) Because of the substantial transactions costs involved in investment, production, and (at least) big ticket consumption decisions, in these areas, agents are necessarily married to their choices; decisions in these areas are normally crucial, and once an action is made, the possible future path is changed. In such a transmutable world, he who hesitates regarding choices in these areas and decides to remain liquid is saved to make a crucial decision another day.

Some economic processes may appear to be ergodic, at least for short subperiods of calendar time, while others are not. The epistemological problem facing every economic decision maker is to determine whether (a) the phenomena involved is currently governed by probabilities that can be presumed ergodic – at least for the relevant future or (b) nonergodic circumstances are involved. It is only in the latter case that entrepreneurship, money, liquidity, and contracts have important and essential roles to play (See Davidson, 1982–3, 1991, 1994). It is only the latter case where important policy decisions need to be made.

A nonergodic (uncertain) environment provides an analytical rationale for the existence of fixed money contracts and nonneutral money. Consequently, it provides an "alternative construction" that meets the "serious challenge ... to the theorist" that Hahn (1981, p. 1) posed.

X. Designing policy

Economists-scientists should "know" that, in some nonroutine domains, discovered empirical regularities in past data cannot be used to predict the future. In these nonergodic sectors of economic science, economists can and should encourage the development of "certain important [institutional] factors that somewhat mitigate in practice the effect of our ignorance of the future" (Keynes, 1936a, p. 163) by guiding the economy towards social objectives. If economists would recognize that nonergodicity is a prevalent property in many important economic situations, they would have to admit there could be a permanent role for the government to work with the private sector to improve the economic performance of markets.

In cooperation with the private sector, the government should be continuously searching for ways to develop economic institutions that attempt to reduce uncertainties by guiding the economic environment via aggregate demand policies and institutions that constrain rent-seeking proclivities, to limit future outcomes to those that are closely compatible with full employment and reasonable price stability.

The moral of this analysis of the ways different theorists deal with knowledge about an uncertain future is provided in a slight paraphrasing of Reinhold Neibuhr's famous "Serenity Prayer": God give us the grace to accept with serenity the things that cannot be changed [immutable realities], courage to change the things which should be changed [transmutable realities], and the wisdom to distinguish the one from the other.

8
World War II and the Postwar Open Economies System

As early as 1931, Keynes began to experience episodes of severe pains in his chest and shortness of breath that "were tell-tale signs of coronary artery insufficiency, with resulting anginal pains" (Skidelsky 1992, p. 627). A little over a year after the publication of *The General Theory of Employment Interest and Money* (1936a), in May 1937, Keynes suffered what today would be diagnosed as an attack of coronary thrombosis (Skidelsky, 1992, p. 634). From May until the end of September 1937, Keynes was confined to a private hospital for convalescence. Even after release from hospital, Keynes was told by his doctors that he must take significant periods of rest each day and even stay in bed one day a week.

This long convalescence limited his professional activities although he did keep up with public events that suggested the coming of war. By February 1938, Keynes had started to make public appearances again and began writing on economic problems that would occur as Britain, preparing for war, approached full employment. By April 1939, Keynes was arguing for low interest rates, control of capital exports, and the government to run fiscal surpluses as aggregate demand exceeded full-employment supply output when the British economy was put on a war footing (Skidelsky, 2003, p. 581).

On September 1, 1939, German troops marched into Poland and World War II began. For the first two years of the war, Keynes

> became chiefly concerned with how to pay for it. Keynes used his General Theory analysis to explain that if rearmament expenditures increased aggregate demand past full employment, then government fiscal policy should run surpluses to rein in the excess demand. These surpluses should include a compulsory savings plan as part of the fiscal policy. Under Keynes's plan the government would impose a

> graduated percentage of all incomes above a stipulated minimum to be turned over to the government. This additional government revenue would be used to pay for military defense expenditures without pushing aggregate demand above the full-employment level. Part of this additional government revenue would be taxes but part would be compulsory savings that would be returned to each income earner after the war so as to offset the lack of effective demand that Keynes expected to occur after the end of hostilities.
>
> (Skidelsky, 2003 p. 588)

In February 1940, Keynes published a pamphlet entitled *How To Pay For The War* (1940). This pamphlet explained in detail his compulsory savings plan proposal. It demonstrated the appropriateness of his *General Theory* for periods of potential boom as well as mass unemployment. In the pamphlet, Keynes proposed a permanent method for regulating aggregate demand to avoid excess aggregate demand induced booms as well as slumps due to a lack of aggregate effective demand.

I. Planning for the postwar open economy system

In August 1940, without being assigned any official duties, Keynes was offered an office at the Treasury. He was to be "a sort of roving commission" (Skidelsky, 2003, p. 603). By 1940, Keynes had already begun to consider the problem of overseas finances for the war effort. The problem that Britain faced was how it could obtain sufficient liquid funds to pay for the import of all the war materials (especially from the United States) that it could not produce at home.

Soon Keynes became a special envoy of the Chancellor of the Exchequer making several trips to Washington to help negotiate the financing of the purchase of war materials that Britain needed to continue to fight the war against Germany.

As early as 1941, Keynes began to think about devising a plan for a postwar international payments system that would lock the United States "into a system that would maintain balance of payments equilibrium between all countries without trade discrimination but without forcing deflation, unemployment and debt-bondage on the deficit countries" (Skidelsky, 2003, p. 672).

To explain Keynes's proposal for a postwar international payments system, we must initially develop some concepts that economists have developed to distinguish between a closed versus an open economy. A closed economy is an economy where the residents of one nation have no trade or financial transactions with residents of any other nation. In a closed economy, all legal contractual commitments between transactors are expressed in terms of a single nation's monetary unit.

In an open economy, some transactions are between parties residing in different nations. Since typically each nation uses a different money to settle its domestic contractual commitments, when a resident of nation A agrees to a contractual commitment with a resident of nation B, then both parties must agree on the use a single money as its means of contractual settlement. The money chosen for denominating the specific contract may be either the domestic money of nation A or the domestic money of nation B, or even the money of a third nation. The use of different monies by parties to international contracts can have important implications for the demand for liquidity in a global economy.

It is conventional wisdom of the mainstream of the economics profession that Keynes's revolutionary book *The General Theory of Employment, Interest, and Money* (1936a) is developed primarily for the analysis of a closed economy. Accordingly, many believe that Keynes's *General Theory* analysis is not applicable to economic problems of nations integrated into the global economy of the 21st century. Nothing can be further from the truth. The principles underlying Keynes's *General Theory* analysis have a direct applicability for discussing the operations and problems of any open economy.

In fact, in *The General Theory* Keynes explicitly introduces into the analysis some important economic complications that can result when the nation under discussion is an open economy. For example, Keynes noted that for any open economy

[1] foreign trade could modify the magnitude of domestic employment (Keynes, 1936a, p. 120),

[2] reductions in either money wages or the exchange rate of the domestic currency for the purpose of increasing the international competitiveness of domestic industries in order to improve the nation's trade balance by expanding exports relative to imports would worsen the terms of trade. A deterioration in the terms of trade signifies a reduction of the real income of the nation's already employed workers, even if the increase in exports stimulates additional hiring of previously unemployed workers (Keynes, 1936a, p. 263), and

[3] stimulating either investment in domestic plant and equipment or investment in other nations by increasing a nation's exports relative to its imports can increase domestic employment growth (Keynes, 1936a, p. 335).

Keynes also noted that if the government of nation A is afraid to use fiscal policy to deliberately increase aggregate demand in order to stimulate the domestic economy because politicians believe that the resulting government deficits will unleash inflationary forces, then a policy that tends to increase nation A's export demand relative to imports will be seen as an alternative path for expanding domestic employment. This export expansion policy at the expense of imports, however, will negatively affect nation A's trading partner (nation B) as B's domestic industries lose domestic sales to A's exporters while B's export industries do not gain sales from nation A. Or as Keynes (1936a, p. 338) put it, a "favorable balance [of trade], provided it is not too large, will prove extremely stimulating" to domestic employment, even if it does so at the expense of employment opportunities abroad.

In a passage that is particularly relevant to today's global economic setting, Keynes (1936a, p. 335) noted that

> in a society where there is no question of direct investment under the aegis of public authority [due to fear of either government deficits *per se* or big governments], the economic objects, with which it is reasonable for the government to be preoccupied, are the domestic interest rate and the balance of foreign trade.

A reduction in domestic interest rates will tend to stimulate additional domestic investment expenditures. If, however, nations with developed financial markets permit free movement of capital funds across national boundaries, then people with funds will, *ceteris paribus*, move their savings from nations with lower interest rates to the nation with the highest interest rate. The result will be a tendency to equalize interest rates across nations, with the nation which sets the highest interest rate calling the interest-rate tune for the rest of the global economy.

With free international financial mobility, therefore, "the authorities had no direct control over the domestic rate of interest or the other inducements to home investment, [and] measures to increase the favorable balance of trade [are] ... the only *direct* means at their disposal for increasing foreign investment" (Keynes, 1936a, p. 336) and therefore increasing domestic employment and income. In other words, if capital is freely mobile internationally, then a nation cannot unilaterally try to reduce its interest rate to stimulate investment and employment. Moreover, if the use of expansionary fiscal deficits is seen as politically unacceptable, then a policy that increases exports relative to imports in order to improve the balance of trade, what can be called an export-led growth policy, will appear to the State to be the only desirable method of promoting domestic economic growth, employment, and prosperity.

The balance of trade is defined as the value of exports minus the value of imports. A nation's balance of trade is said to be "favorable" when the value of exports exceeds the value of imports. An unfavorable balance of trade means the nation is importing more than it is exporting. This import surplus of an unfavorable trade balance will normally be financed by either drawing down the nation's foreign exchange reserves or by borrowing from foreigners.

Keynes was well aware that the domestic employment advantage gained by this export-led growth policy to achieve a more favorable balance of trade "is liable to involve an equal disadvantage to some other country" (Keynes, 1936a, p. 338) for one nation's export surplus must be another nation's unfavorable trade balance involving the value of imports exceeding the value of exports. When countries pursue an "immoderate policy" (Keynes, 1936a, p. 338) of export-led growth (e.g., Japan, Germany, and the Newly Industrializing Countries (NICs) of Asia in the 1980s and China, India, and other Asian nations in the first years of the 21st century), this aggravates their trading partners' unemployment in the import-competing industries as well as the partners' overall unemployment problem. If trading partners finding their unemployment problem increasing due to an unfavorable trade balance, these nations are often forced to engage in a "senseless international competition for a favorable balance which injures all alike" (Keynes, 1936a, pp. 338–9).

The traditional approach for expanding exports and improving the trade balance is to make a nation's domestic industries *more competitive* by either forcing down nominal wages (including fringe benefits) in order to reduce labor production costs, or (and) by a devaluation of the exchange rate,[1] thereby reducing the price of exports in terms of the other nation's money while increasing the domestic price of imports. Since workers and labor unions are likely to resist any reduction in their money wages, rather than attempting to force down domestic money wage rates, a nation often devalues its exchange rate to gain a competitive edge over foreign producers of goods and services. Any competitive gains obtained by manipulating money wages or exchange rates, however, will only foster further global stagnation and recession if one's trading partners attempt to regain a competitive edge by similar policies.

Unlike the classical theorists of his day (and our day as well), Keynes recognized that the 16th-century political economists known as "the mercantilists" were aware of the fallacy of cheapness and the danger that excessive international competition may turn the terms of trade against a country" (Keynes, 1936a, p. 345), thereby reducing domestic living standards so that even if more people are working, they, on average, can be earning less in terms of the goods and services that each hour of labor effort can buy.

Keynes's *General Theory* analysis (1936a, p. 378) recommends that *every* nation should actively undertake a program for public *domestic* investment to generate *domestic* full employment without having to worry about international economic repercussions. Otherwise, a *laissez-faire* philosophy involving "prudent" fiscal policies that either eliminated, or at least resulted in negligible fiscal deficits, in tandem with a system of free international monetary flows, creates a global environment where *each* nation independently sees significant national advantages in a policy of export-led growth, even though pursuit of these policies simultaneously by many nations "injures all alike" (Keynes, 1936a, pp. 338–9). This warning of Keynes, however, has gone virtually unrecognized since the early 1970s, as Keynes's revolutionary analysis was never adopted by mainstream economists.[2]

In a *laissez-faire* world, when governments do not have the political will to stimulate directly any domestic component of aggregate spending to reduce unemployment, "domestic prosperity [is] directly dependent on a competitive pursuit of [export] markets" (Keynes, 1936a, p. 349). This is a competition in which all nations cannot be winners.

For a nation to break out of a global slow-growth or stagnating economic environment, the truth, Keynes insisted, lay in pursuing a

> policy of an autonomous rate of interest, unimpeded by international preoccupations, and a national investment programme directed to an optimum level of employment which *is twice blessed* in the sense that *it helps ourselves and our neighbors at the same time.* And *it is the simultaneous pursuit of these policies by all countries together which is capable of restoring economic health and strength* internationally, whether we measure it by the level of domestic employment or by the volume of international trade.
>
> (Keynes 1936a, p. 349, italics added)

To achieve a policy of being able to set interest rates independent of international forces requires a nation to be able to impose, when necessary, international regulations on the inflow and outflow of international capital funds. This is usually labeled a policy of capital controls.

It should be obvious from the afore cited passages from Keynes's 1936 book that Keynes was well aware of the problems that might arise if any government tried to pursue a full-employment policy if an open, *laissez faire,* global economic system was established after World War II. Accordingly, not long after the World War II began, Keynes's turned his mind to developing a proposal for a New Way to resolved trade problems that did not force nation's into a competitive war to achieve favorable trade balances.

In 1940, a document that stimulated Keynes's thinking about postwar international payments and liquidity problems was the "Funk Plan". Hitler's finance minister, Walter Funk, set out the blueprints for Hitler's New [Economic] Order. The Funk Plan was built on an earlier system devised by Hitler's former finance minister, Hjalmar Schacht. The details of this Schacht-Funk Plan was sent to Keynes by the British Ministry of Information with a request that Keynes make a broadcast to the Americans and the British Dominions in which he would discredit this Hitler plan for a new economic order.

Keynes, however, felt that Funk and Schacht had taken steps in the right direction and that the Allies ought to be thinking about building on the concept of a clearing union that was part of the Funk Plan. Keynes recognized that Germany would use Funk's plan to the detriment of their neighbors, but nevertheless the underlying economic principle was sound and could be built into a desirable postwar system that benefited all the nations of the world since the crucial point was to have a system that maintained trade balances among all nations (Skidelsky, 2003, pp. 672–3).

Following Schacht, the Funk Plan attempted to ensure that goods exchange for goods and therefore made possible a level of trade that might not be undertaken in a system of free markets with flexible exchange rates. As a result of studying the Funk Plan, "the doctrine that exchange controls were superior to currency depreciation became a permanent part of Keynes's thinking" (Skidelsky, 2003, p. 673). It should be noted, however, that as early as 1936, with the emphasis in *The General Theory* on the importance of an autonomous domestic interest rate in an open economy setting, Keynes had already recognized the possibility of the need for international capital funds restrictions.

Keynes recognized that the Funk Plan was not the best possible postwar system but it easily could provide some guidelines for building a new international economic system that was far superior to a policy of *laissez-faire* in international trade and financial transactions. The great innovation that Keynes would provide to the Funk Plan was the idea that in any trading system, if there developed a persistent trade imbalance between nations, there should be a mechanism where the creditor nation, which is experiencing the favorable balance of trade, should recognize its responsibility for solving the trade imbalance by not hoarding (saving) in the form of international liquid assets (i.e., foreign exchange reserves) the value of the nation's earned export surplus. Instead, the creditor nation should spend any excessive trade surplus earnings by buying producibles from deficit nations, thereby permitting the deficit nations to work their way out of debt.[3]

With the Funk Plan in hand, Keynes developed his proposal for a postwar currency system that transferred the major onus of adjustment in international trade from the debtor to the creditor nation. Keynes's plan called for an international currency union whose purpose

> was to secure creditor adjustment without renouncing debtor discipline. Its method was to marry the Schacht-Funk "clearing" approach with the banking principle. All residual international transactions – those giving rise to surpluses and deficits in [nations'] balance of payments position to be settled through "clearing accounts" held by [nations'] member central banks in an International Clearing Bank (ICB).
>
> (Skidelsky, 2003, pp. 267–7)

Keynes envisioned this ICB as a supranational central bank. The balance of each of the national central banks at the ICB was to be called "bancors". Bancors would be the ultimate reserve asset of the international financial system.

In Keynes's system, each nation's central bank would be required to sell its domestic currency to an ICB member nation's central bank when the latter wanted to sell some of its bancor deposit at the ICB to obtain the domestic currency of a nation. There would also be overdraft facilities at the ICB to provide international liquidity for those nations whose bancor deposits were temporarily close to depletion, and therefore the nation might have trouble making payments to foreigners until its bancor reserve position was restored. By May 1942, Keynes's clearing union scheme was accepted by the British government as a plan for a postwar international payments system that could be brought to the table in negotiations with the United States.

A week after the United States entered the war in December 1941, the United States Secretary of Treasury, Henry Morgenthau, instructed his director of monetary research, Harry Dexter White, to develop a proposal for postwar monetary stabilization arrangements (Skidelsky, 2003 p. 695). White's proposal for an international exchange stabilization fund became the American alternative to the British Keynes Plan. The basic difference was that Keynes's plan for a clearing union was based on the banking principle that depositors who held positive balances at a bank (rather than spent them) should still possess the liquidity of these deposits while the bank put these funds to use by making them available to anyone who would borrow these idle funds in order to spend them on the current products of industry. White's plan did not provide any way for a nation subscribing to the exchange stabilization fund could to use, at their own discretion and initiative, their subscribed funds to meet their own liquidity needs when necessary.

Fundamental to Keynes's plan was the desirability of shifting the balance of payments adjustment problems from debtor to creditor nations. This would avoid any deflationary forces that affected both debtor and creditor nations when, under a more conventional international payments system, a debtor nation is forced to make the major balance of payments adjustment by reducing consumers' demand for goods and services for the purpose of reducing imports, and therefore payments, to foreigners.

Keynes designed a system with a built-in mechanism that induced international creditor nations to accept the major responsibility for curing persistent trade imbalances between nations of the world. Since everyone expected that the United States would be the major creditor nation after the war, the Keynes Plan required the United States to accept the responsibility for curing the international financial problems that was bound to occur in the immediate postwar era. It was obvious to all that the war-devastated nations of Europe and Asia would required significant imports from the United States to rebuild their economies, while their ravaged economies would not have the capacity to produce exports to the United States to earn dollars needed to buy American produced goods. The Keynes Plan required the creditor nation to accept the onus of correcting a trade imbalance, thereby implying the possibility that the United States would have to take on an unspecified, but a substantially large financial responsibility to help the rest of the world rebuild from the devastation of World War II.

White's plan was much more modest. It set up an exchange stabilization fund. The function of this fund was to assure that member nations did not engage in an exchange-rate war by devaluing their exchange rate to gain a competitive edge over other nations in international markets. The fund, at its discretion, could make loans to the central banks of nations that were experiencing significant persistent deficits in their international payments position, in order to prevent the deficit nations from having to devalue their currency. With these loans from the International Monetary Fund (IMF), these nations could pay for their excess of imports over exports while the nations tried to adjust their economies to eliminate the unfavorable trade balance. The financing of White's stabilization fund was to be established by specified initial subscriptions of all the nations that became members. This essentially limited the liability of the United States to its initial subscription – a sum of $3 billion that White claimed was the maximum that the United States Congress would accept.

In July 1944, 736 delegates and their staffs from 44 countries journeyed to the Mount Washington Hotel in Bretton Woods, New Hampshire to hammer out a negotiated plan for the postwar international payments system. Since the United States had paid the piper for the Allied war effort, it called the tune. Keynes's plan was rejected and the White Plan was adopted. The IMF was the embodiment of White's stabilization fund plan. As Skidelsky (2003, p. 767) has noted, the Bretton Woods agreement "was shaped not by Keynes's *General Theory* but by the United States's desire of an updated gold standard as a means of liberalizing trade. If there was an underlying ideology it was Morgenthau's determination to concentrate financial power in Washington".

Less than two years after the Bretton Woods meeting, Keynes died on Easter Sunday, April 21, 1946.

In chapter 10, we will discuss Keynes's general theory principles that underlay his plan for a postwar international payments system and show how, despite the defeat of the Keynes Plan at Bretton Woods, the postwar global prosperity was in large part due to the major creditor nation, the United States, accepting, for political rather than economic reasons, the responsibility for solving persistent trade imbalances as in Keynes's plan prescription. In chapter 10, we will also suggest what a Keynes Plan system would involve if one were to institute such a proposal in the 21st century. By explaining the principles underlying Keynes's plan for his international payments system, it is possible to design an international clearing union institution that is more in tune with the economics and politics of the 21st century. For, as Keynes recognized, it was not sufficient to present an economic prescription based on the right principles, but the principles must be cleverly packaged so that they do not appear to be in dramatic conflict with the political views and values of the day.

But before we pursue Keynes's plan for international monetary reform, in chapter 9 we will explain why the classical theory of open economies that most mainstream economists accept as absolute truths can be just as misleading and disastrous as the classical theory of closed economies.

9

Classical Trade Theory versus Keynes's General Theory of International Trade and International Payments

The classical law of comparative advantage and classical theory's presumption of the desirability of freely flexible exchange rates[1] are the foundations of mainstream economists' claim that free trade and unfettered international finance markets are socially desirable since they promote maximum efficiency and prosperity globally. On the other hand, Keynes's analysis of the operation of a monetary economy suggests that, like Say's Law, the conventional wisdom regarding the importance of the classical law of comparative advantage and the desirability of flexible exchange rates can be "misleading and dangerous".

I. The benefits associated with the classical theory of international trade

Every well-trained mainstream economist whose work is logically consistent with classical theory knows that the claimed benefits of free trade with a freely flexible exchange rate are:

1. that it is impossible for any nation to experience a persistent (unfavorable) trade imbalance where the value of imports exceeds that of exports;
2. that each nation can pursue monetary and fiscal policies for full employment without inflation, independent of the economic situation of its trading partners;[2] and
3. that the flow of capital will always be from the rich creditor (i.e., developed) nations to the poor debtor (i.e., less developed) nations. This international capital flow from rich to poor nations depends on a classical belief in the ubiquitous classical theory's "law of variable proportions" that determines the real return per unit of

> effort to both capital and labor as inputs in the production process. Since rich countries are presumed to be capital rich (i.e., possess more real capital goods per worker) while poor nations have less capital per worker, the law of variable proportions states that the real return on capital should be higher in the poor nations where capital is relatively more scarce. In a free-market environment, therefore, capital should flow from where it earns a lower return to where it earns a higher return, i.e., capital should flow from rich nations into the poor nations until the return on capital is equal in each country. The effect of this hypothetical classical international capital flow would be to encourage more rapid development of the poorer LDCs and, in the long run, a more equitable global distribution of income and wealth.

Since capital is scarce in LDCs, investment projects in poor nations financed by this hypothesized free-market capital flows from rich to poor nations should generate sufficient sales and foreign earnings for the LDCs to repay the capital obtained from foreign lenders and investors. Accordingly, this classical conventional wisdom implies that international capital flows are temporary[3] and *self-liquidating.*

It consequently follows from this classical theory way of thinking that government policy should be to ensure that all import and export markets and international financial- and exchange-rate markets should be immediately "liberalized" and made permanently free of any government regulations or restrictions.

II. International trade and liberalized markets: the facts

Since the breakdown of the Bretton Woods international payments system in the early 1970s, there has been a persistent trend toward (1) freeing international trade from government imposed tariff and quota barriers and (2) liberalizing international capital and foreign exchange markets. The economic results have not been consistent with classical theorists' Panglossian promises of the wonderful benefits that automatically occur when government regulations are removed from export, import, and financial markets. Despite widespread liberalization of export, import, and international financial markets since 1973,

1. some Latin American and African non-oil-producing nations have experienced persistent deficits in their balance of payments; and

2. flight capital has drained resources from the relatively poor nations toward the richer ones, resulting in a more inequitable redistribution of income and wealth globally as well as within many nations, and
3. the major trading nations of the developed world have been under increasing pressure to coordinate their monetary and fiscal policies. For example, in September 1987, the United States and Germany publicly clashed over incompatible monetary policies. The great October 1987 crash of world financial markets followed. This frightening experience reinforced the idea among the central bankers of the developed nations that if they don't all hang together, they may all hang separately.

To understand this disjuncture between classical theory and the facts, we begin by examining the implications of the trade and employment patterns implied in the classical law of comparative advantage compared to what really happens in the real world.

III. Trade, the wealth of nations, and the law of comparative advantage

One universal economic "truth" that *all* mainstream economists agree upon is that the "law of comparative advantage" assures that with free trade more goods and services are produced globally. This is accomplished by each nation specializing in producing from its industries that have a "comparative advantage" and exporting some of the products of its comparative advantage industries for imports by other nations, while, it is assumed, *all resources in each trading nation are always fully employed*. As a result, all nations should gain from free trade.

Which industries of each nation have this comparative advantage is determined by supply-side relationships that determine the productivity of capital and labor in the production process. (A hypothetical example of this gain due to the law of comparative advantage is given *infra*.) Any government interference with a free-trading relationship between nations following the law of comparative advantage will reduce the economic prosperity of the nations involved from reaching their potential maximum solution.

Adam Smith (1776), on the other hand, believed that the ability of any nation to produce additional income and wealth is constrained primarily by the extent of the marketplace. By expanding the market for goods, Smith argued, the introduction of trade between regions permitted entrepreneurs to take advantage of economies of scale, thereby producing more from each worker employed, and thereby enhancing the income and the wealth of nations. For Adam Smith, economic growth was primarily demand driven. The key to overcoming existing production constraints was the expansion of market demand. An obvious moral of Smith's analysis is that no nation that aspires to be wealthy can be an island unto itself. Of course, implicit in the Smith analogy is that consumers in the domestic market for the products of domestic industries are already satiated with goods, so that domestic market expansion is unlikely, if not impossible. In any case, supply constraints due to the classical law of diminishing returns, introduced into classical theory by the 19th-century economist David Ricardo, has no significant role to play in Smith's inquiry into what limits the wealth of nations at any point of time.

Ricardo (1817) introduced the law of comparative advantage to justify the importance of free trade among nations. Since Ricardo, advocates of free international trade have invoked the need for each nation to specialize in the industry (industries) in which it has a comparative advantage to increase wealth in the face of supply (significantly large diminishing returns) constraints. Unlike Smith's argument, this Ricardian need for specialization to increase the wealth of nations does not rely on being able to capture the economies of scale by expanding domestic production. In a Ricardian world of trade, production in each nation occurs in the realm of diminishing returns that is due to the operation of the classical law of variable proportions where the added production of hiring an additional worker is less than the addition to output produced by the worker hired previously. In Ricardo's scheme, increases in aggregate demand will not, *per se*, lead to significant increases in the wealth by nations. Rather, it is the law of comparative advantage, where one nation specializes in that industry for which it has the greatest production cost advantage, while that nation's trading partner specializes in the industry that has the smallest cost disadvantage, that permitted the wealth of both trading partners to improve as demand for goods and services increases.

Let us illustrate the law of comparative advantage with the following hypothetical example. Assume there are two economies, e.g., the East (i.e., cheap-labor countries like India and China) and the West (high-cost-labor countries such as the United States or Western Europe). For simplicity, before free trade begins, each economy produces two tradeable products – say bicycles (which uses cheap unskilled labor) and computers (which requires higher paid skilled labor). In the absence of trade, assume that there are a million employed workers in the East and a hundred thousand employed workers in the West engaged in these two industries, and that the global total of these 1,100,000 employed workers produces (and presumably their employers could profitably sell) a total of 375,000 bicycles and 55,000 computers in the market place.

According to classical Ricardian theory, the introduction of free trade between East and West will encourage each economy to specialize in producing the products in which it has a comparative advantage. Suppose the East could produce both bicycles and computers at a lower cost than the West, since even the highly skilled workers in the East are willing to work for a significantly lower wage than that paid to skilled workers in the West. Suppose, however, that the East's low cost of production advantage was greater in the bicycle industry than in the computer industry. Economists would say that although the East had an absolute cost advantage in the production of both bicycles and computers, the East's comparative advantage is in the production of bicycles and the West's comparative advantage is in the production of computers. Then, according to the law of comparative advantage, the East should, by employing all its one million workers and capital, specialize in the production of bicycles, while the West should employ its 100, 000 workers so as to specialize in the production of computers. Assume, because of this specialization, the globally employed 1,100,000 workers would produce more bicycles and more computers, say, 400,000 bicycles and 70,000 computers.

In this hypothetical comparative advantage example, by engaging in free trade, it is assumed that the world gains a total of 25,000 additional bicycles and 15,000 additional computers. Then, the East should sell bicycles to the West and in turn buy computers from the West. Since, with the same employed labor force, more of both goods are produced and available for consumption, the residents of each nation should gain somewhat from this trade in the sense that they will have more bicycles and computers for their use while all the goods are produced with the same amount (real cost) of labor time worked in each nation. Thus, it is claimed that the law of comparative advantage "proves" that the real income of the global economy increases, as with free trade more goods and services are provided to consumers in both the East and the West.

For Ricardo, each nation's comparative advantage was typically associated with its unique supply environment (e.g., availability of minerals deposits, climate differences and its effects on agricultural production, etc) that resulted in differences in production costs. This argument for "free" trade based on the law of comparative advantage is based on the notion of opening the domestic market to a foreign source which has relatively lower costs of production due to productivity advantages (even if the industry is operating under diminishing returns) not available in the domestic economy.

In Ricardo's famous wine-cloth example, it was the climate and a high labor-to-capital ratio which gave Portugal its comparative advantage in the production of wine vis-à-vis England's comparative advantage in the production of cloth. Even if the production of both wine and cloth was cheaper in Portugal than England, if Portugal concentrated its resources on the production of wine, where it had the greatest cost advantage, and England used its resources in the production of cloth, where it had the least cost disadvantage, then, as in our hypothetical bicycle-computer example *supra*, total output of both commodities would be greater than if each country tried to produce both commodities. Consequently, this total increase in output because of the specialization of each nation in its comparative advantage industry makes it possible to increase the quantity of wine and cloth available to the market in both nations.

Divergences in costs are obvious in agriculture and mineral exploitation, where climate and the nonrandom deposits of minerals among nations made certain commodities relatively cheaper to produce in one country than another. In mass production industries, on the other hand, differences in production costs are less likely to reflect differences due to nature's climatic or mineral endowment associated with any particular nation, as the same technology is used in production in any nation.

Keynes (1933c, p. 238) recognized this possibility when he wrote:

> A considerable degree of international specialization is necessary in a rational world in all cases where it is indicated by wide differences in climate, natural resources. ... But over an increasingly wide range of industrial products ... I become doubtful whether the economic costs of self-sufficiency is great enough to outweigh the other advantage of gradually bringing the producer and the consumer within the same ambit of the same national economic and financial organisations [to assure full employment]. Experience accumulates to prove that most modern mass production processes can be performed in most countries and climates with equal efficiency.

In other words, Keynes was arguing, and today's facts tend to demonstrate that, given the existence of multinational firms and the ease with which they can transfer technology internationally, any differences in relative costs of production in any particular industry are more likely to reflect national differences in money wages (per same hour of "real" human labor) plus the costs of providing "civilized" working conditions (measured in terms of a single currency) such as limiting the use of child labor, plus the costs to the enterprise of providing health insurance and pension benefits for employees, etc. In other words, in a *laissez-faire* system today, global industrial-trade patterns are more likely to reflect differences in nominal wage, occupational safety, and other nominal labor expenses that the enterprise must bear, than real costs associated with either national differences in climate, or difference in the availability of natural resources.

In the 21st century, low transportation and/or communication costs make it possible to deliver many goods and services cheaply to distant foreign markets. Consequently, mass-production industries that use low-skilled workers, semi-skilled workers, or even high-skilled workers are likely to locate in those nations where the economic system values human life the lowest, at least as measured by the wage paid per hour of labor and the work environment provided by entrepreneurs. Most developed nations passed legislation long ago that made "sweatshop" production and the use of child labor illegal. Yet such conditions typically still exist in the competitive industries of most less developed nations. Consequently, free competition among mass production industries engaged in international trade usually implies that in developed nations the standard of living of the workers will decline toward that of workers in nations that have large populations of cheap available labor, working in "sweatshops", with little legislation protecting safe and healthy working conditions.

On the other hand, in those production processes (e.g., personal services such as servants, waiters, barbers, etc.) where communication and/or transportation costs are very high, and immigration legislation limits the importation of cheap labor, significant employment opportunities may still exist in the personal service industries of developed nations with legislative regulations requiring civilized working condition standards. If free trade displaces a growing number of workers from previously high-paying mass-production industries in developed nations, then the competition for the existing service jobs in non-tradeable production processes by these displaced workers is likely to depress wages (See Uchitelle, 2006), or at least prevent the real wage of employed workers from rising significantly over time. It is, therefore, no wonder that the share of wages in United States GDP was, in 2005, at its lowest level in decades.

As we cross the threshold into the 21st century, Keynes's analytical framework indicates that the argument for free international trade as a means of promoting the wealth of all nations and their inhabitants cannot be rationalized on the basis of the law of comparative advantage – except perhaps for minerals, agriculture, and other industries where productivity is related to climatic conditions or mineral availability. Today, production in these climate- and natural resource-related industries, however, is often controlled by the market power of cartels (e.g., OPEC) and/or producer nations' governmental policies designed to prevent market prices from falling sufficiently to reflect the "real" costs of production. In other words, many industries for which the law of comparative advantage might still be applicable are often largely sheltered from international competitive forces by cartels.

The growth of multinational corporations in mass production industries and the movement toward a more liberalized free trade in the final decades of the 20th century encouraged business enterprises to "outsource" production, i.e., to search for the lowest-wage foreign workers available in order to reduce production costs. The availability of "outsourcing" also acts as a countervailing power to high-cost, labor-union-organized domestic workers in developed countries. Indeed in the early years of the 21st century, the rapidly developing industrial structure of many nations (e.g., China, India, Southeast Asia) can be largely attributed to the competitive search by multinational firms to utilize low wage foreign workers to compete with the high wage workers in developed nations to produce the identical goods and services under the same technological production processes.

In the early decades after World War II, when transportation and communication costs between nations were high and there were significant restrictions on trade, high domestic unit labor costs acted as a spur to encourage corporate managers in mass production industries to search for innovative domestic investment ways to improve domestic labor productivity, and thereby reduce labor costs per unit of output. With the growth of multinationals and the removal of many restrictions on the international trading of mass-produced manufactured goods, high domestic labor costs now encourage managerial practices such as outsourcing, rather than productivity enhancing investments, to lower unit production costs. Under current conditions, it is cheaper to outsource using existing technical production processes than incur the higher cost of searching for technological improvements in production processes to reduce unit production costs domestically. Accordingly, the higher profits from outsourcing have not been plowed back into research and technological development even if, in the long run, it is technological improvements that raise living standards. Under the rules of free trade today, there is less of an incentive for managers to pursue innovations to improve domestic labor productivity in any industrial sector where inexpensive foreign labor can "do the job", and transportation and/or communication costs are small relative to production costs. The decline in the rate of growth of domestic labor productivity in many developed nations since the 1970s can be, at least partly, related to this phenomena of emphasizing the use of cheap foreign labor vis-à-vis the search for domestic production process improvements by the private sector.

Except for production of some minerals, diminishing returns is, today, rarely an important aspect of production cost of internationally traded goods and services. Consequently, instead of substituting production in a nation with cheap foreign labor for production in a nation with high-cost workers, justification for the desirability of the expansion of international trade must be the result of increasing market demand globally. Demand-driven expansion of trade can explain the growth of the wealth of nations in both the Adam Smith's sense of exploiting economies of scale and in the sense of John Maynard Keynes, who saw the lack of effective demand as the main reason for the inability of economies to provide the flow of production that they were capable of providing.

Nevertheless, rather than arguing that trade provides the opportunity for all nations to expand the effective demand for the products they produce, economic advisors to important policy makers bring out the old chestnut of the classical "law of comparative advantage" to justify liberalizing trade agreements even when the facts do not appear to support this argument. For example, in the spring of 2005, the chairman of President Bush's Council of Economic Advisors, N. Greg Mankiw, defended the practice of "outsourcing" production, where American firms, instead of hiring residents to work in factories located in the United States, shift production to factories overseas where lower wage workers are readily available.

Mankiw claimed that, despite the obvious loss of high-wage jobs by American workers to lower wage foreign workers, outsourcing is beneficial to both the United States economy and the rest of the world. Mankiw argued that, in the long run, free trade will result in more income and wealth for all nations by creating new higher value jobs for workers in the United States as well as the jobs created in the nations to which production has been outsourced.

Unfortunately, the law of comparative advantage upon which Mankiw's claim of the creation of new high-value jobs is based requires at least two basic assumptions that are not applicable to the real world in which we live. First, as in our hypothetical bicycle-computer example *supra*, it is assumed that the hypothesized additional produced supply of 25,000 bicycles and 15,000 computers automatically will create its own additional global demand for these additional products. (Wouldn't the multinational auto companies be glad to know that if they increase global productive capacity by siting plants in countries that have comparative advantage in auto assemblies, then they will sell [at a profit] all the cars they can produce? There can never be surplus capacity – as there seems to be today.)

This assertion that additional supply always creates its own additional market demand implies the applicability of Say's Law to our classical trade theory analysis. But as we have already noted, Keynes demonstrated that Say's Law could not be applied to money-using entrepreneurial economies. Full employment is not an automatic outcome of free market competition domestically or internationally. Consequently, if there is anything economists should have learned since Keynes, it is that one cannot prove that there will automatically be gains from free trade to be shared by all trading economies unless one can be assured that there is full employment in all nations – before and after free trade.

That brings us to a second problem in applying the law of comparative advantage to the real world. The textbook comparative advantage analysis assumes that the gains from trade due to the law of comparative advantage occur only if neither capital nor labor is mobile across national boundaries, while the law of variable proportions determines the productivity of labor in each industry of each nation. If there is no capital or labor mobility across national boundaries, then when the capital rich region [the West] specializes in an industry that is most productive with a very capital intensive use of technology (computer production), while the East region that has plenty of labor but little capital specializes in the labor intensive industry (bicycles), then total output globally will be maximized.

If capital is internationally mobile, however, and if, after trade, there is not global full employment, then the beneficial results stemming from the law of comparative advantage may not materialize. With free international capital mobility and free trade, entrepreneurs will locate plant and equipment investments to produce goods in that nation where it is most profitable to produce, i.e., where unit labor costs are lowest.[4] Thus, if multinational firms can shift technology from nation to nation, then it will take the same number of man-hours of input to produce a unit of output in each country – or as Keynes (1933b, p. 238) wrote, "modern mass production processes can be performed in most countries ... with equal efficiency". The East, therefore, has the absolute advantage in that its unit money labor costs (when denoted in terms of a single currency) are lower for the production of both bicycles and computers at all relevant ranges of production that the global market can absorb. The East will ultimately attract enough foreign capital to produce all the bicycles and computers necessary to meet global demand. In other words, as long as production does not run into significant diminishing returns and total after-trade demand is not sufficient to assure global full employment, international production and trade patterns will be determined by absolute advantage of having a large supply of low money wage workers available and not by the law of comparative advantage. Consequently, in the West production and employment in the tradeable goods industries will decline substantially, if not completely.

Accordingly, the use of comparative advantage analysis as a justification for letting free markets determine outsourcing, trade, and international payments flows can be dangerous to the health of national economies especially those that restrict the use of child labor, provide their workers with civilized working conditions, and simultaneously provide a high wage standard of living. Such civilized nations will not have any absolute cost advantage in the production of tradeable goods and services vis-à-vis nations where child labor and low wages prevail.

In sum, if capital is mobile internationally, as long as the East has an absolute advantage in producing all tradeable goods because it has available an inexpensive large additional supply of both unskilled and skilled cheap labor that can be brought into the production of tradeables, then the argument that the "law of comparative advantage" assures there are gains from trade for all nations is not applicable. Given the East's abundant available cheap labor supply of unskilled and skilled workers, the East will attract foreign capital from the West to employ East's workers to produce most, if not all, the tradeable goods and services that can be profitably sold globally. The West will be left mainly with employment in industries that produce goods and services that are not tradable across national boundaries.

Of course, some proponents of comparative advantage theory, e.g., Mankiw, have a religious belief that despite the loss of high wage semi-skilled manufacturing jobs in the United States due to outsourcing over recent years, the United States will develop (yet unspecified) higher skilled jobs in some advanced technology sector while the labor force in China and India will not have sufficient skills or education to be competitive in this future new technology sector. Mankiw's "long run" qualification that outsourcing is "good for the US economy", assumes that unemployment will not be a significant problem as he has faith that the new, still unforeseen higher skilled jobs will miraculously appear in the United States.

Why then has Uchitelle's displaced workers not found these new high-value jobs that Mankiw argues are coming to America? The conventional wisdom is that it is the displaced workers' own fault for their being eligible only for lower paying less-productive jobs. An unemployed or a displaced worker needs only to pursue more education and he will always get a better job we are told without a smile on the face of the perpetrator of this innocent fraud! A call for better-educated workers as the remedy for workers displaced by outsourcing is a measure of a mind that has not thought through the problems of trade patterns in a freely trading global economy, where child labor, unsafe working conditions, environmental damaging production, and a host of other factors that are devastating to the progress of a good society are permitted. In the long run, given the current international payments system and liberalized trade structure and the obvious lack of full employment among most of the trading nations of the world, most employment in the advanced economies of the world will be concentrated in jobs where transportation and communication costs make foreign trade prohibitive (nontradeables), and niche industries such as defense, etc., where political or social reasons prevent the outsourcing of production.

Unless, the governments of developed nations take deliberate action to secure and maintain full employment in their domestic economies despite their lack of absolute advantage competitiveness in industries producing tradeable goods and services, free trade has the potential to impoverish a significant portion of the population (workers whose income does not include much sharing of enterprise incomes) of the developed nations as either unemployment rates in the West rise dramatically, or the West's workers are forced to accept a real wage that is competitive to wages being paid to the abundant supply of unskilled and skilled workers in the East. Surely, western politicians should be made aware of these potential "disastrous" results that can occur from blindly applying the classical theory to today's problem of job outsourcing with liberalized trade and international financial markets. Unless western governments take strong, positive, direct actions to assure continuous full employment of their domestic labor force, free trade and outsourcing will not be the panacea its advocates claim[5] it to be.

IV. Can a reduction (devaluation) in the exchange rate always cure an unfavorable trade balance?

If nation A runs a persistent unfavorable balance of trade[6] with nation B, then each year nation A's payments to B for imports exceeds the nation's earnings from its sale of exports to A, and A increases its debt obligations to B. This raises the question of how can nation A solve this unfavorable trade balance and end its problem of a growing international debt obligation.

Classical theorists argue that nation A should permit its exchange rate to move freely in the market place since a flexible exchange rate will automatically solve the unfavorable trade balance problem. A declining exchange rate of nation A, it is presumed, assures that the value of A's exports will automatically increase while the value of its imports decrease until exports equals imports. Why?

If the exchange rate of nation A declines, then the costs (in terms of A's currency) of A's imports increase compared to the costs of gross substitutes produced domestically in nation A, so households in A will substitute domestically produced goods for imports, thereby reducing total imports. For households in B, the devaluation of A's currency reduces the costs of purchasing A's exports compared to buying goods produced by B's factories. Thus, households in B should buy more of A's exports and less domestically produced goods than they did before A's exchange rate declined; while households in A buy less of B's exports and more of goods produced in A's factories. If the gross substitution axiom is applicable, then the result of an exchange rate devaluation of A's currency must be to increase the *quantity* of A's exports to foreigners and to reduce the *quantity* of imports for A, and *vice versa* for B. It is an empirical fact that, all other things being equal, any significant decrease in a nation's exchange rate typically reduces the physical volume of imports and increases the physical quantity of exports. Nevertheless, this devaluation-caused change in physical quantities will reduce A's trade payments deficit only if there is a net increase in the *monetary* value of exports minus imports for nation A.

Whether there is a net increase in the monetary value of exports minus imports depends on the magnitude of the absolute sum of the price elasticity of demand for imports plus the price elasticity of demand for exports. The price elasticity of demand measures the percentage change in quantity demanded for any given percentage change in prices.

To illustrate let us take a hypothetical extreme case where the price elasticity of demand for A's exports is 0.5 so that with a devaluation of say 10 percent, foreigners buy 5 percent more physical exports from A while paying 10 percent less (say in terms of dollars) on all of A's exports purchased. In this case, the total monetary value of A's exports in dollars actually declines by 5 percent even as the physical volume of exports increases. Suppose also that the price elasticity of A's imports is 0.4, so that A's residents buy 4 percent less exports from B but pay 10 percent more in terms of dollars for all imports purchased. In that case, the monetary costs of imports in terms of dollars would have declined by only 4 percent. Accordingly, with the sum of the price elasticities equal to 0.9 (= 0.5 + 0.4) the monetary value of export falls by 5 percent, while the monetary value of imports decreases by 4 percent. Accordingly, the devaluation creates a greater deficit in the export-import balance when measured in terms of a common currency such as dollars than that which existed before devaluation.

Assuming no change in aggregate income, only if the sum of these price elasticities of a nation's exports and imports exceeds unity (what economists call the Marshall-Lerner condition), will the total monetary value of A's exports minus imports increase and the trade balance improve as the result of an exchange rate devaluation.[7] Empirical studies typically suggest that the sum of these price elasticities for most developed nations is less than unity in the short run, and hence a devaluation does not improve the trade balance. Classical theorists, however, presume that the Marshall-Lerner condition will always prevail in the long run when everything becomes a good substitute for everything else.

Nevertheless, even if the sum of the price elasticities is only slightly greater than unity (and so the Marshall-Lerner condition is applicable), then it may take a huge depreciation of A's currency to significantly reduce A's unfavorable trade balance. Any large devaluation of the exchange rate will have a significant deleterious effect on the real income of the residents of the nation at least partly by creating inflation in the prices of all imports. Accordingly, as Keynes (1941, p. 29) explicitly noted, requiring the nation with an unfavorable trade balance to adjust by reducing its exchange rate may force the nation into an endless and difficult "Sisyphus task" that makes for the "most disruptive of social order, and to throw the burden on the countries least able to support it, making the poor poorer".

In Keynes's analytical framework, therefore, if a nation permits its exchange rate to fall freely even if this ultimately reduces the unfavorable trade balance, the policy results are likely to be truly disruptive to the civilized society of the nation.

In most economic textbooks, however, there is the presumption that price elasticities for both imports and exports are close to infinite so that only a minuscule change in the exchange rate is necessary to cure any trade imbalance. This presumption of almost infinite price elasticities underlies the classical theory's claim that flexible exchange rates always cure international payments imbalances without unduly affecting the long run global real income of the nations engaged in international trade. Thus, mainstream theorists assume, rather than prove, that freely flexible exchange rates assure there will never be any trade balance payments problems.

In a textbook that he co-authored, however, Federal Reserve Chairman Ben Bernanke admitted that in the short run the Marshall-Lerner conditions may not hold, and hence flexible exchange rates can exacerbate a trade imbalance. Bernanke wrote, "a fall in the exchange rate tends to reduce [the value] of net exports in the very short run. ... After consumers and firms have had more time to change the quantities of imports bought and exports sold, the Marshall-Lerner condition is more likely to hold, and a fall in the exchange rate is likely to lead to an increased net exports" (Abel and Bernanke, 1992, p 508).

In this textbook, Abel and Ben Bernanke indicate that the typical short-run response of net exports to an exchange rate depreciation is in the form of a "J-curve", where for an unspecified length of calendar time that Bernanke calls the short run, the deficit in the trade balance of payments worsens and the economy moves along the downward slope of the J-curve. After some unspecified period of calendar time passes, this textbook analysis suggests, a trade balance payment improvement along the upward portion of the J-curve can be expected.

From a Keynes analysis, however, in a world of uncertainty, the initial short-run J-curve worsening in the trade balance can induce expectations of a further fall in the exchange rate that might generate a new J-curve that signifies a further immediate decline in the value of net exports. In a series of short runs, it is possible then that a J-curve fall in the exchange rate merely provokes further J-curves and a continued falling exchange rate, so that for any acceptable reduction in the exchange rate, an improved trade balance is never achieved. Who knows how long a period of calendar time is required, so that consumers and businesses make sufficient adjustments that Bernanke calls for, so that the Marshall-Lerner conditions finally prevail?

To avoid this perverse and unsettling possibility, Abel and Bernanke (1992, p. 508) merely "assume that the time period is long enough so that

Marshall-Lerner conditions holds". In other words, orthodox economists such as Bernanke solve the problem of an unfavorable trade deficit by *assuming* conditions exist where gross substitution effects are sufficiently strong to solve the problem without creating any deleterious effects on either of the trading nations. In a moment of candor, however, Abel and Bernanke (1992, p. 508) remind the reader: "Keep in mind, though, that this assumption [that the Marshall-Lerner conditions prevail] may not be valid for shorter periods – and in some cases, even for several years".

In 1985, after three years of large import surpluses, mainstream economists in the United States claimed that only a devaluation of the United States dollar would resolve this seemingly persistent unfavorable trade balance problem. In late September 1985, under public pressure fermented by the persistent demands of mainstream United States economists for a devaluation, Treasury Secretary James Baker launched an initiative to "talk down" the value of the dollar in the foreign exchange market. Secretary Baker's economic advisers spoke about a "soft landing" where a 35 percent devaluation of the dollar would cure the United States trade deficit without unleashing any inflationary or depressionary forces.

One week before this Baker initiative, I presented testimony[8] to the Joint Economic Committee of the United States Congress where I argued the "Keynes case" of why a deliberate lowering of the dollar exchange rate by 35 percent would not, by itself, significantly reduce the United States trade deficit. Rather than supporting the conventional wisdom that a 35 percent devaluation would provide a soft-landing solution to the persistent United States trade deficit, the facts have supported my "Keynes case" testimony presented to the Joint Economic Committee.

The facts are that in 1986, despite a drop of more than 30 percent in the value of the dollar, the value of imports grew by 11 percent, while the value of exports rose by less than 2 percent, and the trade deficit increased. In 1987, with another 10 percent drop in the dollar, exports and imports both expanded by 11 percent and the merchandise trade deficit grew to almost $160 billion while the trade deficit in goods and services grew to more than $140 billion. In 1988, the dollar dropped again, bottoming out at more than 40 percent below its 1985 peak value, while the United States trade deficit finally appeared to peak before "turning around" in 1989. Thus, it took more than three years after the dollar was "talked down" by more than 40 percent *plus a fall in the dollar price of imported crude oil*, before there was *any* reduction in the United States trade deficit.

Since the world price of oil is quoted in United States dollars, the reduction of the United States dollar exchange rate did not impact the quantity of imported oil. In fact, despite the decline in the United States dollar, from 1985 to 1988 the number of barrels of crude oil imported into the United States increased by more than 45 percent. Nevertheless, the total dollar value of oil imports declined by more than $7 billion between 1985 and 1988, as the dollar price of imported oil fell by approximately 50 percent.

Table 9.1 indicates that between 1985 and 1988, the total United States payments for goods and services trade deficit increased by $3 billion (from $98.8 to $101.8 billion) despite the decrease of $7 billion in the value of petroleum imports between 1985 and 1988 that was a result of the dramatic drop in the dollar price of crude oil.

Table 9.1 United States international payments balances (in billions of dollars)

Year	Merchandise Balance	Goods + Services Balance	Current account[9] Balance
1981	−28.0	16.7	5.0
1982	−36.5	5.6	−11.4
1983	−67.1	−25.9	−43.6
1984	−112.5	−78.2	−98.8
1985	−122.2	−98.8	−121.7
1986	−145.1	−123.4	−147.5
1987	−159.6	−140.4	−163.5
1988	−127.0	−101.8	−126.7
1989	−115.7	−75.5	−101.1
1990	−108.8	−57.5	−90.4
1991	−74.0	−28.3	+3.8
1992	−96.1	−35.6	−48.5
1993	−132.6	−68.9	−82.7
1994	−166.1	−97.0	−118.6
1995	−173.7	−95.9	−109.5
1996	−191.0	−104.1	−124.8
1997	−198.1	−107.9	−140.4
1998	−246.7	−164.6	−213.5
1999	−346.0	−263.3	−399.8
2000	−452.4	−377.6	−415.2
2001	−427.2	−362.8	−389.0
2002	−482.3	−421.7	−472.5
2003	−547.3	−494.9	−527.5
2004	−665.4	−611.3	−665.3
2005	−782.7	−716.7	−791.5

Source: *Economic Indicators*, Council of Economic Advisers (May 1993, May 2001, July 2006).

In 1991, the United States experienced a big improvement in its trade balance and an actual small positive sum in its current account balance. This 1991 improvement was due to two factors that are not directly related to any decline in the United States dollar exchange rate. First, the United States experienced a recession in 1991, while the rest of the world's major economies continued to grow. As Americans experienced a rise in unemployment and a decline in income due to the recession, their consumption spending on both domestic goods and imports declined, while United States exports continued to grow, thereby reducing the trade deficit. Second, the current account balance improved dramatically, as Japan, Germany, and some other nations' governments made large unilateral payments to the United States as their contribution to financing the first President Bush's 1991 one-week war again Iraq.

By mid-1992 the United States had recovered from its recession while Europe and Japan slipped toward recession. The result was that both the United States trade balance and the current international payments account balance significantly worsened. With United States economic growth of approximately 3 percent per annum between 1992 and 2000, while the rest of the developed world grew at a slower rate, the United States trade balance again worsened. Since 2000, the United States trade balance has deteriorated further as China and other Asian nations have become big exporters of merchandise produced by an almost unlimited supply of relative low-wage workers, while India, given its large English speaking low-wage population has exported a significant amount of services (e.g., international call centers) as well as merchandise to the United States.

This historical record suggests that the substitution effects in the classical theory assumption that the Marshall-Lerner holds, if not immediately, within a very few years has not been applicable in ultimately resolving the unfavorable trade balance that the United States has experienced since the 1980s. In the real world, trade between nations does not always involve the large gross substitution effects presumed by classical theory. Income effects can have major impacts on a nation's international payments balance. Sole reliance on changes in exchange rates to solve persistent international trade imbalance can be misplaced even in the long run.

Changes in income can have significant effects on trade. Income effects on the payments balance are immediate, direct, and unambiguous (unlike substitution effects that rely on Marshall-Lerner conditions prevailing).[10] As a Keynes view would suggest, it is income effects (different phases of the business cycle among nations and/or differential rates of economic growth between the countries such as the United States and its major trading partners) that appear to have a more significant impact on the payments balance than substitution effects especially in the decade of the 1980s and early 1990s.

Keynes's general theory analysis implies there should be a better way to resolve international payments imbalances than leaving the matter to a freely flexible exchange rate market.

10
Reforming the World's Money

I. A lesson from the early post–World War II history

In *The General Theory*, Keynes argued that if an economy was operating at less than full employment, then the nation's central bank, while maintaining the stability of financial markets, should focus primarily on providing all the liquidity that the economy can absorb in order to reach full employment. For more than a quarter century following World War II, the major central banks around the world tried to meet the role that Keynes had prescribed for them in his *General Theory*.

From the end of the war until the early 1970s, most central banks tended to provide increases in the money supply in response to any domestic or international increase in demand for the nation's money, while maintaining interest rates at historic lows for prosperous times. This endogenous increase in the money supply tended to support expansion of aggregate demand that resulted in a golden age of economic growth and development for both developed and less developed capitalist economies.

While exchange rates were fixed under the Bretton Woods Agreement, in the early years after World War II, the United States avoided amassing surplus international reserves by providing grants to the war torn nations, initially via the Marshall Plan and then via other foreign grants and aid programs. In essence, the United States accepted the Keynes Plan's suggestion that it is in the best interest of all nations if the major creditor nation bears the major burden of reducing trade imbalances and international payments adjustments. As a result of the Marshall Plan, for the first time in modern history, not only was a postwar depression avoided, but the United States and its major trading partners experienced unprecedented long-run rates of real economic growth until the early 1970s.

When, in the early 1970s, the United States withdrew from the Bretton Woods Agreement, the last vestiges of Keynes's enlightened monetary approach were lost, apparently without regret or regard as to

[1] why the Bretton Woods system had been developed in the first place and
[2] how well it had helped the free world to recover from a devastating war which had destroyed much of the productive stock of capital in Europe and Asia.

In the decades since the breakdown of Bretton Woods, the world's economic performance has been unable to match what became almost routine economic success in the quarter century after the end of World War II in terms of low rates of global inflation accompanied by high rates of employment and real growth. Since 1973, however, international economic problems have multiplied, while significantly high rates of unemployment in many nations have again become the norm.

Under any traditional international free trade system, any nation that attempts to improve its economic growth performance by pursuing Keynes's policies for increasing domestic effective demand via easy monetary and fiscal policies will almost immediately face an international payments problem. Expanding domestic aggregate demand will increase the demand for imports relative to the value of exports. When a nation's imports persistently exceed its exports, the nation typically requires foreign loans to finance this import surplus that is encouraging increased economic growth in the trading partners' export industries.

Since 1981, the United States has been the "engine of growth" for most of the rest of the world, since the United States has run an unfavorable trade balance as United States imports have tended to grow more rapidly than its exports In so doing, as Table 9.1 indicates, the United States has been saddled by increasing international deficits almost every year for its laudatory efforts.

II. The Bretton Woods experience and the Marshall Plan

Too often economic discussions on the requirements for a good international payments system that would eliminate persistent trade and international payment imbalances have been limited to the question of the advantages and disadvantages of fixed vs. flexible exchange rates. As the last chapter suggested, in championing the argument for flexible exchange rates most mainstream economists merely assume that the price elasticities of the demand for imports and exports will meet the Marshall-Lerner condition. The facts of experience since the end of World War II, plus Keynes's revolutionary liquidity analysis, indicates that more is required, if a mechanism is to be designed to resolve persistent trade and international payments imbalances while simultaneously promoting global full employment, rapid economic growth, and a long-run stable international standard of value.

Since World War II, the economies of the capitalist world have conducted experiments with the different types of exchange rate systems. For approximately a quarter of a century (1947–73) after the war, nations operated under the Bretton Woods Agreement with a fixed, but adjustable, exchange rate system where, when necessary, nations could invoke widespread limitations on international financial movements (i.e., capital controls). Since 1973, the conventional wisdom of economists and politicians is that nations should liberalize all financial markets to permit unfettered international capital flows to operate under a freely flexible exchange rate system.

In contrast to the classical view of the desirability of liberalized markets, Keynes's position at the 1944 Bretton Woods conference suggested an incompatibility thesis. Keynes argued that free trade, flexible exchange rates and free capital mobility across international borders is likely to be incompatible with the economic goal of global full employment and rapid economic growth.

Between 1947 and 1973, policy makers in their actions implicitly recognized Keynes's "incompatibility thesis". This period was, as already noted, an era of sustained economic growth in both developed and developing countries. Moreover, during this period, there was "a much better overall record of price level stability" with very high levels of employment compared to either the post-1973 period or the earlier gold standard (1879–1914) era of fixed exchange rates (McKinnon, 1990, p. 10).

The free world's economic performance in terms of both real growth *and* price level stability during the Bretton Woods period of fixed, but adjustable, exchange rates was unprecedented. Moreover, economic growth rates during the earlier gold standard–fixed exchange rate period, although worse than the Bretton Woods record, was better than the global experience during the post-1973 period when liberalizing exchange rate markets to achieve flexible exchange rates has been the conventional wisdom. The disappointing post-1973 experience of persistent high rates of unemployment in many nations, bouts of inflationary pressure and slow growth in many OECD countries, plus debt-burdened growth and/or stagnation (and even falling real GNP per capita) in some developing countries contrasts sharply with the experience during the Bretton Woods period.

The significantly superior performance of the free world's economies during the Bretton Woods fixed exchange rate period compared to the earlier gold standard fixed exchange rate period suggests that there must have been an additional condition besides exchange rate fixity that contributed to the unprecedented growth during the 1947–73 period. That additional condition, as Keynes explained in developing his Plan for the Bretton Woods Conference, required that any creditor nation that runs persistent favorable trade payments must accept the major responsibility for resolving these trade imbalances. The postwar Marshall Plan (see *infra*) was an instance where the creditor nation adopted the responsibility that Keynes had suggested was required.

III. Keynes, free trade, and an international payments system that promotes full employment

To reduce entrepreneurial uncertainties and the possibility of massive currency misalignments in any fixed exchange rate system, Keynes recommended the adoption of a fixed, but adjustable, exchange rate system. More importantly, Keynes argued that the "main cause of failure" of any traditional international payments system – whether based on fixed or flexible exchange rates – was its inability to actively foster continuous global economic expansion whenever persistent trade payment imbalances occurred among trading partners. This failure, Keynes (1941, p. 27) wrote:

> can be traced to a single characteristic. I ask close attention to this, because I shall argue that this provides a clue to the nature of any alternative which is to be successful.
> It is characteristic of a freely convertible international standard that it throws the main burden of adjustment on the country which is the *debtor* position on the international balance of payments – that is, on the country which is (in this context) by hypothesis the *weaker* and above all the *smaller* in comparison with the other side of the scales which (for this purpose) is the rest of the world.

Keynes concluded that an essential improvement in designing any international payments system requires transferring the *onus* of adjustment from the debtor to the creditor position. This transfer would substitute an expansionist, in place of a contractionist, pressure on world trade

(Keynes, 1941, pp. 29–30). To achieve a golden era of economic development Keynes recommended combining a fixed, but adjustable, exchange rate system with a mechanism for requiring the nation "enjoying" a favorable balance of trade to initiate most of the effort necessary to eliminate this balance, while "maintaining enough discipline in the debtor countries to prevent them from exploiting the new ease allowed them" (Keynes, 1941, p. 30).

After World War II, the war-torn capitalist nations in Europe did not have sufficient undamaged resources available to produce enough to feed its population and rebuild its economy. Economic rebuilding would require European nations to run huge import surpluses with the United States in order to meet their economic needs for recovery. During the war, the European nations had run down their foreign reserves to extremely low levels. To obtain the necessary imports from the United States, under a *laissez-faire* system, it would be necessary for the United States to provide enormous loans to finance the required United States export surplus to Europe. The resulting European indebtedness would be so burdensome that it was unlikely that, even in the long run, the European nations could ever service such debt obligations.

Private lenders in the United States were mindful that German reparation payments to the victorious Allied nations after World War I were primarily financed by United States investors lending to Germany (e.g., the Dawes Plan). Germany never repaid these loans. Given this history and existing circumstances it was obvious that private lending facilities could not be expected to provide the credits necessary for European recovery after World War II.

The Keynes Plan, presented at the 1944 Bretton Woods Conference, would require the United States, as the obvious major creditor nation, to accept the major responsibility for curing the international financial problems that would be associated with the postwar European nations need for United States exports. Keynes estimated that the European nations might require imports from the United States in excess of $10 billion to rebuild their economies. The United States representative to the Bretton Woods Conference, Harry Dexter White, rejected the Keynes Plan. As we have already noted, Dexter White argued that Congress would be willing to provide, at most, $3 billion as the United States contribution to solving this postwar international financial problem.

The White Plan created the International Monetary Fund (IMF), whose function it would be to provide short-term loans to nations running unfavorable balances of trade. These loans were supposed to give the debtor nation time to get its economic house in order. The White Plan had the United States subscribing a maximum of $3 billion as its contribution to the IMF lending facilities. White's plan also developed another lending institution, now called the World Bank, that would borrow funds from the private sector. These funds would then be used to provide long-term loans for rebuilding capital facilities and making capital improvements initially in the war-torn nations and later in the less developed countries. White's plan was basically the institutional arrangements adopted at the Bretton Woods Conference.

Under the White Plan, international loans from the IMF or the World Bank were the only available sources for financing the huge volume of imports from the United States that the war-torn nations would require immediately after the war. This would result in a huge international indebtedness of these nations. Even if the nations could obtain a sufficient volume of loans to finance their import necessities for rebuilding, servicing the resultant immense debt of these nations would require them to accept the main burden of adjustment by "tightening their belt". To tighten the nation's belt is a euphemism to indicate that the debtor nations have to reduce dramatically their need for imports.[1] The ultimate result would be a significant decline in the standard of living in these countries which might lead to political and social unrest in these nations.

Even, if after World War II, the deficit trading nations had abandoned the Bretton Woods fixed exchange rate mechanism and opted for a depreciating currency under a flexible exchange rate system to force the deficit nations to "tighten their belts", the result would have reduced Europeans to almost a starvation level of income. Accordingly, any conventional free market solution available to the European nations after World War II to obtain United States imports for rebuilding their economy would so depress the standard of living as to possibly induce political revolutions in most of Western Europe.

To avoid the possibility of many European nations facing a desperate electorate that might opt for a communist system when faced with the dismal future that the conventional Bretton Woods system offered, the United States produced the Marshall Plan and other foreign grants and aid programs to ensure that Communism did not spread West from the Soviet Union. Despite White's argument that the United States would not be willing to give more than $3 billion to solving this international payments problem, the Marshall Plan provided $5 billion in foreign aid in 18 months and a total of $13 billion in four years. (Adjusted for inflation, this sum is equivalent to approximately $135 billion in 2006 dollars.) The Marshall Plan was essentially a four-year gift of $13 billion worth of United States exports to the war-devastated nations.

The Marshall Plan gift gave the recipient nations claim to approximately 2 percent of the total output (GDP) of the United States for four years from 1947 to 1951. Yet no United State resident felt deprived of goods and services even as the Marshall Plan recipients essentially siphoned off $2 out of every $100 worth of goods produced in the United States. Real gross national income (or GNP) per capita in the United States (a measure of the United States standard of living) during the first year of the Marshall Plan was still 25percent higher than it had been in the last peacetime year of 1940. Per capita GNP continued to grow throughout the 1950s.[2]

Despite Americans giving away 2 percent of their national income per annum, there was no real sacrifice for Americans associated with the Marshall Plan as the remaining income was significantly greater than prewar levels. The resulting United States exports that the recipients of Marshall Plan aid were able to purchase created significant increases in employment in United States export industries just as several million men and women were discharged from the United States armed forces and entered the United States labor force looking for jobs. For the first time in its history, the United States did not suffer from a severe recession immediately after the cessation of a major war. The United States and most of the rest of the world experienced an economic "free lunch" as both the potential debtor nations and the creditor nation experienced tremendous real economic gains resulting from the Marshall Plan and other foreign aid programs.

By 1958, however, although the United States still had an annual goods and services export surplus of over $5 billion, United States governmental foreign and military aid exceeded $6 billion, while there was a net private capital outflow of $1.6 billion.[3] The postwar United States potential surplus on international payments balance was at an end.

As the United States current international payments account swung into deficit in 1958, other nations began to experience payments surpluses. These credit surplus nations did not spend their entire payments surpluses. Instead, they used a portion of their annual dollar surpluses to purchase international liquid assets in the form of gold reserves from the United States Federal Reserve System. For example, in 1958, the United States lost over $2 billion in gold reserves to foreign central banks. These trends accelerated in the 1960s, partly as a result of increased United States military and financial aid responses to the construction of the Berlin Wall in 1961 and later because of the United States's increasing involvement in Vietnam. At the same time, a rebuilt Europe and Japan became important producers of exports so that the rest of the world became less dependent on the United States exports.

Still the United States maintained a positive merchandise trade balance until the first oil price shock in 1973. More than offsetting this merchandise trade surplus during most of the 1960s, however, were foreign and military aid plus net capital outflows from the United States so that the United States experienced an annual unfavorable balance of international payments. The Bretton Woods system had no way of automatically forcing the emerging surplus nations to stop accumulating dollars and instead step into the creditor adjustment role that the United States had been playing since 1947. Instead the surplus nations continued to convert some portion of their annual dollar surpluses into calls on United States gold reserves. The seeds of the destruction of the Bretton Woods system and the golden age of economic development were being sown as surplus nations drained gold reserves from the United States.

When the United States closed the gold window and unilaterally withdrew from Bretton Woods in 1971, the last vestige of Keynes's enlightened international monetary approach was lost.

IV. Changing the international payments system

The 1950–73 golden age of economic development required international institutions and United States government foreign aid policies that operated on principles inherent in the Keynes Plan, with the creditor nation accepting the major responsibility for solving international payments imbalance. The formal Bretton Woods Agreement, however, did not require creditor nations to take such actions. Since 1973, the international payments system has been one where international payments considerations often impede the rapid economic growth of many of the developed nations of the world while severely constraining the growth of the LDCs.

Utilizing Keynes's general theory principles, it is possible to update Keynes's original plan for a postwar international monetary scheme that will promote global economic prosperity. For "to suppose [as the conventional wisdom does] that there exists some smoothly functioning automatic [free market] mechanism of adjustment which preserves equilibrium if only we trust to methods of *laissez-faire* is a doctrinaire delusion which disregards the lessons of historical experience without having behind it the support of sound theory" (Keynes, 1941, pp. 21–2).

In the 21st-century interdependent global economy, a substantial degree of economic cooperation among trading nations is essential. The original Keynes Plan for reforming the international payments system called for the creation of a single supranational central bank. The clearing union institution suggested *infra* is a more modest proposal than the Keynes Plan, although it operates under the same economic principles laid down by Keynes. Our proposal is aimed at obtaining an acceptable international agreement (given today's political climate in most nations) that does not require surrendering national control of either local banking systems or domestic monetary and fiscal policies. Each nation will still be able to determine the economic destiny that is best for its citizens without fear of importing deflationary repercussions from their trading partners. Each nation, however, will not be able to export any domestic inflationary forces to their international neighbors.

What is required is a closed, double-entry bookkeeping clearing institution to keep the payments 'score' among the various trading nations plus some mutually agreed upon rules to create and reflux international liquidity while maintaining the purchasing power of the created international currency of the international clearing union. The eight provisions of the international clearing system suggested in this chapter meet the following criteria. The rules of the proposed system are designed

1. to prevent a lack of global effective demand[4] due to a liquidity problem arising whenever any nation(s) holds either excessive idle reserves or drain reserves from the system,
2. to provide an automatic mechanism for placing a major burden of correcting international payments imbalances on the surplus nations,
3. to provide each nation with the ability to monitor and, if desired, to control movements of flight capital, tax evasion money movements, earnings from illegal activities, and even funds that finance terrorist operations,[5] and finally
4. to expand the quantity of the liquid asset used in settling international contracts (the asset of ultimate redemption) as global capacity warrants while protecting the purchasing power of this asset.

There are eight major provisions in this clearing system proposal. They are

1. The unit of account and ultimate reserve asset for international liquidity is the International Money Clearing Unit (IMCU). All IMCUs can be held *only* by the central banks of nations that abide by the rules of the clearing union system. IMCUs are not available to be held by the public.

2. Each nation's central bank, or in the case of a common currency (e.g., the Euro) a currency union's central bank, is committed to guarantee one way convertibility from IMCU deposits at the clearing union

to its domestic money. Each central bank will set its own rules regarding making available foreign monies (through IMCU clearing transactions) to its own bankers and private sector residents.[6]

Since central banks agree to sell their own liabilities (one-way convertibility) against the IMCU only to other central bankers via the international clearing union while they simultaneously hold only IMCUs as liquid reserve assets for international financial transactions, there can be no draining of reserves from the international payments system. Ultimately, all major private international transactions clear between central banks' accounts in the books of the international clearing institution.

The guarantee of only one-way convertibility permits each nation to institute controls and regulations on international capital flows if necessary. The primary economic function of these international capital flow controls and regulations is to prevent rapid changes in the bull-bear sentiment from overwhelming the market maker and inducing dramatic changes in international financial market price trends that can have devastating real consequences.

There is a spectrum of different capital controls available. At one end of the spectrum are controls that primarily impose administrative constraints either on a case-by-case basis or an expenditure category basis. Such controls may include administrative oversight and control of individual transactions for payments to foreign residents (or banks) often via oversight of international transactions by banks or their customers. Other capital controls might include the imposition of taxes (or other opportunity costs) on *specific* international financial transactions, e.g., the 1960s United States Interest Equalization Tax.

Finally there can be many forms of monetary policy decisions undertaken to affect net international financial flows, e.g., raising the interest rate to slow capital outflows, raising bank reserve ratios, limiting the ability of banks to finance purchases of foreign securities, and regulating interbank activity as suggested by Mayer (1998).[7]

The IMF, as lender of last resort during the 1997 East Asian contagion crisis, imposed the same conditions on all nations requiring loans for international liquidity purposes. The resulting worsening of the situation should have taught us that in policy prescriptions one size does *not* fit all situations. Accordingly, the type of capital regulation a nation should choose from the spectrum of tools available at any time will differ depending on the specific circumstances involved. It would be presumptuous to attempt to catalog what capital regulations should be imposed for any nation under any given circumstances. Nevertheless, it should be stressed that regulating capital movements may be a necessary *but not a sufficient* condition for promoting global prosperity. Much more is required.

If any government objects to the idea that the IMCU provision #2 provides governments with the ability to limit the free movement of "capital" funds, then this nation is free to join other nations of similar attitude in forming a regional currency union (UMS) and thereby assuring a free flow of funds among the residents of the currency union.

3. Contracts between private individuals in different nations will continue to be denominated in whatever domestic currency permitted by local laws and agreed upon by the contracting parties. Contracts to be settled in terms of a foreign currency will therefore require some publicly announced commitment from the central bank (through private sector bankers) of the availability of foreign funds to meet such private contractual obligations.

4. The exchange rate between the domestic currency and the IMCU is set initially by each nation or currency union's central bank – just as it would be if one instituted an international gold standard. Since private enterprises that are already engaged in trade have international contractual commitments that would span the changeover interval from the current system, then, as a practical matter, one would expect, but not demand, that the existing exchange rate structure (with perhaps minor modifications) would provide the basis for initial rate setting.

Provisions #7 and #8 *infra* indicate when and how this nominal exchange rate between the national currency and the IMCU would be changed in the future.

5. An overdraft system should be built into the clearing union rules. Overdrafts should make available short-term unused creditor balances at the Clearing House to finance the productive international transactions of others who need short-term credit. The terms will be determined by the *pro bono publico* clearing union managers.

6. A trigger mechanism to encourage any creditor nation to spend what is deemed (in advance) by agreement of the international community to be "excessive" credit balances accumulated by running current account surpluses. These excessive credits can be spent in three ways: (1) on the products of any other member of the clearing union, (2) on new foreign direct investment projects, and/or (3) to provide unilateral transfers (foreign aid) to deficit members. Spending via (1) forces the surplus nation to make the adjustment directly by way of the trade balance on goods and services. Spending by way of (3) permits adjustment directly by the capital account balance, while (2) provides adjustment

by the capital accounts (without setting up a contractual debt that will require reverse current account flows in the future).

These three spending alternatives force the surplus nation to accept a major responsibility for correcting the payments imbalance. Nevertheless, this provision gives the surplus country considerable discretion in deciding how to accept the onus of adjustment in the way it believes is in its residents' best interests. It does not permit the surplus nation to shift the burden to the deficit nation(s) via contractual requirements for debt service charges independent of what the deficit nation can afford.[8] The important thing is to make sure that continual oversaving[9] by the surplus nation in the form of international liquid reserves are not permitted to unleash depressionary forces and/or a building up of international debts so encumbering as to impoverish the global economy of the 21st century.

In the unlikely event that the surplus nation does not spend or give away these credits within a specified time, then the clearing agency would confiscate (and redistribute to debtor members) the portion of credits deemed excessive.[10] This last resort confiscatory action (a 100% taxes on excessive liquidity holdings) would make a payments adjustment via unilateral transfer payments in the current accounts.

Under either a fixed or a flexible rate system with each nation free to decide on how much it will import, some nations will, at times, experience persistent trade deficits merely because their trading partners are not living up to their means – that is because other nations are continually hoarding a portion of their foreign export earnings (plus net unilateral transfers). By so doing, these oversavers are creating a lack of global effective demand. Under provision #6, deficit countries would no longer have to deflate their real economy in an attempt to reduce imports and thereby reduce their payment imbalance because others are excessively oversaving. Instead, the system would seek to remedy the payment deficit by increasing opportunities for deficit nations to sell abroad and thereby work their way out of their deteriorating debtor position.

7. A system to stabilize the long-term purchasing power of the IMCU (in terms of each member nation's domestically produced market basket of goods) can be developed. This requires a system of fixed exchange rates between the local currency and the IMCU that changes only to reflect permanent increases in efficiency wages.[11] This assures each central bank that its holdings of IMCUs as the nation's foreign reserves will never lose purchasing power in terms of foreign produced goods. If a foreign government permits wage-price inflation to occur within its

borders, then, the exchange rate between the local currency and the IMCU will be devalued to reflect the inflation in the local money price of the domestic commodity basket. For example, if the rate of domestic inflation was 5 percent, the exchange rate would change so that each unit of IMCU could purchase 5 percent more of the nation's currency.

If, on the other hand, increases in productivity lead to declining production costs in terms of the domestic money, then the nation with this decline in efficiency wages (say of 5 percent) would have the option of choosing either [a] to permit the IMCU to buy (up to 5 percent) less units of domestic currency, thereby capturing all (or most of) the gains from productivity for its residents while maintaining the purchasing power of the IMCU, or [b] to keep the nominal exchange rate constant. In the latter case, the gain in productivity is shared with all trading partners. In exchange, the export industries in this productive nation will receive an increasing relative share of the world market.

By devaluing the exchange rate between local monies and the IMCU to offset the rate of domestic inflation, the IMCU's purchasing power is stabilized. By restricting use of IMCUs to Central Banks, private speculation regarding IMCUs as a hedge against inflation is avoided. Each nation's rate of inflation of the goods and services it produces is determined solely by the local government's policy toward the level of domestic money wages and profit margins vis-à-vis productivity gains, i.e., the nation's efficiency wage. Each nation is therefore free to experiment with policies for stabilizing its efficiency wage to prevent inflation as long as these policies do not lead to a lack of global effective demand. Whether the nation is successful or not in preventing domestic goods price inflation, the IMCU will never lose its international purchasing power in terms of any domestic money. Moreover, the IMCU has the promise of gaining in purchasing power over time, if productivity grows more than money wages and each nation is willing to share any reduction in real production costs with its trading partners.

Provision #7 produces a system designed to, at least, maintain the relative efficiency wage parities amongst nations. In such a system, the adjustability of nominal exchange rates will be primarily (but not always, see Provision #8) to offset changes in efficiency wages among trading partners. A beneficial effect that follows from this proviso is that it eliminates the possibility that a specific industry in any nation can be put at a competitive disadvantage (or secure a competitive advantage) against foreign producers solely because the nominal exchange rate changed independently of changes in efficiency wages and the real costs of production in each nation.

Consequently, nominal exchange rate variability can no longer create the problem of a loss of competitiveness due solely to the overvaluation of a currency as, for example, experienced by the industries in the American "rust belt" during the period 1982–5. Even if temporary, currency appreciation independent of changes in efficiency wages can have significant permanent real costs as domestic industries abandon export markets and lose domestic market business to foreign firms and the resultant existing excess plant and equipment is cast aside as too costly to maintain.

Provision #7 also prevents any nation from engaging in a beggar-thy-neighbor, export-thy-unemployment policy by pursuing a real exchange rate devaluation that does not reflect changes in efficiency wages. Once the initial exchange rates are chosen and relative efficiency wages are locked in, reduction in real production costs which are associated with a relative decline in efficiency wages is the main factor (with the exception of provision #8) justifying an adjustment in the real exchange rate.

Although provision #6 prevents any country from piling up persistent excessive surpluses, this does not mean that it is impossible for one or more nations to run persistent deficits. Consequently, provision #8 *infra* provides a program for addressing the problem of persistent international payment deficits in any one nation.

8. If a country is at full employment and still has a tendency toward persistent international deficits on its current account, then this is *prima facie* evidence that it does not possess the productive capacity to maintain its current standard of living. If the deficit nation is a poor one, then there is a case for the richer nations who are in surplus to transfer some of their excess credit balances to support the poor nation.[12] If the deficit nation is a relatively rich country, then the deficit nation must alter its standard of living by reducing its relative terms of trade with its major trading partners. Rules, agreed upon in advance, would require the trade deficit rich nation to devalue its exchange rate by stipulated increments per period until evidence becomes available to indicate that the export-import imbalance is eliminated without unleashing significant recessionary forces.

If, on the other hand, the payment deficit persists despite a continuous positive balance of trade in goods and services, then there is evidence that the deficit nation might be carrying too heavy an international debt service obligation. The *pro bono* officials of the clearing union should bring the debtor and creditors into negotiations to reduce annual debt service payments by (1) lengthening the payments period, (2) reducing the interest charges, and/or (3) debt forgiveness.[13]

It should be noted that provision #6 embodies Keynes's innovative idea that whenever there is a persistent (and/or large) imbalance in current account flows, whether due to capital flight or a persistent trade imbalance, there must be a built-in mechanism that induces the surplus nation(s) to bear a major responsibility for eliminating the imbalance. The surplus nation must accept this burden for it has the wherewithal to resolve the problem.

In the absence of provision #6, under any conventional system, whether it has fixed or flexible exchange rates and/or capital controls, there can ultimately be an international liquidity crisis (as any persistent current account deficit can deplete a nation's foreign reserves) that unleashes global depressionary forces. Thus, provision #6 is necessary to ensure that the international payments system will not have a built-in depressionary bias. Ultimately then it is in the self-interest of the surplus nation to accept this responsibility, for its actions will create conditions for global economic expansion some of which must accrue to its own residents. Failure to act, on the other hand, will promote global depressionary forces, which will have some negative impact on its own residents.

11
Inflation

Classical theory assumed a Say's Law full-employment economy where money was neutral and increases in the supply of money could not affect employment and real output. Thus, as the 18th-century Scottish philosopher and classical economist David Hume argued, any increase in the quantity of money in the economy must directly increase the price level (i.e., cause inflation). Nobel Prize winner and classical monetarist theorist Milton Friedman is usually credited with coining the statement "inflation is always and everywhere a monetary phenomenon" where inflation is merely too many dollars chasing too few goods.

Keynes's general theory analysis was developed in the 1930s after Britain had suffered more than a decade of high unemployment and depression. It is not surprising therefore that Keynes devoted most of his theoretical analysis to curing the unemployment problem and relegated his discussion of the threat of inflation to some side comments on "bottlenecks" and "changes in the wage unit" (Keynes, 1936a, pp. 300–3). In Keynes's analysis money is, neither in the short run or the long run, neutral. Consequently, Keynes's general theory suggests that any monetary policy that affects the quantity of money in the system will impact directly on real economic outcomes rather than on the price level.

As early as 1930, Keynes suggested (1930, ii, p. 220) that bank "credit is the pavement along which production travels, and the bankers if they knew their duty, would provide the transport facilities to just the extent that is required in order that the productive powers of the community can be employed at their full capacity". Thus, the function of any central bank, as controller of the banking system, is to encourage bankers to make credit (liquidity) available as cheaply as possible to investors as long as the economy has significant idle resources that could be usefully employed. In Keynes's world of nonergodic uncertainty where money is never neutral, the central bank has the primary function of providing sufficient liquidity to facilitate economic expansion and growth, and not the targeting of a rate of inflation before full employment is achieved.

I. Contracts, prices, and inflation

Our earlier discussion of the importance of money and spot and forward contracts provides us with the platform for explaining the cause(s) of inflation in the real world. In all modern money-using economies, production and exchange processes are organized via money contracts in either a spot market or a forward (or futures) market. Accordingly, at any point of calendar time two sets of prices potentially exist simultaneously. These are spot prices[1] for immediate delivery and payment and forward prices[2] which are today's contractual prices specified to be paid at a future date when delivery is made.

Alfred Marshall, the teacher of Keynes and a famous economist in his own right, noted that spot market prices could be at any level that cleared the market – even if the spot price did not cover the costs of production. Marshall's short-run (or forward) prices are the offer prices of sellers that buyers must be willing to pay in order to place the forward contractual orders that induce sellers to undertake the productive activity necessary to assure delivery at a specific future date. The forward offer prices of sellers will equal the necessary money costs of production (including profits) associated with the seller achieving a specific production output target at a specific point of time.

In his *Treatise on Money* (1930, vol. 2, pp. 155–6), Keynes identified two types of inflation: *Commodity Inflation* and *Incomes Inflation*. The former inflation type is identified with rising spot market prices over time where at any point of time only pre-existing stocks of goods can be traded. Since production takes some period of calendar time to occur, if there is a sudden increase in spot market demand, there can be no available augmentation of existing stocks for immediate delivery to constrain this spot market inflation. (Holders of the pre-existing durable producibles can sell at a higher spot price and thereby obtain a capital gain on their holdings.)

The second form of inflation, *Incomes Inflation*, is associated with the rise in the money costs of production associated with each unit of goods produced. These money costs of production represent the income payments to wage and salary earners, material suppliers, lenders, and profit recipients. In other words, if the money costs of production increase, then owners of the inputs to the production process receive higher money incomes that are not offset by productivity increases. This incomes inflation terminology highlights the obvious but oft-neglected fact that, given productivity relations, inflationary increases in the prices of domestic producible goods are always associated with (and the result of) an increase in someone's money income earned in the production process. Accordingly, if one is to target the rate of inflation of domestically producible goods, one must limit the rise in the money income of owners of inputs per unit of output.

II. The inflation process in a Keynes world

Spot prices, by definition, move in step with immediate changes in the market demand for existing products (ignoring changes in reservation demand[3]). Thus, at any moment in calendar time every unexpected sudden increase in demand for products and/or services for immediate delivery will produce an increase in spot prices. Nevertheless, it is the effect on forward – not spot – prices which are important for a continuing (over calendar time) inflation problem. No matter how high spot prices go at any point of calendar time, if buyers are willing to wait the gestation period for the production of additional output, then buyers can always order today newly produced goods and services for delivery at a future date at today's forward (supply) price offered by entrepreneurs. If, despite any hypothetical increase in spot demand, the forward prices remain stable over time, then the spot price inflation can only be a temporary (market period) phenomena. Moreover, to the extent that the spot price of commodities with long gestation periods is the inflation problem, and there is no spillover causing a rise in the money costs of production, then the policy solution for inflation is the holding by the government of buffer stocks.

Since a spot or commodity price inflation occurs whenever there is a sudden and unforeseen change in demand or available supply *for immediate delivery*, this type of inflation can easily be avoided if there is some institution that is not motivated by self-interest, but instead maintains a "buffer stock" to prevent unforeseen changes in spot demand and supply from inducing significant spot price movements. A buffer stock is nothing more than some commodity shelf-inventory that can be moved into and out of the spot market to buffer the market from disorderly price disruptions by offsetting the unforeseen changes in spot demand or supply.[4]

For example, since the oil price shocks of the 1970s, the United States has developed a "strategic petroleum reserve" stored in underground salt domes on the coast of the Gulf of Mexico. These oil reserves are designed to provide emergency market supplies to buffer the domestic oil spot market if there is a sudden decrease in oil supplies imported from the politically unstable Middle East. The strategic use of such a petroleum reserve means that the spot price of oil will not increase as much as it otherwise would if, for example, a political crisis broke out in the Middle East. In other words, a spot oil-price inflation could be avoided as long as the buffer stock remained available to offset any immediately available commodity shortage. Thus, during the short Desert Storm war against Iraq in 1991, United States government officials made strategic petroleum reserves available to the market to offset the possibility of disruptions (actual or expected) from affecting the spot price of crude oil. The Department of Energy estimated that this use of a buffer stock prevented the price of gasoline at the pump from rising about 30 cents per gallon during the brief Desert Storm war period.

Use of buffer stocks as a public policy solution to spot price inflation is as old as the biblical story of Joseph and the Pharaoh's dream of seven fat cows followed by seven lean cows. Joseph – the economic forecaster of his day – interpreted the Pharaoh's dream as portending seven good harvests where production would be much above normal and prices paid to farmers below normal; followed by seven lean harvests where annual production would not provide enough food to go around while prices farmers received would be exorbitantly high. Joseph's civilized policy proposal was for the government to buy and store up a *buffer stock* of grain during the good years and release the grain to market, without profit, during the bad years. This would maintain a stable price over the 14 harvests and avoiding inflation in the bad years while protecting farmers' incomes in the good harvest years. The Bible records that this civilized buffer stock policy was a resounding economic success.

III. Incomes inflation

Rises in money wages, salaries and other material costs in production contracts always imply the increase in someone's money income. The costs of production of a firm are the other side of the coin of the income of people who provide labor or property for use by the firm in the production process.

With slavery illegal in civilized societies, the money-wage contract for hiring labor is the most universal of all production costs. Labor costs account for the vast majority of production contract costs in the economy, even for such high-technology products as NASA spacecraft. That is why, especially since World War II, inflation associated with production prices is usually associated with money-wage inflation.

Wage contracts specify a certain money-wage per unit of time. This labor cost plus a profit margin or mark-up to cover material costs, overheads, and profit on the investment become the basis for managerial decisions as to the prices they must receive on a sales contract to make the undertaking worthwhile. If money wages rise relative to the productivity of labor, then the labor costs of producing any quantity of output increases. Consequently, firms must raise their sales (forward) contract price if they are to maintain profitability and viability. When any production costs and therefore contract prices for orders are rising throughout the economy, we are suffering a forward contract or *incomes inflation.*

Clearly, then, to prevent incomes inflation there must be some constraint on the rate of increase of money incomes relative to productivity.

IV. Incomes policy

Why, at least since World War II, has rising wage rates in most developed nations been a major factor in ongoing incomes inflation? To understand that, we must recognize the change in the nature of the industrial society that came after World War II. As John Kenneth Galbraith noted, "The market with its maturing of industrial society and its associated political institutions ... loses radically its authority as a regulatory force ... [and] partly it is an expression of our democratic ethos" (Galbraith, 1978, pp. 8–9).

After the devastating experience most households endured during the Great Depression of the 1930s, the emerging ethos of the common man in democratic nations held that people should have more control of their economic destiny. The Great Depression had taught that individuals cannot have control of their economic lives if they leave the determination of their income completely to the tyranny of the free market. Consequently, after World War II in societies with any democratic tendencies, people not only demanded economic security from their economic system but they also demanded to play a controlling role in determining their economic life. This required power to control one's income. The result was an institutional power struggle for higher incomes between trade unions, political coalitions, economic cartels and monopolistic industries. When these power struggles lead to demands for higher incomes at any level of production, the result is incomes inflation.

As long as the government guarantees that it will pursue a full-employment policy, each self-interested worker, union, and business entrepreneur has little fear that their demand for higher prices and money income will result in lost sales and unemployment. As long as the government accepts the responsibility for creating sufficient aggregate effective demand to maintain the economy close to a full-employment level of output, there will be no market incentive to stop this recurring struggle over the distribution of income. Full-employment policies without some deliberate announced incomes constraint policy assure that there would no longer exist what Marx called "the industrial reserve army" of the unemployed. In a *laissez-faire* market environment, however, this industrial reserve army of the unemployed is a major force that can constrain organized workers' demand for higher money wages.

Since the 1990s, with globalized free trade, the almost unlimited supply of unskilled and semi-skilled workers in countries such as China and India willing to work at much lower wages than those that prevail in the West have acted similar to a Marxist "industrialized army of the unemployed" in limiting western workers' ability to even maintain, on average, the existing wage rate.

For those classical economists who believe in the beneficence of the "invisible hand" of free markets, there is only one way to combat any incomes inflation that may occur in our economy. In a free society where people are motivated solely by self-interest, workers and entrepreneurs are free to demand any price for their services, even if such demands are inflationary. As the former prime minister of England, Mrs. Thatcher, was often quoted as saying, "One of the rights of a free society is the right to price oneself out of the market".

To ensure that inflationary income demands of workers, entrepreneurs, commodity producers, and other enterprises, can prices themselves out of the market requires that the central bank ensures that the banking system will not finance these inflationary income demands. The central bank must constrain liquidity sufficiently so that there will be a lack of sufficient effective demand to effectively prevent any significant inflationary wage or other income demands being validated in the marketplace.

If an independent central bank adamantly refuses to increase the money supply to finance inflationary income demands of owners of domestic factors of production, then the resultant slack demand in the market place for domestic goods will discipline *all* workers and firms with the fear of loss of sales and income. The hope is that this fear will keep wage and price increases in check. To make this fear credible, a central bank doing inflationary targeting, must institute a restrictive monetary policy so that all firms and workers feel threatened. Nothing closely approaching full-employment prosperity is possible as long as there is a reliance on the free market's incomes policy of threatening unemployment and enterprise failure. Thus, those who advocate "inflation targeting" monetary policy by the central bank are implicitly endorsing an incomes policy based on "fear" of loss of jobs, sales revenues, and profits for firms that produce goods and services domestically. Fear, it is believed, will keep owners of the domestic factors of production in their place. The amount of slack demand necessary to enforce this *incomes policy of fear* will depend on what some modern classical economists call the domestic *natural rate of unemployment* and, in a globalized economy, the existence of large-population nations whose workers willingly accept wages much below that of the industrialized developed nations.

Accordingly, proponents of this inflation-targeting incomes policy of fear are implicitly suggesting that the natural unemployment rate will be smaller if governments "liberalize" labor markets by reducing, if not completely eliminating, long-term unemployment benefits or other money income supports including minimum wages, employer contributions to pension funds, health insurance for their employees, legislation protecting working conditions, etc. Then workers will be less truculent.

A permanent social safety net is seen as mollycoddling casualties in the war against inflation so that others may think there is little to fear if they join the ranks of the unemployed. A ubiquitous and overwhelming fear instilled in all members of society is a necessary condition for the barbarous inflation-targeting program to work. The result is inevitably that the civil economic society is the first casualty.

With the integration of populous nations such as China, India, etc., into the global economy of the 21st century, as we have already suggested, another "industrial reserve army" has been introduced into the economies of many OECD nations. Given the almost unlimited supply of idle and underemployed workers in these populous nations who are willing to accept jobs at wages much below those prevailing in the major OECD nations, and the growing phenomenon of outsourcing of manufacturing jobs and services (where transportation and communication costs are relatively small), the labor forces of major industrial nations have been significantly constrained in their income demands in the last two decades. As a result, incomes inflation has been limited to those domestic service occupation and industries and manufacturing industries (e.g., national defense) where outsourcing is not a possible alternative. The result has been a growing inequality of income between the unskilled and semi-skilled workers in Western industrial nations and the domestic managers and owners of multinational corporations who can engage in outsourcing of their lower end jobs and demanding higher profit margins on the segment of their integrated chain that provide goods and services domestically.

What anti-inflation incomes policy can be developed from Keynes's revolutionary analytic approach? In 1970, Sidney Weintraub, basing his analysis on Keynes's analytical framework (Weintraub, 1958), developed a "clever" anti-inflation policy which he called TIP, or a tax-based incomes policy. TIP required the use of the corporate income tax structure to penalize the largest domestic firms in the economy if they agreed to wage-rate increases in excess of some national productivity improvement standard. Thus, the tax system would be used to penalize those firms that agreed to inflationary wage demands. The hope of TIP was that if wage increases could be limited to overall productivity increases, then workers and owners of all other inputs to the domestic production process would willingly accept noninflationary monetary income increases.

There were two conditions that Weintraub believed were necessary if TIP was to be an effective policy that did not rely on "fear" of loss of income to constrain incomes inflation. These conditions are

(1) TIP was to be a permanent policy institution, and
(2) TIP must be a penalty system, not a reward (subsidy) tax system.

Once instituted, TIP could never be removed, for otherwise it would become an impotent policy as it reached its termination date. (Weintraub indicated that the magnitude of the tax penalties could be altered as conditions warranted, but there must always be the existence of a threat of penalties to insure compliance.) Secondly, a reward tip, i.e., one which reduced people's taxes if they adhered to the national wage standard, would be administratively unworkable, as everyone would claim the reward and it would be up to the government to prove which claimants were not entitled to the reduction in taxes. Weintraub suggested that TIP was similar to the way government enforces speed limits on the nation's highways. If one exceeds the speed limit – which is always in place – one paid a speeding fine. Governments never paid good drivers for not exceeding the speed limit.

Unfortunately, the United States and many other nations have never seriously attempted to develop a permanent, penalty-oriented TIP. Instead, inflation has been fought via the typical monetarist "incomes policy of fear", i.e., restricting the growth of the money supply so as to create slack markets via recession. Those who raise their wages above productivity growth will then find themselves priced out of the marketplace.

The real cost of such a monetarist incomes policy to many industrialized nations in the recent past has been significant. For countries such as Germany and France, close to double-digit unemployment rates – previously unseen since the Great Depression – have become the norm.

Weintraub, the perpetual believer in the use of human intelligence rather than brute (market) forces to encourage socially compatible civilized behavior, believed that ultimately some form of civilized incomes constraint policy would be seen as a more humane policy to control inflation without the necessary depressing side effects of traditional monetarist policy.

Words and concepts are important weapons in the fight against inflation. One of the most important functions of government in this anti-inflationary struggle is to educate the public of the major industrialized nations that the income distribution struggle is (in the aggregate) a no-win, actual lose game, although there may be relative winners for periods of time. In the absence of a sensible policy about the distribution of income nationally and internationally, the result is not a zero-sum game, but a real loss in aggregate income nationally and internationally as governments pursue restrictive monetary and/or fiscal policies.

12

Keynes's Revolution: The Evidence Showing Who Killed Cock Robin

In his 1935 New Year's Day letter to George Bernard Shaw, Keynes indicated that he was writing a book that would revolutionize economic theory through its real-world description of an economy where liquidity and money contracts played a dominant role in the organization of production and exchange processes. For several decades after World War II economists spoke about this Keynesian Revolution in economic theory and policy. In 1971, even an American president, Richard M. Nixon, announced, "now I am a Keynesian". Today, however, the teaching of Keynes's revolution in theory and policy is dead, at least in economics textbooks, the writings of mainstream economists, and speeches of government policy makers, whether they be "liberal" or "conservative".

How can we explain the deathblow given to this revolutionary analysis developed by the greatest thinker in economics of the 20th century? In this concluding chapter, we shall show it was due to a strange confluence of forces occurring after World War II, namely, economics becoming a mathematical science, the new Bourbakian mathematical economist philosophy as to what should be regarded as a correct general theory, and the anti-communist political forces that permeated many aspects of life in America – including witch-hunting in academia.

Keynes believed that his revolution involved questioning, and, as he says on page 16 of *The General Theory*, throwing out fundamental axioms underlying classical theory. In the German language edition of *The General Theory*, Keynes (1936b, p. ix) specifically noted, "This is one of the reasons which justify my calling my theory a *general* [emphasis in the original] theory ... it is based on *fewer restrictive assumptions* ['weniger enge Voraussetzunger stutz'] than the orthodox theory, it is also more easily adopted to a large area of different circumstances" [second emphasis added]. Keynes was searching for a theory that provided the maximum level of generality while describing the circumstances of important real-world monetary economic processes.

All mainstream theories – e.g., General Equilibrium Theory, Neoclassical Synthesis Keynesianism, Monetarism, New Classical Theory, New Keynesian Theory, post-Walrasian Theory, and Behavioral Economics – impose additional restrictive axioms into their foundations. The result is these theories become special cases of Keynes's general theory, for the latter has the maximum generality. From a logical standpoint the onus is on those who add restrictive axioms to the maximum general theory to justify these additional axioms. Those theorists who invoke only Keynes's general theory's lesser axiomatic foundation are not required, in logic, to prove a general negative, i.e., they are not required to prove the additional restrictive axioms are unnecessary.

The conventional wisdom of mainstream economists has been that it is not necessary to justify the additional restrictive axioms of any variant of classical general equilibrium theory, including highly mathematical computer based models known as dynamic stochastic general equilibrium (DSGE) models. These general equilibrium theories involve "thousands of variables" and an equation for each variable that, at any point of time, simultaneously determines the price and output of every item that is traded in the economic system (Samuelson, 1947, p. 8). The foremost proponent for using this mathematical general equilibrium theory approach as the mother of all economic analysis is Nobel Prize winner Gerard Debreu.

Beginning in the 1930s in France, a small group of mathematicians (who became known as the Bourbaki school) attempted to "purify" scientific discourse in all disciplines. Debreu was educated as a mathematician in France during World War II. The philosophy of this Bourbaki school of mathematics captured mathematical economics in the 1950s, primarily through the work of Gerard Debreu. In his Nobel Museum (Internet) autobiography, Debreu states that during his formative years at school "Bourbaki ... fashioned my mathematical taste".

In his book *How Economics Became a Mathematical Science*, E. Roy Weintraub (2002, p. 102) noted that by World War II, "the predominant view in American mathematical circles was the same as Bourbaki's: mathematics is an autonomous abstract subject, with no need of any input from the real world. ... Thus Bourbaki came to uphold the primacy of the pure over the applied, the rigorous over the intuitive".

This Bourbaki philosophy created an unbridgeable chasm between math and its applications in real world science, between the rigor of axiomatization and the rigor in the old 19th and early 20th century sense of basing argumentation on observable real world phenomena. According to Weintraub (2002, p. 103) this Bourbaki desire for purity and isolation from the real world did not unleash a vigorous backlash among natural scientists until the 1990s, and it is now often claimed that the hold of "the Bourbaki plague is dying out" in the physical sciences. Unfortunately, the Bourbakian philosophical view still infects mainstream economic theory.

In economics, the Bourbaki philosophy was transplanted into postwar American economics by Debreu, and the seed bed that encouraged the domination of this non-real-world view of economic theory was the Cowles Commission for economic research of the early 1950s (Weintraub, 2002, p. 104). Debreu argued that all economic theory had to start from Leon Walras's 19th-century general equilibrium model (Walras, 1874). Weintraub (2002, p. 113 emphasis added) has noted that Debreu, in his Bourbakian mathematical approach to economics, has argued that "*good general theory does not search for the maximum generality, but for the right generality*". In other words, the Bourbaki mathematical view of how to do economic theory would not accept Keynes's search for the "maximum" generality to provide a general theory that has the smallest axiomatic foundation while still "adaptable to a large area of different circumstances" regarding the world of experience.

According to the Bourbakian view of economics, Keynes's general theory, which was based on fewer axioms than Debreu's general equilibrium theory, is not "good" theory even though Keynes's keen intuition led him to provide this realistic description of the economic system in which we live. Instead, Debreu's general equilibrium theory of value, which expresses itself in terms that few, if any, would readily recognize as an apt description of a real-world economy (Weintraub, 2002, p. 114), provides the Bourbakian "right" level of generality – even if this theory is not realistic. Unfortunately, Debreu (and other general equilibrium theorists) does not provide any criteria for what is the "right" level of generality. They merely claim their general equilibrium approach is the right level of generality. Weintraub notes that this Bourbakian case for the right level of generality is merely a matter "of style ... and politics ... and taste" (Weintraub, 2002, p. 125) and not of logic.

Weintraub (2002, p. 114) has written that Debreu's 1959 monograph *The Theory of Value* "still stands as the benchmark axiomatization of the Walrasian general equilibrium model. In retrospect, the 1959 book wore its Bourbakist credentials on its sleeve, though there may have been few economists at this juncture who would have understood the implications of the following statement:

> The theory of value is treated here with the standards of rigor of the contemporary formalist school of mathematics. The effort towards rigor substitutes correct reasoning and results for incorrect ones ... leads to a deeper understanding of the problems to which it is applied. ... Alliance to rigor determines the axiomatic form of analysis where the theory, in the strict sense, is logically disconnected from its interpretation. In order to bring out fully this disconnection from its interpretations, all the definitions, all the hypothesis, and the main results of the theory ... are distinguished by italics; moreover, the transformation from the informal discussions of interpretation to the formal construction of the theory ... reveals all the assumptions and the logical structure of the analysis.
>
> (Debreu, 1959)

Here is Debreu's clear declaration of independence of theory from real-world descriptive restraints. Debreu is indicating there is no need for the elements of a rigorous economic theory to have exact counterparts in the real world of experience. Debreu considered that

> "the model of Walrasian equilibrium was the root structure [the right level of generality] from which all further work in economics would eventuate. ... The objective was no longer to represent the economy ... but rather to codify the very essence of ... the Walrasian system. This fundamental shift in objective explains ... his [Debreu's] disdain for attempts (like that of Kenneth Arrow and Frank Hahn) to forge explicit links between the Walrasian model and contemporary theoretical concerns in macroeconomics".
>
> (Weintraub, 2002, p. 121)

In his bold leap of faith, Debreu believed his work to be "the definitive mother-structure from which all further work in economics would start, primarily by weakening its assumptions or else superimposing new interpretations upon the existing formalism. But this required one very crucial manoeuver that was never stated explicitly: namely, that the Walrasian general equilibrium approach was the root structure from which all further scientific work in economics would eventuate" (Weintraub, 2002, p. 121).

When after World War II, economics became a mathematics-based "science", mainstream economists, in their desire to be seen as hard-headed scientists, signed on to this Bourbakian philosophy even if most did not recognize or comprehend the implications. In recent years, the post-Walrasian school (see Colander, 2006) is merely the latest group to be enamored with the challenge of weakening, but not overthrowing, the axiomatic foundation of the basic mathematical Walrasian model by assuming some level of epistemological uncertainty due to the complexity of the mathematical relationships. Nevertheless, these complexity models still assume the existence of a "long-run [equilibrium] state of the system" (Durlauf, 2005, p. F226).

But why after Keynes's revolutionary analysis, the reader might ask, have mainstream economists resurrected this classical theory with its additional restrictive axioms as the only valid basis for developing policy prescriptions for the major economic problems of the 21st century? This chapter will provide the evidence to explain that this apparent deification of classical theory was actually not a rising from the dead. Keynes's analysis was never understood by the established leaders and trendsetters of the economics profession. Instead, almost immediately after Keynes published his revolutionary monetary theory it was aborted for two reasons: (1) the inability of mainstream economists, especially those who called themselves Keynesians, to comprehend Keynes's message regarding liquidity and the importance of money contracts in organizing production and exchange transactions and (2) the political anti-communist atmosphere (McCarthyism) that was rampant in the United States in the years immediately after World War II.

The failure of Keynes's analysis to revolutionize the way mainstream economists build theories to explain the real world ultimately would not have surprised Keynes. In his inaugural lecture before the British Academy on April 22, 1971, Austin Robinson, quoting from an unpublished early draft of Keynes's *General Theory*, indicated that Keynes wrote:

> "In economics you cannot *convict* your opponent of error, you can only *convince* him of it. And even if you are right, you cannot convince him ... if his head is already filled with contrary notions that he cannot catch the clues to your thought which you are throwing to him".

We shall show that not only Keynes's generation of economic theorists, but, more importantly, younger economists such as Paul Samuelson (who later became a Nobel laureate), had their heads so full of the contrary notions of classical theory that they could not catch the thoughts that Keynes was throwing to all who would listen.

I. Fixed wages and the problem of unemployment

As we have already noted, Keynes's biographer, Lord Skidelsky (1992, p. 512), made the point "that mainstream economists after the Second World War treated Keynes's theory as a 'special case' of the classical theory, applicable to conditions where money wages ... were 'sticky'. Thus his theory was robbed of its theoretical bite, while allowed to retain its relevance for policy".

If Keynes was merely arguing that unemployment was the result of price and wage rigidities, then Keynes was not providing a revolutionary theoretical analysis of the major economic problem of the failure of a money using *laissez-faire* economy to provide a full-employment environment. 19th-century economists had argued already that the lack of flexible wages and prices (what modern mainstream economists call supply side imperfections) is the sole cause of unemployment.

We have already noted that in *The General Theory of Employment, Interest and Money*, Keynes (1936a, p. 257) specifically stated that his theory of unemployment did not rely on the assumption of wage (and/or price) rigidities. His theory relied on a different analysis. Nevertheless, after World War II, university economics students were taught that the Keynesian Revolution required the assumption of sticky wages and/or prices to explain the existence of involuntary unemployment.

Some mainstream Keynesians attempted to bolster their wage and price rigidity argument by adding, as an additional cause of unemployment equilibrium, the existence of an interest rate stickiness or fixity. This fixed interest rate argument is called the "liquidity trap", where at some low, but positive, rate of interest the demand to hold money for speculative reasons is assumed to be perfectly elastic (i.e., horizontal). Thus, according to liquidity trap theorists, interest rates could not decline further and therefore monetary policy would be unable to induce any further increase in investment expenditures necessary to expand the economy toward a full-employment outcome. After World War II, however, econometric studies could not find any evidence of the existence of a liquidity trap in the form of a perfectly elastic demand for money segment.

Had mainstream economists read *The General Theory*, however, they would have known that on page 202, Keynes specifies the speculative demand for money as a rectangular hyperbola – a mathematical function that never has a perfectly elastic segment. Moreover, eyeball empiricism led Keynes (1936a, p. 207) to indicate that he knew of no historical example where the liquidity preference function became "virtually absolute", i.e., perfectly elastic. In sum, both from a theoretical and an empirical view, Keynes had already denied the existence of a liquidity trap.

Postwar mainstream "Keynesian" economists either never read or never understood Keynes's book. In fact, in most prestigious universities' economics departments students have been taught that Keynes's book *The General Theory of Employment, Interest and Money* is an obscure and confusing book, and therefore they need not read it or comprehend it. For example, N. Greg Mankiw, a self-proclaimed "New Keynesian" economist, a Harvard University Professor, and a former chairman of President George W. Bush's Council of Economic Advisers has written that the "*General Theory* is an obscure book … [it] is an outdated book. … We are in a much better position than Keynes was to figure out how the economy works. … Few macro economists take such a dim view of classical economics [as Keynes did] … Classical economics is right in the long run. Moreover, economists today are more interested in the long-run equilibrium. … [There is] widespread acceptance of classical economics" (Mankiw, 1992, pp. 560–1).

When distinguished professors such as Mankiw say such things it is obvious that students of economics will neither read nor try to comprehend Keynes's "obscure" message. Instead, these students are told that the "Keynesian" argument boils down to the classical theory view that it is primarily supply side imperfections – especially due to the rigidity of money wages in the labor market of the last half century, where the "welfare" state has coddled workers by legislating minimum wages, encouraging labor union organization, providing "lavish" unemployment benefits, etc. – that are the basic causes of observed unemployment in the world in which we live.

Consequently, it should not be surprising that graduates of distinguished economic departments who are advisors to government policymakers suggest that if a nation is ever to fight the persistent levels of unemployment that plague many developed nations in today's globalized economy, labor markets must be "liberalized", i.e., completely deregulated, and the social safety net that prevents unemployment from being an unmitigated disaster for workers must be reduced, if not completely removed. If labor market "liberalization" is taken to its theoretical extreme, this would imply no government rules regarding minimum workshop safety conditions or even the prohibition of child labor.

According to orthodox classical theory, full employment can only be approached by making labor unions impotent, dismantling any existing social safety net, etc., until labor market conditions in the developed nations are equivalent to those in the less developed nations such as India, China, and other Asian countries that possess large numbers of workers who are willing to work at extremely low wages, as well as send their children out to work, in unsafe "sweatshop" working conditions.

II. Who actually aborted Keynes's revolution?

Debreu's Bourbakian mathematical economic approach might not have captured mainstream economics after World War II but for the fact that few economists actually understood Keynes's different revolutionary analysis. Immediately after World War II, however, leading economists ignored Keynes's claim that classical theory was a special case requiring additional restrictive, unrealistic axioms and instead taught their students that Keynes's theory was a special case of classical theory (where there were rigidities in wages and/or prices).

To explain why Keynes's revolutionary claim that the explanation of unemployment was nested in the desire of people to use liquid assets as a store of value never had a chance of becoming the foundation of macroeconomic analysis, we will use primarily the example of Paul Samuelson's attempt to propagate Keynesianism immediately after World War II. After that, we will show that John Hicks, who won the Nobel Prize in 1972 for his "pioneering contributions to general equilibrium theory", ultimately recognized that his classical general equilibrium explanation of Keynes's analysis, Hicks's IS-LM version of Neoclassical Keynesianism, was not representative of Keynes's general theory framework.

III. Samuelson's Neoclassical Synthesis Keynesianism

For most students who studied economics during the last half of the 20th century, Samuelson was thought to be a disciple of Keynes and his revolutionary general theory analysis. Samuelson is usually considered the founder of the American Keynesian school, which he labeled Neoclassical Synthesis Keynesianism because of the classical microeconomic theory that Samuelson believed was the microfoundation of Keynes's macroeconomic analysis.

Samuelson's 1937 Ph.D. thesis won the Wells Prize at Harvard and was published as *Foundations of Economic Analysis* (1947). In this volume, Samuelson spelled out in precise mathematical terms the basis of early

20th-century classical (often called neoclassical) microeconomic theory. Accordingly, it should not be surprising that, in the 1940s, Samuelson made his presentation of neoclassical theory as the microfoundations for his brand of Keynesianism. Unfortunately, Samuelson's Neoclassical Synthesis Keynesianism is not analytically compatible with the theoretical framework developed by Keynes in *The General Theory of Employment Interest and Money*.

Given Samuelson's dominance of the American macroeconomic scene after World War II, the different axiomatic foundation of Samuelson's popularization of Keynesianism vis-à-vis Keynes's *General Theory* aborted Keynes's truly revolutionary analysis from being adopted as mainstream macro economics. Consequently, in the 1970s academic literature, true classical economists such as the monetarist school leader Professor Milton Friedman of the University of Chicago easily defeated Samuelson's 'Keynesianism" on the grounds of the logical inconsistencies between Samuelson's microfoundations and his "Keynesian" macroeconomic policy prescriptions. The effect of this victory of classical theory monetarists was to change the domestic and international choice of economic policies deemed socially acceptable (1) to prevent unemployment, (2) to promote economic development, and even (3) the method to finance government social security systems away from prescriptions that were compatible with Keynes's *General Theory* and toward the age-old *laissez-faire* policies advocated by the classical theory that had dominated 19th and early 20th century thought.

Since the 1970s, socially acceptable policies to prevent unemployment have regressed, with the result that, as Table 7.1 *supra* indicated, the "golden age of economic development", experienced by both OECD nations and LDCs during the more than quarter century between World War II and 1973, disappeared despite the technological advances in the study of economics. Prior to the monetarist victory over Neoclassical Synthesis Keynesianism, postwar governments, whether they be liberal or conservative, actively pursued the types of economic policies that Keynes had advocated in the 1930s and 1940s.

The effect of following Keynes's prescriptions until 1973, (if not his theory during the period when Neoclassical Synthesis Keynesianism dominated economic textbooks), was that per capita economic growth in the capitalist world proceeded at a rate that has never been reached in the past nor matched since. The *average* annual per capita economic growth rate of OECD nations from 1950 till 1973 was almost precisely double the previous *peak* growth rate of the industrial revolution period. Productivity growth in OECD countries was more than triple (3.75 times) that of the industrial revolution era.

The resulting prosperity of the industrialized world was transmitted to the less developed nations through world trade, aid, and direct foreign investment. From 1950–73, average per capita economic growth for all LDCs was 3.3 percent, almost triple the average growth rate experienced by the industrializing nations during the industrial revolution. Aggregate economic growth of the LDCs increased at almost the same rate as that of the developed nations, 5.5 percent and 5.9 percent respectively. The higher population growth of the LDCs caused the lower per capita income growth. (See Davidson, 2002, pp. 1–3).

As a result of the monetarist theory's academic victory over Samuelson's Neoclassical Synthesis Keynesianism in the 1970s, New Keynesian theory was developed and tended to replace Samuelson's Neoclassical Keynesianism. Just as Friedman's monetarism had conquered Samuelson's brand of Keynesianism by exploiting the latter's logical inconsistencies, New Classical theory and its rational expectations hypothesis easily made a mockery of the New Keynesians approach which relied on the rigidity of wages and prices to achieve Keynesian-like results. Rational expectations requires the ergodic axiom as a logical foundation and therefore presumed that with free markets there already existed a long-run full employment economic future that human actions and government policies could not alter. Accordingly, the New Classicists could argue that our economic problems were associated with short-run supply-side problems primarily due to government interference with competition in the labor and product market place. If markets could be liberated of government interference, New Classical theorists could demonstrate that even in the short run the economy could achieve full employment prosperity. If these government restrictions were not removed, then it might take a longer period of time until the classical theory provided the right conclusions (as the previously cited quote from New Keynesian Mankiw noted). The result of the classical victory over both Neoclassical Synthesis and New Keynesians, was to lead policy makers to adopt policies for liberalizing all markets in the mistaken belief that "all is for the best in the best of all possible worlds provided we let well enough alone".

Accordingly, as we entered the 21st century, only the Post Keynesian school of economists remain to carry-on in Keynes's analytical footsteps and develop Keynes's theory and policy prescriptions for a 21st-century real world of economic globalization.

IV. The coming of Keynesianism to America

In their wonderful book *The Coming of Keynesianism to America*, Colander and Landreth (1996, p. 23) credit Paul Samuelson with saving the textbook pedagogical basis of the Keynesian Revolution from destruction by the anti-communist spirit (McCarthyism) that ravaged American academia in the years immediately following the World War II.

Lori Tarshis, a Canadian who had been a student attending Keynes's lectures at Cambridge during the early 1930s had, in 1947, published an introductory economics textbook that incorporated Tarshis's lecture notes' interpretation of Keynes's *General Theory*. Colander and Landreth (1996, p. 69) note that despite the initial popularity of the Tarshis textbook, its sales declined rapidly as it was attacked, by trustees of, and donors to, American colleges and universities, as preaching an economic heresy. The frenzy about Tarshis's textbook reached a pinnacle when William F. Buckley, in his book *God and Man at Yale* (1951), devoted one chapter to attacking the Tarshis textbook that was in use at Yale as communist inspired (Colander and Landreth [hereafter C-L], 1996, pp. 69–70).

In August 1986, Colander and Landreth interviewed Paul Samuelson, (C-L, 1996, pp. 145–78) about his becoming an economist and a "Keynesian". Samuelson indicated that he recognized the "virulence of the attack on Tarshis" and so he wrote his textbook "carefully and lawyer like" (C-L, 1996, p. 172). The term "neoclassical synthesis Keynesianism" did not appear in the first edition of Samuelson's textbook, *Economics: An Introductory Analysis* (1948), published after the early attacks on Tarshis's text. This Neoclassical Synthesis terminology, however, does appear prominently in the later editions of Samuelson's textbook. With hindsight it would appear that Samuelson's assertion and belief that his brand of Keynesian macroeconomics is synthesized with (and based on) traditional classical theory assumptions made the Samuelson version of Keynesianism less open to attacks of bringing economic heresy into university courses in economics compared to Tarshis's Keynesian analysis.

Unlike Tarshis's analysis, which was based on separate aggregate supply and demand functions, the analytical foundation of Samuelson's Keynesianism was imbedded in Samuelson's 45-degree Keynesian cross. Samuelson derived this cross-analysis from a single equation aggregate demand function. This mathematical derivation in conjunction with the claimed synthesis of neoclassical theory made it more difficult to attack the Samuelson version of textbook Keynesianism as politically motivated. Thus, for several generations of economists educated after World War II, Samuelson's name was synonymous with Keynesian theory as various editions of Samuelson's neoclassical Keynesian textbook were best sellers for almost half a century. Even those younger economists who broke with the Old Neoclassical Synthesis Keynesianism and developed their own branch of New Keynesianism based their analytical approach on Samuelson's *Foundation of Economic Analysis* (1947) and its classical microeconomic axiomatic foundations.

From a historical perspective, it appears that Samuelson may have saved the textbook pedagogical basis of the Keynesian Revolution from McCarthyism destruction simply by ignoring the less restrictive axiomatic foundation of Keynes's analytic revolution.

V. How did Samuelson learn Keynes's theory?

In his 1986 interview, Samuelson indicated that in the period before World War II, "my friends who were not economists regarded me as very conservative" (C-L, 1996, p. 154). Samuelson graduated from the University of Chicago in June 1935 and were it not for the Social Science Research Council fellowship that he received upon graduation, he would have done his graduate studies at the University of Chicago (C-L, 1996. p. 154–5). Consequently, it was the visible hand of a fellowship offer that placed Samuelson at Harvard when Keynes's *General Theory* was published in 1936. What information about Keynes's *General Theory* was Samuelson exposed to at Harvard?

Robert Bryce, a Canadian, had attended Keynes's Cambridge lectures between 1932 and 1935. In a 1987 interview with Colander and Landreth (1996, pp. 39–48), Bryce indicated that in spring of 1935 he (Bryce) spent half of each week at the London School of Economics (LSE) and half at Cambridge University. At the London School, Bryce used his notes taken during Keynes's lectures at Cambridge to write an essay on Keynes's revolutionary ideas – without having read *The General Theory* – for the people at the LSE. Bryce's essay so impressed LSE Professor Frederick Hayek, a world famous Austrian classical theorist, that Hayek let Bryce have four consecutive weeks of Hayek's LSE seminar to explain Keynes's ideas as Bryce had written them out in this essay. Bryce's LSE presentations were a huge success (C-L, 1996, p. 43).

In the fall of 1935, Bryce went to Harvard and stayed for two years. During that time, an informal group met during the evenings to discuss Keynes's book. Bryce, using the same pre-*General Theory* essay that he had used as the basis for his talks at the LSE, presented to this group what he believed was Keynes's *General Theory* analysis – although he still had not read *The General Theory*. As Bryce put it, "In most of the first academic year [1935–6] I was the only one who was familiar enough with it [Keynes' theory] to be willing to argue in defense of it." (C-L, 1996, p. 45–6). So in 1936, Bryce's essay became the basis of what most economists at Harvard, probably including Samuelson, thought was Keynes's analysis – even though Bryce had not read *the* book when he made his presentations. Even in 1987, Bryce stated that, " anyone who studies that book is going to get very confused. It was ... a difficult, provocative book" (C-L, 1996, p. 44–6).

The immediate question therefore is: "Did Bryce ever really comprehend the basis of Keynes's analytical framework?" And if he did not, how did that affect how the young Samuelson and others at Harvard in 1936 learnt about Keynes's analytical framework. Bryce's presentations at the LSE and Harvard were supposed to make Keynes's ideas readily understandable – something that Bryce believed Keynes did not do in *The General Theory*. Bryce indicated that at Harvard "I felt like the only expert on Keynes's work around" (C-L, 1996, p. 45).

Samuelson has indicated that his first knowledge of Keynes's *General Theory* was gained from Bryce (C-L, 1996, p. 158). Moreover, even after reading *The General Theory* in 1936, Samuelson, perhaps reflecting Bryce's view of the difficulty of understanding Keynes's book, found the *General Theory* analysis "unpalatable" and not comprehensible (C-L, 1996, p. 159). Samuelson finally indicated that "The way I finally convinced myself was to just stop worrying about it [about understanding Keynes's analysis]. I asked myself: why do I refuse a paradigm that enables me to understand the Roosevelt upturn from 1933 till 1937? ... I was content to assume that there was enough rigidity in relative prices and wages to make the Keynesian alternative to Walras operative" (C-L, 1996, pp. 159–60).

Obviously, Samuelson's mind was already so filled with contrary notions of Walrasian general equilibrium theory that he never made any attempt to catch the clues to Keynes's general theory analytical foundation that rested on removing three classical axioms: (1) the neutral money axiom, (2) the gross substitution axiom, and (3) the ergodic axiom, for, in 1986 Samuelson was still claiming that "we [Keynesians] always assumed that the Keynesian underemployment equilibrium floated on a substructure of administered prices and imperfect competition" (C-L, 1996, p. 160). When pushed by Colander and Landreth as to whether this requirement of rigidity was ever formalized in his work, Samuelson's response was, "There was no need to" (C-L, 1996, p. 161).

Yet specifically in chapter 19 of *The General Theory*, and even more directly in his published response to Dunlop and Tarshis, Keynes (1939b) had already responded in the negative to this question of whether his analysis of underemployment equilibrium required imperfect competition, administered prices, and/or rigid wages. Dunlop and Tarshis had argued that the purely competitive model was not empirically justified, therefore it was monopolistic and administered pricing and wage rigidities that was the basis of Keynes's unemployment equilibrium. Keynes reply was simply: "I complain a little that I in particular should be criticized for conceding a little to the other view" (Keynes, 1939b, p. 411). In chapters 17–19 of his *General Theory*, Keynes explicitly demonstrated that even if a purely competitive economy with perfectly flexible money wages and prices existed ("conceding a little to the other view"), there was no automatic mechanism that could restore the full-employment level of effective demand. In other words, Keynes's *General Theory* could show that, as a matter of logic, less than full-employment equilibrium could exist in a purely competitive economy with freely flexible wages and prices.

Samuelson, who became the premier American Keynesian of his time, had either not read, or not comprehended (1) Keynes's response to Dunlop and Tarshis or even (2) chapter 19 of *The General Theory*, which was entitled "Changes in Money Wages". As we have already noted, in chapter 19 Keynes explicitly indicates that the theory of unemployment equilibrium did not require "a rigidity" in money wages (Keynes, 1936a, p. 257).

Keynes (1936a, p. 259) indicated that to assume that rigidity was *the* sole cause of the existence of an unemployment equilibrium lay in accepting the argument that the micro-demand functions "can only be constructed on some fixed assumption as to the nature of the demand and supply schedules of other industries and as to the amount of aggregate effective demand. It is invalid, therefore to transfer the argument to industry as a whole unless we also transfer the argument that the *aggregate effective demand is fixed*. Yet, this assumption reduces the argument to an *ignoratio elenchi*".

An *ignoratio elenchi* is a fallacy in logic of offering a proof irrelevant to the proposition in question. Unfortunately, Samuelson invoked the same classical *ignoratio elenchi* when he argued that Keynes's *General Theory* was simply a Walrasian general equilibrium system where, if there is an exogenous shock to effective demand, rigid wages and prices created a temporary disequilibrium that prevented full employment from being restored in the short-run.

As Keynes went on to explain, "whilst no one would wish to deny the proposition that a reduction in money wages *accompanied by the same aggregate effective demand as before* will be associated with an increase in employment, the precise question at issue is whether the reduction in money wages will or will not be accompanied by the same aggregate effective demand as before measured in term of money, or, at any rate, by an aggregate effective demand which is not reduced in full proportion to the reduction in money-wages" (Keynes, 1936a, pp. 259–60; see also Davidson, 1998). Keynes then spent the rest of chapter 19 explaining why and how a general theory analysis must look at the relationship between changes in money wages and/or prices and changes in aggregate effective demand – an analysis that, by assumption, is not relevant to either a Walrasian system or Samuelson's neoclassical synthesis Keynesianism.[1]

At the same time that Samuelson became a Keynesian by convincing himself not to worry about Keynes's actual analytical framework, Tarshis had obtained a position at Tufts University, a mere half-hour of travel from Harvard. Tarshis would often meet with the group at Harvard, including Bryce, that was discussing Keynes. Tarshis notes that "Paul Samuelson was not in the Keynesian group. He was busy working on his own thing. That he became a Keynesian was laughable" (C-L, 1996, p. 64).

Yet, Paul Samuelson has called himself a "Keynesian" and even a "Post Keynesian" in several editions of his famous textbook. Nevertheless, Samuelson's theoretical "neoclassical synthesis" axiomatic foundation is logically not the general theory spelled out by Keynes.

VI. The axiomatic differences between Samuelson's Neoclassical Keynesianism and Keynes/post-Keynesian theory

At the same time that Samuelson was developing his Neoclassical Synthesis Keynesianism, he was working on his masterful *Foundations of Economic Analysis* (1947). In his *Foundations* Samuelson asserts certain specific classical axioms are the basis of classical micro theory and therefore by extension, his Neoclassical Synthesis Keynesian macroeconomic analysis. For example, Samuelson noted that (1) utility functions are homogeneous of degree zero (Samuelson, 1947, pp. 119–21) and in a purely competitive world (2) it would be foolish to hold money as a store of value as long as other real assets had a positive yield (Samuelson, 1947, pp. 122–4). Statement (1) means that money is neutral and (2) means that any real producible capital goods that produce a positive yield are assumed to be *gross substitutes* for money. Samuelson's *Foundations of Economic Analysis* (1947) required that *all* demand curves be based on a ubiquitous gross substitution axiom, so that everything is a substitute for everything else. Thus, contrary to Keynes's liquidity preference theory, Samuelson's *Foundations* implies that producibles are gross substitutes for any existing nonproducible liquid assets (including money) when the latter are used as stores of savings. Accordingly, Samuelson's *Foundation of Economic Analysis* denies the logical possibility of involuntary unemployment as long as all prices are perfectly flexible.[2]

Furthermore, in an article published in 1969 Samuelson argued that the "ergodic hypothesis [axiom]" is a necessary foundation of economic theory if economics is to be a hard science (Samuelson, 1969, p. 184). As already explained, Keynes also rejected this ergodic axiom.

In chapter 4, we explained that in an ergodic stochastic world, in the long run, the equilibrium future is predetermined and cannot be changed by anything human beings or governments do. It follows that any government market regulation or interference into normal competitive market (assumed ergodic) processes, may, in the short run, prevent the system from achieving the full employment level assured by the axioms of a classical Walrasian system. In an ergodic system where the future can be reliably predicted so that future positive yields of real assets can be known with actuarial certainty, and where the gross substitution axiom underlies all demand curves, then as long as prices are flexible, money must be neutral, and the system automatically adjusts to a full employment general equilibrium.

If, on the other hand, in such an ergodic world prices are sticky in the short run, then it will take a longer time for the gross substitution theorem to work its way through the system but, at least in the long run, a full employment general equilibrium is still assured since in the long run it is assumed that all prices are flexible. Samuelson (C-L, 1996, p. 163) has explicitly stated that in his view Keynes's analysis is a "very slow adjusting disequilibrium" system where the "full Walrasian [classical theory] equilibrium was not realized" in the short run because prices and wages do not adjust rapidly enough to an exogenous shock. Nevertheless, the economic system would, if left alone, achieve full employment in the long run as all prices adjusted, as Professor Mankiw also has suggested.

In Keynes's general theory analysis, on the other hand, a full-employment equilibrium is not assured in either the short run or the long run. Keynes argued that in a money-using entrepreneur economy where the future is uncertain (and therefore could not be reliably predicted), money (and all other liquid assets) would always be nonneutral as they are used as a store of savings. In essence, Keynes viewed the economic system as moving through calendar time from an irrevocable past to an uncertain, not statistically predictable, future. This required Keynes to reject the ergodic axiom.

In sum, his book, *Foundations for Economic Analysis* (Samuelson, 1947) plus his 1969 article on "Classical and Neoclassical Theory"(where he embraces the ergodic axiom), Samuelson specifies that good "scientific" economic theory must be founded on the three classical axioms that Keynes's argued were the equivalent of the axiom of parallels in Euclidean geometry. Clearly, then, Samuelson's macroeconomics is not applicable to the "non-Euclidean" economics of a money-using entrepreneurial system that Keynes developed in his *General Theory*.

VII. What about Hicks's IS-LM model?

Hicks wrote (1946, pp. 1–4) that he "had the fortune to come upon a method of analysis. ... The method of General Equilibrium ... [that] was specially designed to exhibit the economic system as a whole ... [With this method] we shall thus be able to see just why it is that Mr. Keynes reaches different results from earlier economists". Hicks (1937) used this general equilibrium method to develop his famous IS-LM model, which he claimed explained Keynes's analytical approach. In Hicks's IS-LM system, the real and monetary aspects of the economy are divided into independent subsets of equations. For these subsets to be independent requires the assumption of neutral money. Accordingly, this IS-LM model is merely another classical theory version of Samuelson's Neoclassical Synthesis Keynesianism.

In 1971, I met John Hicks at a six-day International Economics Association conference on the microfoundations of macroeconomics. At the conference my participation (Davidson, 1977, pp. 313–17) emphasized the importance of contracts, the existence of spot and forward markets, and the need for liquidity. In the discussion at the end of the conference, I emphasized the fact that a classical "general equilibrium model was not designed to, and could not answer the interesting macroeconomic questions of money, inflation and unemployment. ... If we [economists] insist on balancing Keynes's macroeconomic analysis on an incompatible general equilibrium base we would not make any progress in macroeconomics; we would also regress to the disastrous pre-Keynesian solutions to the macro-political-economic problems"[3] (Davidson, 1977, p. 392). By the end of the conference, Hicks informed me that the microfoundations of his approach to macroeconomics was closer to mine than to any one else at the conference (where other participants included future Nobel Prize winners Tjalling Koopmans and Joseph Stiglitz).

Over the next few years, Hicks and I met privately several times in the UK to continue our discussions regarding the microfoundation of Keynes's general theory. By the mid-1970s, Hicks (1976, pp. 140–1) was ready to admit that his IS-LM model was a "potted version" of Keynes. By 1979, Hicks (1979, p. 38) was arguing that economics is embedded in calendar time and a relationship that held in the past could not be assumed to hold in the future. In an article in the *Journal of Post Keynesian Economics* entitled "ISLM: An Explanation", Hicks (1980–1, p. 139) recanted his IS-LM model when he wrote: "As time has gone on, I have myself become dissatisfied with it [the IS-LM apparatus]". In this article, Hicks admitted that the IS-LM formulation did not describe Keynes's general theory approach at all.

Finally, after reading my paper on the fallacy of rational expectations (Davidson, 1982–3), Hicks wrote to me in a letter dated February 12, 1983,[4] "I have just been reading your RE [rational expectations] paper. ... I do like it very much. ... You have now *rationalized* my suspicions, and shown me that I missed a chance of labeling my own point of view as *nonergodic*. One needs a name like that to ram a point home".

Thus, the author of the IS-LM analysis renounced his famous formulation of Keynes's framework and accepted the Post Keynesian view of what was the basic analytical foundation of Keynes's *General Theory*.

Finally, I should note that the importance of rejecting the ergodic axiom has been recognized finally by several other Nobel Prize winners as relevant to the analysis of the economic system in which we live. For example in a letter dated May 21, 1985, Nobel Prize Winner Robert M. Solow wrote to me, "let me first say that I have always admired that article of yours on nonergodic processes and thought it was right on the button. ... I usually think of it in terms of Knightian uncertainty and all that, but yours is a good way of putting it". Nobel Prize winner Douglas North also cites my argument in his emphasis on recognizing the importance of nonergodicity in *Understanding The Process of Economic Change* (North, 2005, p. 19). So perhaps there is still hope that mainstream economists will rediscover Keynes's *General Theory* as the starting point for all economic analysis.

VIII. Conclusion

Paul Samuelson saved the term "Keynesian" from being excoriated from post–World War II textbooks by the McCarthy anti-communist movement at the time. But the cost of such a saving was to sever the meaning of Keynes's theory in mainstream economic theory from its *General Theory* analytical roots. Keynes's revolutionary monetary theory demonstrated that in a money-using, market-oriented economy, supply-side market imperfections including the fixity of money wages or prices or a liquidity trap are not necessary conditions for the existence of involuntary unemployment equilibrium, while flexible wages and prices and pure competition are not sufficient conditions to assure full-employment equilibrium, even in the long run.

Samuelson's view of Keynesianism resulted in aborting Keynes's revolutionary analysis from altering the foundation of mainstream macroeconomics. Samuelson's use of math to formulate his Neoclassical Synthesis Keynesianism, coming at the same time as Debreu's Bourbakian general equilibrium approach was becoming popular, provided a double whammy that aborted Keynes's revolutionary theory. Consequently, what passes as conventional macroeconomic wisdom of mainstream economists at the beginning of the 21st century is nothing more than a high-tech and more mathematical version of 19th-century classical Walrasian theory.

In winning the battle against the forces trying to prevent the teaching of suspected communist-inspired "Keynesian" economics in our universities, Samuelson ultimately lost the war that Keynes had launched to eliminate the classical theoretical analysis as the basis for real-world economic problems of employment, interest, and money. In 1986, Lorie Tarshis recognized this when he noted, "I never felt that Keynes was being followed with full adherence or full understanding of what he had written. I still feel that way" (C-L, p. 72).

Mainstream economics – whether espoused by Old Neoclassical Keynesians, New Keynesians, Old Classical or New Classical theorists, Walrasians, post-Walrasians, Behavioral Theorists, etc.[5] – relies on the three classical axioms that Keynes discarded in his general theory attempt to make economics relevant to the real-world problems of unemployment and international trade and international payments. As a result, these problems still plague much of the real world in the globalized economy of the 21st century.

Until mainstream journals of economics open their pages to the revolutionary (small axiomatic) basis of Keynes's general theory of a monetary economy, mainstream economists will not be able to provide policy prescriptions for resolving the major economic problems (e.g., outsourcing, persistent United States current account deficits, increasing inequality of income and wealth within nations as well as between nations, etc.) of the global economy of the 21st century.

Unfortunately, it would appear that in the absence of a global economic calamity equivalent to the Great Depression of the 1930s, mainstream economists will ignore Keynes's *General Theory* and will instead continue to play with more and more complicated mathematical, statistical, and computer generated games to develop Walrasian and post-Walrasian foundations for classical theories. Advocates for these theories claim to "simulate" real-world economic behavior, despite the fact that the restrictive classical axioms are buried in their theory foundations. For example, economist Alan Kirman, a member of the prestigious Institute For Advanced Studies at Princeton and a contributor to a class of macroeconomic models that some have called post-Walrasian, claims that "although prices are constantly changing and never settle to any steady state, we [post-Walrasians] can show that the time average of prices will converge, that *the process is ergodic*" (Kirman, 2006, p. xx). Yet, since the 1990s empirical investigators (e.g., Christiano and Eichenbaum, 1990) have recognized that macroeconomic time series statistics are nonstationary, just as Keynes (1939) claimed in his criticism of "Mr. Tinbergen's method". Since nonstationary time series is a sufficient condition for nonergodic systems, therefore Kirman's claim appears to be inconsistent with the empirical evidence.

Apparently, rather than utilizing a Keynes's relevant analytical framework, these post-Walrasians prefer playing analytical tractability games so they can be precisely wrong rather than roughly right. The increasingly sophisticated mathematical and statistical tools used in complex post-Walrasian models that only modern day computers can manipulate to achieve "precise" answers have become the black box (magicians' hat) from which classical rabbits are pulled to help design real world economic policies. Those who criticize these post-Walrasian computer "simulations" as GIGO – garbage in garbage out – are typically ridiculed as technological Luddites who fail to appreciate the beauty of such complex computer-generated models. But underneath all the complex post-Walrasian equational specifications, there still lie the three fundamental classical axioms (neutral money, gross substitution, and ergodicity) that Keynes claimed must be overthrown in order to understand the operation of the economic system in which we live.

As long as developed economies such as the United States, the United Kingdom, Euroland, etc., continue to muddle through with the economic performance similar to that experienced in the last two decades, mainstream economists will be able to continue to play their irrelevant computer simulations from which governments and central banks will make policy decisions. But when, not if, the next Great Depression hits the global economy, then perhaps economists will rediscover Keynes's general theory analytical system that contributed the golden age of the post–World War II. For Keynes, however, that will be a Pyrrhic victory.

Notes

Chapter 2

1. Skidelsky provides evidence that suggests that Keynes had a conscientious objection propensity (1983, pp. 320–4).
2. Keynes, according to Skidelsky (1992, p. xxviii), longed to be a creative artist but did not have the capacity to create works of art.

Chapter 4

1. Joan Robinson designated this Neoclassical Synthesis "Bastard Keynesianism" to warn readers that the resulting analytical system was a perversion of Keynes's own analytical framework.
2. At the same time there was a group of Keynes's younger colleagues, the so called "Cambridge Circus" that consisted of Richard Kahn, Piero Sraffa, Joan Robinson, Austin Robinson, and James Meade, who began regular meetings after the publication of Keynes's *Treatise of Money*. The circus engaged in informal discussions of Keynes's theoretical ideas. Although the members of the circus have since claimed to have been influential in Keynes's development of his *General Theory*, his biographer, Robert Skidelsky, indicates that the "circus seems to have played relatively minor part in the development of *The General Theory*"(Skidelsky 1992, p. 447).
3. See chapter 12 for a further discussion of this "*ignoratio elenchi*".
4. Especially Nobel Prizes in economics.
5. A religious person who accepts as a fundamental truth the Bible's story of creation where a Divine Being created humans and all the animals in six days must reject any "scientific" evolutionary evidence that purports to demonstrate that humans evolved from lower life forms over millions of years. Similarly, a true believer in the axiomatic foundations of classical theory will deny that money can be shown to be ultimately nonneutral in the long run. This is not to deny that some members of the "New Keynesian" school and even some Old Classical school Monetarists accept the notion that money may be nonneutral in the short run, because of some "temporary" supply-side failure of the free market. Nevertheless, all mainstream economists believe in the long run that money is neutral.
6. After reading my paper on the fallacy of rational expectations, Hicks wrote to me in a letter dated February 12, 1982, "I have just been reading your RE [rational expectations] paper. ... I do like it very much. ... You have now *rationalized* my suspicions, and shown me that I missed a chance of labeling my own point of view as *nonergodic*. One needs a name like that to ram a point home".
7. Keynes argued that Tinbergen's econometric analysis was not applicable to the economic system because economic data are not homogeneous through

time. The nonhomogeneity of data is a sufficient, but not a necessary condition, for a nonergodic process.

8. Nobel Prize winner Paul Samuelson (1969, pp. 184–5) argued that invoking the ergodic axiom was the only way to make economics a "hard science".
9. As we will explain in the following chapters, Lucas's 1981 and Samuelson's (1969) claim to having the only "scientific" methodology is based on the conflating of the axiom of ergodicity with scientific methodology. This claim, however, is not correct. Modern physics as well as other "hard sciences" have, in recent years, recognized that some processes that they deal with are nonergodic. The question of economics as a nonergodic science is discussed in later chapters of this volume (also see Davidson, 1982–3).

Chapter 5

1. This sticky interest rate argument is called the "liquidity trap" where at some low, but positive, rate of interest the demand to hold money for speculative purposes is assumed to be perfectly elastic (i.e., horizontal). After World War II, econometric investigations could find no evidence of a liquidity trap. Had mainstream economists read the *General Theory*, however, they would have known that on page 202 Keynes specifies the speculative demand for money as a rectangular hyperbola – a mathematical function that never has a perfectly elastic segment. Moreover, eyeball empiricism led Keynes (1936a, p. 207) to indicate that he knew of no historical example where the liquidity preference function became "virtually absolute", i.e., perfectly elastic. In sum, both from a theoretical and an empirical view, Keynes denied the existence of a liquidity trap.
2. For the derivation of the aggregate supply and demand curves, and the point of effective demand, see the Appendix to chapter 6 *infra*.
3. In an intertemporal setting with gross substitutability over time, agents plan to spend a lifetime's income on the products of industry over their life cycle. Thus, the long-run tendency of classical life-cycle theories is that income earners will spend all their income earned on the products of industry. A minute before his/her death, a rational utility maximizing income earner would spend the last penny of income earned sometime during his/her life cycle. In economist jargon, in a classical theoretical world, at least in the long run, all earned income is spent on the products of industry.
4. The negligible production elasticity applies to those economies that adopt a commodity form of money. The commodity chosen will be one where even if the demand for the commodity increases, additional production of the commodity will be difficult if not impossible. For example, Keynes (1930, *2*, p. 259) suggested that the commodity "Gold is, and always has been, an extraordinary scarce commodity. A modern liner could convey across the Atlantic in a single voyage all the gold which has been dredged or mined in seven thousand years".
5. A zero elasticity of substitution implies that the gross substitution axiom is not universally applicable to all demand functions (i.e., specifically the demand function for liquidity), and therefore, as Arrow and Hahn (1971, p. 361) have demonstrated, in the absence of ubiquitous gross substitution all existence proofs of general equilibrium are jeopardized.

6. This may help explain the preponderance of mainstream economists (and politicians who listen to them) for policies that promote current savings (in the Keynes sense) over consumption.

Chapter 6

1. As our chapter 5 example of our vacation skier and hotel investor illustrated.
2. In his famous book *The Affluent Society*, Galbraith (1957) makes the important point that economies should worry, not only about the level of employment, but also whether the output of workers is directed toward improving the social welfare; or merely providing more consumption goods that might actually degrade the environment.
3. If one could dichotomize government budgets into an operating budget and a capital (investment) budget, Keynes tendency was to prefer that government operating budgets always to be balanced while government capital budgets run deficits when the economy is at less than full employment, and surpluses when aggregate demand tends to exceed full-employment aggregate supply.

Chapter 7

1. Keynes (1036a, p. 222) emphasized spot and forward markets in his discussion of "The Essential Properties of Money". Also see Keynes's *Treatise on Money* (1930, vol. 1, p. 282 and vol. 2, pp. 127–9).
2. Keynes (1933b, p. 88) defined consumption goods as finished "when they are ready for sale to the consumer, or to a Capitalist for the purpose of holding them in stock for speculation [for later sale on a spot market]" while capital goods are "finished" when they are ready for use by consumers as consumption-capital (e.g., houses) or by producers as instrumental capital.
3. There is never involuntary unemployment of slaves.
4. Fixed money forward contracts are an essential aspect of all production processes organized by entrepreneurs. As Arrow and Hahn (1971, pp. 356–7) have demonstrated that classical theory is not applicable to systems using money contracts and that if "a serious monetary theory' is to be developed, the importance of money contracts must be explained. Accordingly, it should be obvious that classical theory, despite its popularity among mainstream New Classical and New Keynesian economists alike, is not a useful tool for resolving the real economic problems that our entrepreneurial, contract-oriented system faces, nor does it provide a serious theory of money.
5. Or in some cases when intervention cannot minimize market-price movements, the market maker may shut down the market so that no transactions can take place until the market maker can organize enough resources to stabilize the price in a reopened market. During the period when the market is shut down, the asset has lost its liquidity property.
6. Since A. A. Berle and G. C. Means (1932), applied economists have recognized this separation of ownership from control as an important problem for developed capitalist economies. Since classical theory does not make the distinction between time preference and liquidity preference, it is not surprising

that mainstream economic theorists have proved to be of little guidance on this ownership versus management problem. Recent scandals involving corporate executives increasing their wealth at the expense of stock holders (e.g., Enron) is an obvious result of this separation of ownership and management problem.

7. As long as some income earners save in the form of liquid assets, then, in order to achieve full employment, there must be others who will spend sufficiently to offset the propensity to save at full employment.
8. In July 1963, the United States introduced the Interest Equalization Tax (IET) on purchases by residents of foreign countries' (other than Canadian residents), fixed-rate securities. The tax rate varied from zero to 150 basis points, depending on maturity date of the foreign country's security. In August 1971, dollar convertibility was suspended, and in 1973, Nixon closed the gold window. In 1974, the IET was formally abolished.
9. The huge growth rate recorded for developing nations since 1998 has been strongly influenced by the opening up of China and other nations of southeast Asia to world trade, plus an explicit Chinese government policy of strictly limiting population growth.
10. Only in the nonergodic world that is our entrepreneurial economic system is it sensible to organize complex and lengthy production and exchange processes via the use of nominal contracts (Davidson, 1994) in order to give entrepreneurs some control of cash flows over an otherwise uncertain future. In such a world, the primary function of organized financial markets is to provide liquidity by permitting the resale of assets in an orderly market. Only secondarily do modern "super-efficient" financial markets affect the allocation of new capital amongst industries and to the extent these markets apportion capital, this distribution is not predetermined by some long-run immutable real economic fundamentals.
11. Samuelson (1969, pp. 104–5) and Lucas and Sargent (1981, p. xii) have made the assumption of the ergodic axiom and therefore a predetermined reality a necessary condition for scientific methodology in economics. Walras 1874 and Debreu 1959 required either a full set of spot and forward markets for every commodity for every date in the future from today to eternity or, in a stochastic (probability) setting, a full set of probabilistic conditional markets to determine all future outcomes.
12. Subject to various states of the world.
13. Axiomatic general equilibrium theories that are presented in a non-stochastic format normally impose on the economic processes the properties of a conservative system. The intrinsic stability of such conservative systems is linked with the theory of ergodic processes by Liouville's Theorem (See Wikipedia, the free encyclopedia, Internet).
14. Proper classification can be, at least, conceptually discovered. *A priori* all observations should be lumped into the same class as long as the only difference in the value of each observation can be attributed solely to experimental error. When the difference in magnitudes among observations can be attributed to a systematic difference either *a priori* or by a statistical analysis of variance, then separate classes must be set up for observations that are "known" to be due to systematic differences. A truly unique occurrence, i.e., the only conceptually possible occupancy in a class, can occur only if the

analyst *knows the entire universe* of outcomes and therefore can dogmatically state that this observation is systematically different from *all* other possible conceivable observations obtainable from an infinity of realizations. For Knight, however, unique events are associated with "partial knowledge" of the universe, and consequently, the analyst can never know when an occurrence is unique.

15. Does the butterfly have free will to decide if, and when, to flutter its wings or is that also determined by some immutable nature law?
16. See O'Driscoll and Rizzo (1985, pp. 38–40) for a description of a "vague Darwinian process" operating in a free market economy.
17. Savage (1954, pp. 83–4) admits that he finds "it difficult to say with any completeness how such isolated situations are actually arrived at and justified" and he suggests, "tongue in cheek ... that the fact that what are often thought of as consequences ... in isolated decision situations are in reality highly uncertain. ... I therefore suggest that we must expect acts with actually highly uncertain consequences to play the role of sure consequences in typical isolated decision situations" where EUT is applicable.
18. It is here that Shackle's concept of the crucial experiment is relevant. For Shackle, an agent engages in a crucial decision when "the person concerned cannot exclude from his mind the possibility that the very act of performing the experiment may destroy forever the circumstances in which" the choice was made (Shackle, 1955, p. 6).
19. Cass and Shell (1983, p. 194) state that they "adopt the strong version of the rational expectations hypothesis: Consumers share the same beliefs about sunspot activity. This allows the interpretation that subjective probabilities are equal to objective probabilities". I would have thought that the relevant objective probabilities involved the random variables depending on the unchanging economic (deep) parameters regarding tastes, endowments and production possibilities of *the immutable external economic reality* – what Cass and Shell (1983, p. 196) call the "basic parameters defining an economy", and not the objective probability of sunspot activity.
20. A "shock" is defined as an exogenous force. If the shocked system has a tendency to return to its predetermined equilibrium position (or rate of growth), then the system is immutable.
21. Blanchard (1990, p. 828) states, "All the models we have seen impose long-run neutrality of money as a maintained assumption. This is very much a matter of faith, based on theoretical considerations, rather than on empirical evidence".
22. If important decisions regarding the accumulation of wealth, the possession of liquidity, the commitment to a production process with significant set-up costs and gestation period, etc., are crucial, then the future "waits, not for its contents to be discovered, but for that content to be *originated*" (Shackle, 1980, p. 102).
23. An error-learning model implies that there are ergodic objective probability distributions, and that as we make errors in our subjective probabilities, we learn how to zero in on the objective probability function.
24. Any economic choice which once undertaken cannot be undone without significant (income or capital) costs must mean that the initial circumstances in all its relevant attributes cannot be replicated. Crucial decisions

involve such costly actions which alter current probability structures, if they exist at all, in unpredictable ways; hence the ordering axiom is violated and no probability function can be defined. Rational expectations equilibrium models, on the other hand, presume given and unchanging subjective probability distributions. These models can be a useful analytical tool for studying noncrucial decision making involving small (i.e., almost costless) differences in outcomes, for then choice can be easily replicated, e.g., the choice of whether to purchase a winesap or a delicious apple, based on rational expected utilities. In the view of Keynes, Shackle and the Post Keynesians, it is very doubtful that choices between expensive and far-reaching commitments (e.g., at the microlevel the purchase of durables which cannot be resold without significant costs, or at the macrolevel choices between public policies) can be represented by such probabilistic analogies.

25. See Lesourne, The Economics of Order and Disorder (1992).

Chapter 8

1. For example, to stimulate United States exports in 1977, President Carters Administration's attempted to "talk down the dollar". In the spring of 1993, Secretary of the Treasury Bentsen tried to talk up the yen. In 2005, Secretary of the Treasury John Snow tried to induce China to appreciate its exchange rate to help the United States reduce its dependence on imports from China while increasing American exports to China.
2. In the 1980s, mainstream economists waxed enthusiastically about the export-led economic miracles of Japan, Germany, and the Pacific Rim Newly Industrialized Countries (NICS) without noting that these miraculous performances were at the expense of the rest of the world.
3. In chapter 10, a proposal for an international clearing union for the 21st century that incorporates this vital proviso will be discussed.

Chapter 9

1. A freely flexible exchange rate requires a free market unfettered by government intervention to determine the purchase price of a foreign currency in terms of the domestic money.
2. Professor Harry Johnson once declared (in *The Times of London*, December 9, 1968) "the basic argument for floating exchange rates is so simple that most people have considerable difficulty in understanding it ... a floating exchange rate would save a country from having to reverse its full employment policies because they lead to inflation and deficit".
3. Classical economists do not conceive of "flight capital" as an economic problem. Indeed naive classicists claim that those with wealth have the right in any circumstance to choose when and where they move their reserves independent of the damage such moves may inflict on the national and international economy. But all the rights of the individual always are, and should be, constrained by the potential impacts on society that the exercise of these rights can have in particular circumstances. For example, no one would defend someone shouting "Fire" in a crowded auditorium as indisputably

protected under an individual's right of free speech. In many circumstances, flight capital can cause more damage then yelling fire in an auditorium.

4. Assuming transportation costs do not completely offset the lower labor costs per unit.
5. Since 2003, the Iraqi war plus the Bush Administration tax cuts have created a close to full employment economy for the United States so that the impact on living standards has been muted as unemployment rates are low even though real wages per worker have hardly increased in recent years. More and more working class families have required two or more employed workers to maintain the real income of the family.
6. Since 1982, the United States has been running an unfavorable balance of trade (see table 9.1 *infra*).
7. If instead the price elasticity of imports was 0.6, while the price elasticity of exports was 0.5, then the monetary value of imports would fall by 6 per cent – a greater amount than the value of exports – and the trade deficit in monetary terms would diminish.
8. Testimony of Professor Paul Davidson, Joint Economic Committee, September 18, 1985.
9. The current account is defined as the sum of (exports minus imports) plus net investment income plus unilateral transfer payments. Net investment income is income received by United States residents from production abroad minus income payments to foreigners from production occurring in the United States. A unilateral transfer payment is a payment made from a person (or government) of country A to another person (or government) of another country without any offsetting sales of goods, services, or assets.
10. In a letter to dated 5 December 1941 (UK Public Office Document 7247/116), Keynes explicitly noticed this problem when he wrote: "If therefore we take into account the terms of trade effects there is an optimum level of exchange [rate] such that any movement either way would cause a deterioration in the country's merchandise [trade] balance".

Chapter 10

1. The "scarce currency" clause of the Bretton Woods Agreement would permit European nations to discriminate against American imports. But this would not resolve the problem since there was no other major source of the goods necessary to feed and rebuild Europe.
2. Only in the small recessions of 1949 and 1957 did per capita GNP stop growing. But even during these brief periods, it never declined.
3. Figures obtained from *Statistical Abstract of the United States*, 1959, United States Bureau of Census, Washington (1959, p. 870).
4. Williamson (1987) recognizes that when balance of payments "disequilibrium is due purely to excess or deficient demand", flexible exchange rates *per se* cannot facilitate international payments adjustments.
5. This provides an added bonus by making tax-avoidance, profits from illegal trade, and funding terrorist operations more difficult to conceal.
6. Correspondent banking will have to operate through the International Clearing Agency, with each central bank regulating the international relations and operations of its domestic banking firms.

Small scale smuggling of currency across borders, etc., can never be completely eliminated. But such movements are merely a flea on a dog's back – a minor, but not debilitating, irritation. If, however, most of the residents of a nation hold and use (in violation of legal tender laws) a foreign currency for domestic transactions and as a store of value, this is evidence of a lack of confidence in the government and its monetary authority. Unless confidence is restored, all attempts to restore economic prosperity will fail.

7. Mayer has argued that the 1997 East Asian currency contagion problem that almost brought down the global financial system was due to the interbank market that created the whirlpool of speculation. Mayer (1998. pp. 29–30) has stated that what was needed was "a system for identifying ... and policing interbank lending" including banks' contingent liabilities resulting from dealing in derivatives. Echoing our nonergodic theme, Mayer (1998, p. 31) declares "The mathematical models of price movements and covariance underlying the construction of these [contingent] liabilities simply collapsed as actual prices departed so far from 'normal' probabilities".
8. Some may fear that if a surplus nation is close to the trigger point it could short circuit the system by making loans to reduce its credit balance *prior* to setting off the trigger. Since preventing unreasonable debt service obligations is an important objective of this proposal, a mechanism which monitors and can restrict such pretrigger lending activities may be required.

   One possible way of eliminating this trigger avoidance lending loophole is as follows: An initial agreement as to what constitutes sensible and flexible criteria for judging when debt servicing burdens become unreasonable is established. Given these criteria, the clearing union managers would have the responsibility for preventing additional loans which push debt burdens beyond reasonable servicing levels. In other words, loans that push debt burdens too far, could not be cleared though the clearing union, i.e., the managers would refuse to release the IMCUs for loan purposes from the surplus country's account. (I am indebted to Robert Blecker for suggesting this point.)

   The managers would also be required to make periodic public reports on the level of credits being accumulated by surplus nations and to indicate how close these surpluses are to the trigger point. Such reports would provide an informational edge for debtor nations permitting them to bargain more successively regarding the terms of refinancing existing loans and/or new loans. All loans would still have to meet the clearing union's guidelines for reasonableness.

   I do not discount the difficulties involved in setting up and getting agreement on criteria for establishing unreasonable debt service burdens. (For some suggestions, however, see the second paragraph of provision #8.) In the absence of cooperation and a spirit of goodwill that is necessary for the clearing union to provide a mechanism assuring the economic prosperity of all members, however, no progress can ever be made.

   Moreover, as the international debt problem of African and Latin American nations in the 1980s and 1990s clearly demonstrated, creditors may ultimately have to forgive some debt when they previously encourage excessive borrowings. Under the current system, however, debt forgiveness is a last resort solution acceptable only after both debtor and creditor nations suffer from faltering economic growth. Surely a more intelligent option is to develop an institutional arrangement which prevents excessive debt servicing burdens from ever occurring.

9. Oversaving is defined as a nation persistently spending less on imports plus direct equity foreign investment than the nation's export earnings plus net unilateral transfers.
10. Whatever "excessive" credit balances that are redistributed shall be apportioned among the debtor nations (perhaps based on a formula which is inversely related to each debtor's per capita income and directly related to the size of its international debt) to be used to reduce debit balances at the clearing union.
11. The efficiency wage is related to the money wage divided by the average product of labor; it is the unit labor cost modified by the profit mark-up in domestic money terms of domestically produced GNP. At the preliminary stage of this proposal, it would serve no useful purpose to decide whether the domestic market basket should include both tradeable and nontradeable goods and services. (With the growth of tourism more and more nontradeable goods become potentially tradeable.) I personally prefer the wider concept of the domestic market basket, but it is not obvious that any essential principle is lost if a tradeable only concept is used, or if some nations use the wider concept while others the narrower one.
12. This is equivalent to a negative income tax for poor fully employed families within a nation. (See Davidson, 1987–8).
13. The actual program adopted for debt service reduction will depend on many parameters including: the relative income and wealth of the debtor vis-à-vis the creditor, the ability of the debtor to increase its per capita real income, etc.

Chapter 11

1. Spot prices are equivalent to what the economist Alfred Marshall labeled market period prices.
2. Forward prices are Marshall's short-run flow-supply prices.
3. Reservation demand is the demand by current holders to hold their preexisting producibles off the market in order to obtain a higher price in the future. Such speculation can occur as long as expectations of future higher spot prices exceed the costs of carrying these existing durables to the future date.
4. In 1942, as a companion to his suggested Clearing Union for international payments, Keynes proposed a "Commod Control" international agency charged with the stabilization of prices (in terms of bancors) of internationally traded commodities by engaging in a buffer stock program. Keynes also argued this would stabilize the income of commodity producers.

Chapter 12

1. The particular proof that Keynes claimed was irrelevant was the classical assertion that a fixed and unchanging downward sloping marginal product curve of labor was the demand curve for labor and so that falling wages must increase employment. In chapter 20 of *The General Theory*, Keynes specifically develops an "employment function" that is not the marginal product of labor curve and does not assume that aggregate effective demand is fixed.

What the marginal productivity of labor curve indicates is that if in response to an expansion of aggregate effective demand, private sector entrepreneurs hire more workers to produce an additional flow of output per period, then in the face of diminishing returns (with no change in the degree of competition), the rise in employment will be associated with a fall in the real wage rate. In other words, the marginal product of labor curve is, for any given the level of effective demand and employment, the real wage-determining curve. For a complete analysis of this point see Davidson (1998, 2002).

2. To overthrow the axiom of gross substitution in an intertemporal context is truly heretical. It changes the entire perspective as to what is meant by "rational" or "optimal" savings, as to why people save or what they save. It would deny the life-cycle hypothesis. Indeed, Danziger *et al.* (1982–3) have shown that the facts regarding consumption spending by the elderly are incompatible with the notion of intertemporal gross substitution of consumption plans which underlie both life cycle models and overlap generation models currently so popular in mainstream macroeconomic theory.
3. Unfortunately, my prediction concerning the progress in macroeconomics has come true.
4. This letter is available in the collection of my correspondence that is on deposit at the Duke University Library Archives of economists' correspondence and writings.
5. Some economists, e.g., behavioral theorists and some post-Walrasians, have tried to erect *ad hoc* models suggesting that agents may not always act with the economic rationality of classical theory's decision makers because often the decision makers do not have the computational power to process sufficient information about the future.

David Colander (2006, p. 2) notes that "Post Walrasians assume low-level information processing capabilities and a poor information set". Nevertheless, underlying this post-Walrasian analytical approach is the belief that the "true structure" governing the economic future is a Walrasian economic system (see Mehrling, 2006, p. 78; Kirman, 2006, p. xx; Brock and Durlauf, 2006, p. 116). Unfortunately, such theories have no unifying underlying general theory to explain why such "irrational" behavior exists. Behavioral theorists cannot explain why those who undertake non-rational behavior have not been made extinct by a Darwinian struggle with those real-world decision makers who take the time to act rationally or who, at least, make decisions that are consistent with those they would make "as if" they knew the underlying Walrasian system.

Had behavioral theorists adopted Keynes's *General Theory* as their basic framework, irrational behavior can be explained as sensible if the economy is a nonergodic system. Or as Hicks (1977, p. vii) succinctly put it, "One must assume that the people in one's models do not know what is going to happen, and know that they do not know just what is going to happen". In conditions of true uncertainty, people often realize they just don't have a clue as to what rational behavior should be.

Bibliography

Abel, A. B. and Bernanke, B. S. (1992) *Macroeconomics*, New York, Addison-Wesley Publishing Company.

Adelman, I. (1991) "Long Term Economic Development" (Working Paper No. 589), California Agricultural Experiment Station, Berkeley, California, March.

Arestis, P. and Sawyer, M. (1998) "Keynesian Economic Policies for the New Millennium", *The Economic Journal, 108*, pp. 181–95.

Arrow, K. J and Hahn, F. H. (1971) *General Competitive Equilibrium*, San Francisco, Holden-Day.

Azariadis, Costas. (1981) "Self-Fulfilling Prophecies", *Journal of Economic Theory, 25*, pp. 380–96.

Baumol, W. J. and Benhabib, J. (1989) "Chaos: Significance, Mechanism, and Economic Applications", *Journal of Economic Perspectives, 3*, pp. 77–106.

Berle, A. A. and Means, G. C. (1932) *The Modern Corporation and Private Property*, New York, Commerce Clearing House.

Bernstein, P. L. (1996) *Against the Gods*, New York, Wiley.

Bernstein, P. L. (1998a) "Stock Market Risk in a Post Keynesian World", *Journal of Post Keynesian Economics, 21*, Fall, pp. 15–24.

Bernstein, P. L. (1998b) "Why Efficient Markets Offer Hope to Active Management", Keynote address to the European Federation of Financial Analysts Societies, Brussels, September 28.

Blanchard, O. (1990) "Why Does Money Affect Output?", in *Handbook of Monetary Economics, 2*, edited by B. M. Friedman and F. H. Hahn, New York, North Holland.

Blinder, A. (1992) "A Keynesian Restoration is Here", *Challenge, 35*, September–October, pp. 19–24.

Brock, W. A. and Durlauf, S. N. (2006) "Macroeconomics and Model Uncertainty", in *Post Walrasian Macroeconomics*, edited by D. Colander, Cambridge, Cambridge University Press.

Buckley, W. F. (1951) *God and Man at Yale*, Chicago, Henry Rigney.

Cass, David and Shell, Karl (1983) "Do Sunspots Matter?", *Journal of Political Economy, 91*, pp. 193–227.

Clower, R. W. (1967) "Foundations of Monetary Theory", reprinted in *Monetary Theory*, edited by R. W. Clower (1969), London, Penguin Books.

Colander, D. (2006a) "Introduction", in *Post Walrasian Macroeconomics*, edited by D. Colander, Cambridge, Cambridge University Press.

Colander, D. (2006b) "Post Walrasian Macroeconomics: Some Historical Links", in *Post Walrasian Macroeconomics*, edited by D. Colander, Cambridge, Cambridge University Press.

Colander, D. C. and Landreth, H. (1996) *The Coming of Keynesianism to America*, Cheltenham, Elgar.

Danziger, S., Van der Gaag, J., Smolensky, E. and Taussig, M. K. (1982–3) "The Life Cycle Hypothesis and the Consumption Behavior of the Elderly", *Journal of Post Keynesian Economics, 5*, pp. 208–27.

Davidson, P. (1972) *Money and the Real World*, London, Macmillian.
Davidson, P. (1977) "Discussion of the Paper by Professor Leijonhufvud", in *The Microfoundations of Macroeconomics*, edited by G. C. Harcourt, London, Macmillan.
Davidson, P. (1982–3) "Rational Expectations: A Fallacious Foundation for Studying Crucial Decision-Making Processes", *Journal of Post Keynesian Economics, 5*, pp. 182–97.
Davidson, P. (1984) "Reviving Keynes's Revolution", *Journal of Post Keynesian Economics, 6*, pp. 561–75.
Davidson, P. (1987–8) "A Modest Set of Proposals for Solving the International Debt Crisis", *Journal of Post Keynesian Economics, 10*, pp. 323–38.
Davidson, P. (1988) "A Technical Definition of Uncertainty and the Long Run Non-Neutrality of Money", *Cambridge Journal of Economics, 12*, pp. 329–37.
Davidson, P. (1991) "Is Probability Theory Relevant for Uncertainty: A Post Keynesian Perspective", *Journal of Economic perspectives, 5*, pp. 29–43.
Davidson, P. (1992–3) "Reforming the World's Money", *Journal of Post Keynesian Economics, 15*, pp. 153–79.
Davidson, P. (1994) *Post Keynesian Macroeconomic Theory*, Cheltenham, Edgar.
Davidson, P. (1997) "Are Grains of Sand in the Wheels of International Finance Sufficient to Do the Job When Boulders are Often Required?", *The Economic Journal, 107*, pp. 671–86.
Davidson, P. (1998a) "Volatile Financial Markets and the Speculator", *Economic Issues, 3*, pp. 1–18.
Davidson, P. (1998b) "Post Keynesian Employment and Analysis and the Macroeconomics of OECD Employment", *The Economic Journal, 108*, pp. 817–31.
Davidson, P. (2002) *Financial Markets Money and the Real World*, Cheltenham, Elgar.
Davidson, P. (2003) "Is Mathematical Science an Oxymoron When Describing Economics?" *Journal of Post Keynesian Economics, 25*, pp. 527–45.
Debreu, G. (1959) *Theory of Value, An Axiomatic Analysis of Equilibrium*, New York, Wiley.
Durlauf, S. (2005) "Complexity and Empirical Economics", *The Economic Journal, 115*, pp. 225–43.
Eichengreen B., Tobin, J., and Wyplosz, C. (1995) "The Case for Sand in the Wheels of International Finance", *The Economic Journal, 105*, pp. 162–72.
Felix, D. (1997–8) "On Drawing Policy Lessons from Recent Latin American Currency Crises", *Journal of Post Keynesian Economics, 20*, pp. 191–222.
Friedman, M. (1957) *A Theory of the Consumption Function*, Princeton, Princeton University Press.
Friedman, M. (1974) "Comments on the Critics", in *Milton Friedman's Monetary Framework: A Debate with His Critics*, edited by R. J. Gordon, Chicago, University of Chicago Press.
Friedman, M. (1998) "Markets to the Rescue", *Wall Street Journal*, October 12, p. A22.
Galbraith, J. K. (1957) *The Affluent Society*, New York, Houghton Mifflin.
Galbraith, J. K. (1978) "On Post Keynesian Economics", *Journal of Post Keynesian Economics, 1*, pp. 8–11.
Galbraith, J. K. (1996) "Keynes, Einstein, and the Scientific Revolution", in *Keynes, Money and the Open Economy*, edited by P. Arestis, Cheltenham, Elgar.
Grandmont, Jean-Michel and Malgrange, Pierre (1986) "Non-Linear Dynamics Introduction", *Journal of Economic Theory, 40*, pp. 1–15.

Greer, W. N. (2000) *Ethics and Uncertainty*, Cheltenham, Elgar.
Hahn, F. H. (1977) "Keynesian Economics and General Equilibium Theory: Reflections on Some Current Debates", in *The Microfoundations of Macroeconomics*, edited by G. C. Harcourt, London, Macmillan.
Hahn, F. H. (1981) *Money and Inflation*, London, Basil Blackwell.
Harrod, R. F. (1951) *The Life of John Maynard Keynes*, London, MacMillan.
Hayek, F. A. (1931) *Prices and Production*, London, Routledge.
Hicks, J. R. (1937) "Mr. Keynes and the Classics: A Suggested Interpretation", *Econometrica, 5* (April), pp. 147–9.
Hicks, J. R. (1946) *Value and Capital*, 2nd ed., Oxford, Oxford University Press.
Hicks, J. R. (1976) "Some Questions of Time in Economics", in *Evolution, Welfare and Time in Economics*, edited by A. M. Tang, F. Westerfield, and J. S. Worley, Lexington, Heath Books.
Hicks, J. R. (1977) *Economic Perspectives*, Oxford, Clarendon Press.
Hicks, J. R (1979) *Causality in Economics*, New York, Basic Books.
Hicks, J. R. (1980–1) "ISLM: An Explanation", *Journal of Post Keynesian Economics, 3*, pp. 139–54.
Hoover, H. (1952) *The Memoirs of Herbert Hoover; The Great Depression 1929–1941*, New York, Macmillan.
Keynes, J. M. (1919) *The Economic Consequences of the Peace*, reprinted as *The Collected Writings of John Maynard Keynes, 2* (1971), London, Macmillan. All references are to the reprint.
Keynes, J. M. (1923) *A Tract On Monetary Reform*, reprinted as *The Collected Writings of John Maynard Keynes, 4* (1971), London, Macmillan. All references are to the reprint.
Keynes, J. M. (1924) "Does Employment Need a Drastic Remedy?", reprinted in *The Collected Writings of John Maynard Keynes, 19* (1981), London, Macmillan. All references are to the reprint.
Keynes, J. M. (1930) *A Treatise on Money*, London, Macmillan.
Keynes, J. M. (1931) "The Pure Theory of Money: A Reply to Dr. Hayek", *Economica*, reprinted in *The Collected Writings of John Maynard Keynes, 13* (1973), edited by D. Moggridge, London, Macmillan. All references are to the reprint.
Keynes, J. M. (1933a) "A Monetary Theory of Production", reprinted in *The Collected Writings of John Maynard Keynes, 13* (1973), edited by D. Moggridge, London, Macmillan. All references are to the reprint.
Keynes, J. M. (1933b) "The Monetary Theory of Employment", reprinted in *The Collected Writings of John Maynard Keynes, 29* (1979), edited by D. Moggridge, London, Macmillan. All references are to the reprint.
Keynes, J. M. (1933c) "National Self-Sufficiency", reprinted in *The Collected Writings of John Maynard Keynes, 21* (1982), edited by D. Moggridge, London, Macmillan. All references are to the reprint.
Keynes, J. M. (1934) "Poverty in the Midst of Plenty: Is the Economic System Self-Adjusting?", reprinted in *The Collective Writings of John Maynard Keynes, 13*, edited by D. Moggridge (1973, p. 486), London, Macmillan. All references are to the reprint.
Keynes, J. M. (1935a) Letter on 1 January 1935 to George Bernard Shaw, reprinted in *The Collected Writings of John Maynard Keynes, 13* (1971), London, Macmillan. All references are to the reprint.

Keynes, J. M. (1935b) Letter of 20 February 1933 to D. H. Robertson, reprinted in *The Collected Writings of John Maynard Keynes, 13* (1971), London, Macmillan. All references are to the reprint.

Keynes, J. M. (1935c) "A Monetary Theory of Production", reprinted in *The Collected Works of John Maynard Keynes, 13* (1973a), London, Macmillan. All references are to the reprint.

Keynes, J. M (1936a) *The General Theory of Employment, Interest and Money*, New York, Harcourt, Brace, reprinted as *The Collected Writings of John Maynard Keynes, 7* (1973), London, Macmillan. All references are to the reprint.

Keynes, J. M (1936b) *The General Theory of Employment, Interest and Money*, German language edition, Berlin, Dunker and Humboldt.

Keynes, J. M. (1937) "The General Theory of Employment", *Quarterly Journal of Economics*, reprinted in *The Collected Writings of John Maynard Keynes, 14* (1973), edited by D. Moggridge, London, Macmillan. All references are to the reprint.

Keynes, K. M. (1938) Letter of 4 July 1938 to R. F. Harrod, reprinted in *The Collected Writings of John Maynard Keynes, 14* (1973), edited by D. Moggridge, London, Macmillan. All references are to the reprint.

Keynes, J. M. (1939a), "Professor Tinbergen's Method", *Economic Journal, 49*, reprinted in *The Collected Writings of John Maynard Keynes, 14* (1973b), edited by D. Moggridge, London, Macmillan. All references are to the reprint.

Keynes, J. M. (1939b), "Relative Movements of Real Wages and Output", *The Economic Journal, 49*, reprinted in *The Collected Writings of John Maynard Keynes, 14* (1973b), edited by D. Moggridge, London, Macmillan. All references are to the reprint.

Keynes, J. M. (1940) "How to Pay for the War", reprinted in *The Collected Writings of John Maynard Keynes, 9* (1973), edited by D. Moggridge, London, Macmillan. All references are to the reprint.

Keynes, J. M. (1941) " Post-War Currency Policy" reprinted in *The Collected Writings of John Maynard Keynes, 25* (1980), edited by D. Moggridge, London, Macmillan. All references are to the reprint.

Keynes, J. M. (1949) *Two Memoirs: Dr. Melchior: A Defeated Enemy and My Early Beliefs*, New York, August M. Kelley.

Kirman, A (2006) "Foreword", in *Post Walrasian Macroeconomics*, edited by D. Colander, Cambridge, Cambridge University Press.

Knight, F. N. (1921) *Risk, Uncertainty, and Profit*, New York, Houghton Mifflin.

Kreps, D. M. (1988) *Notes on A Theory of Choice*, Boulder, Westview Press.

Lawson, T. (1988) "Probability and Uncertainty in Economic Analysis", *Journal of Post Keynesian Economics, 11*, pp. 38–65.

Lerner, A. P. (1933–4) "The Concept of Monopoly and the Measurement of Monopoly Power", *Review of Economic Studies, 3*, pp. 157–73.

Lerner, A. P. (1955) "Functional Finance and the Federal Debt", in *American Economics Association Readings in Fiscal Policy*, edited by A. Smithies and J. K. Butters, Chicago, Illinois, Irwin Publishers.

Lesourne, Jacques (1992) *The Economics of Order and Disorder*, Oxford, Clarendon Press.

Lucas, R. E. (1977) "Understanding Business Cycles", in *Stabilization of the Domestic and International Economy*, edited by K. Brunner and A. H. Meltzer, Carnegie Mellon Conference on Public Policy, 5, Amsterdam, North-Holland.

Lucas, R. E. (1981) "Tobin and Monetarism: A Review Article", *Journal of Economic Literature, 19*, pp. 558–67.

Lucas, R. E. and Sargent, T. J. (1981) *Rational Expectations of Econometric Practices*, Minnesota, University of Minnesota Press.

Mankiw, N. G. (1992) "The Reincarnation of Keynesian Economics", *European Economic Record, 36*, pp. 560–8.

Marshall, A. (1890) *Principles of Economics*, London, Macmillan.

Mayer, M. (1998) "The Asian Disease: Plausible Diagnoses, Possible Remedies", *Levy Institute Public Policy Brief No. 44*, pp. 2–5.

McKinnon, R. I. (1990) "Interest Rate Volatility and Exchange Rate Risk: New Rules for a Common Monetary Standard", *Contemporary Policy Studies, 8*, pp. 79–91.

Mehrling, P. (2006) "The Problem of Time in the DSGE Model and the Post Walrasian Alternative", in *Post Walrasian Macroeconomics*, edited by D. Colander, Cambridge, Cambridge University Press.

Moore, G. E. (1903) *Principia Ethica*, Cambridge, Cambridge University Press.

North, D. C. (2005) *Understanding the Process of Economic Change*, Princeton, Princeton University Press.

O'Driscoll, G. P. and Rizzo, M. J. (1985) *The Economics of Time and Ignorance*, New York, Blackwell.

Porter, R. (2005) *John Kenneth Galbraith, His Life, His Politics, His Economics*, New York, Farrar, Straus and Giroux.

Ricardo, D. (1817) *On the Principles of Political Economy and Taxation*, London, Macmillan.

Robertson, D. H. (1926) *Banking Policy and the Price Level*, London, P. S. King and sons.

Samuelson, P. A. (1947) *Foundations of Economic Analysis*, Cambridge, Harvard University Press.

Samuelson, P. A. (1948) *Economics: An Introductory Analysis*, New York, McGraw-Hill.

Samuelson, P. A. (1969) "Classical and Neoclassical Theory", in *Monetary Theory*, edited by R. W. Clower, London, Penguin.

Sargent, T. (1993) *Bounded Rationality in Macroeconomics*, Oxford, Clarendon Press.

Savage, L (1954) *The Foundation of Statistics*, New York, John Wiley.

Shackle, G. L. S. (1955) *Uncertainty in Economics*, Cambridge, Cambridge University Press.

Shackle, G. L. S. (1980) *Epistemics and Economics*, Cambridge, Cambridge University Press.

Shiller, R. J. (1981) "Do Stock Prices Move Too Much to be Justified by Subsequent Changes in Dividends?", *American Economic Review, 71*, pp. 421–36

Shiller, R. J. (2000) *Irrational Exuberance*, Princeton, Princeton University Press.

Skidelsky, R. (1983) *John Maynard Keynes Hopes Betrayed 1883–1920*, London, Macmillan.

Skidelsky, R. (1992) *John Maynard Keynes The Economist As Saviour 1920–1937*, London, Macmillan.

Skidelsky R. (1996) *Keynes*, Oxford, Oxford University Press.

Skidelsky, R. (2000) *John Maynard Keynes Fighting For Britain*, London, Macmillan.

Skidelsky, R. (2003) *John Maynard Keynes Economist, Philosopher, Statesman 1883–1946*, London, Macmillan.

Smith, A. (1776) *An Inquiry into the Wealth of Nations*, reprinted as *An Inquiry into the Wealth of Nations* (1937, p. 14), New York, Modern Library. All references are to the reprint.

Solow, R. M. (1985) "Economic History and Economics", *American Economic Review Papers and Proceedings, 75*, pp. 328–31.

Stiglitz, J. E. (1989) "Using Tax Policy to Curb Speculative Short-Term Trading", *Journal of Financial Services, 3*, pp. 101–13.

Summers, L. H. and Summers, V. P. (1989) "When Financial Markets Work Too Well: A Cautious Case for a Securities Transactions Tax", *Journal of Financial Services, 3*, pp. 163–88.

Tobin, J. (1974) "The New Economics One Decade Older", *The Janeway Lectures on Historical Economics*, Princeton, Princeton University Press.

Uchitelle, L. (2006) *The Disposable American: Layoffs and Their Consequences*, New York, Knopf.

Walras, L. (1874) *Elements of Pure Economics*, reprinted (1954), edited by W. Jaffe, London, Allen and Unwin.

Weintraub, E. R. (2002) *How Economics Became a Mathematical Science*, Durham, Duke University Press.

Weintraub, S. (1958) *An Approach to the Theory of Income Distribution*, Philadelphia, Chilton.

Weintraub, S. (1981) "Flexible Exchange Rates", *Journal of Post Keynesian Economics, 3*, pp. 467–78.

Williamson, J. (1987) "Exchange Rate Management: The Role of Target Zones", *American Economic Review, Papers and Proceedings, 77*, pp. 200–4.

Index

Printed in the United States
151123LV00001B/69/P